ALL HANDS ON TECH

YOUR HOW-TO GUIDE FOR BUILDING GREAT TECH ORGANIZATIONS AT SCALE

MATTHIAS PATZAK

SOPHIE SEIWALD-HØJER

CONTENTS

ISBN-13: 978-3-9826812-0-7 English e-Book
ISBN-13: 978-3-9826812-1-4 English textbook

INTRODUCTION

Many organizations strive to become more efficient, adaptable, and productive by adopting agile methodologies and copying cultural practices from tech giants like Spotify, Netflix, and Google. These efforts often fall under buzzword initiatives such as "Digital Transformation," "DevOps," "Agile," or "Product-Led Organization." This is where the problem often starts: Many of these buzzword initiatives remain on the headline level, failing to adopt and implement these concepts effectively. As a result, transforming traditional IT organizations remains a significant challenge in today's business environment. Needless to say, the emergence of new market players and the relentless pace of technological advancement demand a fresh perspective on how organizations tackle complex tech challenges. No longer can enterprises afford to embark on multi-year projects that risk becoming obsolete before they even deliver results.

The book you are holding in your hands represents a unique blend of perspectives from both the corporate and entrepreneurial worlds of technology transformation. Sophie brings almost two decades of experience from Mercedes-Benz, where she led the challenging journey from a project-driven to a product-driven approach. Her first-hand experience of the complexities of transforming a traditional corporate giant - including emotional challenges, team dynamics and technical hurdles - provides invaluable insights for organizations embarking on similar journeys.

Matthias complements Sophie's expertise with over two decades of experience across the technology spectrum. As an early adopter of agile methodologies, implementing a large-scale continuous integration pipeline in 2002, and later as CTO and CDO of several scale-ups, he has demonstrated how lean-agile practices and cloud-native architecture can dramatically improve both team performance and business outcomes. His experience, ranging from hands-on development to C-level leadership, provides a comprehensive view of successful digital transformation at all organizational levels.

Together, we aim to provide a comprehensive how-to guide for implementing a holistic approach to creating a great and modern technology organization. Whether you are building a new all-digital business model or working within a large organization tackling the good old mainframe to cloud transformation, our book *All Hands on Tech* is based on some simple core beliefs that go hand in hand and go far beyond any single methodology or framework.

What we believe in:

- Customer outcomes OVER feature checklists
- Balanced speed and stability OVER reckless acceleration
- Strong and capable teams OVER Top-down hierarchies
- Data-driven decisions OVER gut feelings alone
- Cross-functional collaboration OVER siloed departments

- Fostering in-house skills and valuable partnerships OVER outsourcing
- Honest communication OVER information hiding
- Critical thinking OVER "Play By The Book" methods

While we acknowledge and understand the right side, we prefer the left side more.

We have been deeply involved in transforming both traditional corporate entities and purely digital business models. Whether starting from scratch or, like most of us, navigating a legacy approach, the challenges we've encountered were complex and multi-layered. In this book, we aim to go beyond the conventional idea of 'agile teams.' Drawing from our personal experience, we believe the key lies in a holistic approach.

Our journey into the realm of great tech organizations has been filled with obstacles, but also with valuable insights and lessons learned, which we've set out to share chapter by chapter. We are aware that many chapters could be a book by itself, so we aimed at giving you the "best of" our knowledge. Feel free to follow us on LinkedIn, subscribe to our Newsletter, or reach out to us via email to dive into the various topics.

In case you are wondering how to read this book: We created a how-to guide. In case you struggle with a specific topic, you can dive right into the chapter itself. To follow our holistic approach, we recommend reading the book end-to-end.

With *All Hands on Tech,* we want you to join us as we explore the fundamental principles, best practices, and real-world examples that help you build better software. We invite you to engage actively with the ideas presented. Take notes, reflect on your experiences, and consider how these concepts might apply to your organization. Your insights and feedback are valuable not only to us but to the wider community of tech leaders.

Once you've finished the book, as self-publishing authors, **we'd be grateful if you could share your thoughts in a review**. Your perspective can help shape the conversation around building great tech organizations and guide other readers in their journeys.

Now, let's dive in and explore the art and science of scaling great tech organizations!

Matthias Patzak & Sophie Seiwald-Højer

1

WHAT DOES A GREAT TECH ORGANIZATION LOOK LIKE?

BUILDING A TRULY great tech organization is both an art and a science, but what does such an organization look like? How can leaders be sure they're leading their teams in the right direction?

Throughout our careers and in our work with diverse organizations, we've seen a common challenge: many leaders and teams lack a clear compass for excellence. They diligently implement new methodologies, invest in cultural initiatives, and chase the latest trends, but often without a concrete vision of their destination. This can lead to premature satisfaction with "good enough" results, using the wrong benchmarks, or losing sight of the truly transformative potential within their grasp.

In this chapter, we aim to provide a comprehensive outline of what makes a truly great technology organization. We'll explore the key characteristics that set exceptional teams apart, going beyond superficial metrics to examine the fundamental qualities that drive sustainable success and innovation. We will only describe what a great tech organization looks like, not how to implement these concepts. That will be done in the more detailed chapters.

The Traditional Approach and Why It Falls Short

Traditional IT organizations have long relied on established practices to manage software development projects. While these methods aim to ensure predictability and control, they often fall short in today's fast-paced, customer-centric digital landscape.

One of the primary issues lies in the rigid adherence to the project management triangle of scope, time, and budget. Success is narrowly defined as delivering software according to an initial plan, often based on vague and incomplete specifications. This approach, reinforced by outsourcing practices, prioritizes documentation and negotiation over adaptability and value creation. Consequently, innovations are sidelined to avoid jeopardizing predefined parameters, resulting in solutions that may no longer address evolving business needs.

Another significant problem is the disconnect between project outcomes and actual business value. While extensive effort goes into creating business cases, these are often grounded in estimates and assumptions rather than concrete data. Post-deployment measurement of benefits is rarely conducted effectively, leaving organizations unable to quantify the real impact of their investments. This disconnect is exacerbated by a focus on internal stakeholder satisfaction rather than true customer needs, with layers of intermediaries obstructing direct communication between developers and end-users.

Furthermore, traditional approaches often set misaligned incentives and metrics. Progress is measured by person-days spent or features completed rather than by meaningful business outcomes like user adoption or revenue growth. This focus on quantitative outputs over qualitative value can lead to the delivery of features that fail to address actual user needs or contribute to business objectives.

These practices result in IT organizations that struggle to adapt to changing market conditions and customer expectations. The emphasis on predefined plans, internal metrics, and stakeholder opinions creates a system that is more focused on completing projects than delivering real value. As technology continues to evolve rapidly, it's clear that a new approach is needed—one that prioritizes flexibility, customer-centricity, and measurable business outcomes.

The General Blueprint

High Ambition, Curiosity, and a Growth Mindset

Great companies set bold goals that inspire and challenge their teams. They promote a culture of curiosity that encourages continuous learning and exploration of new technologies and ideas.

Employees at all levels embrace a growth mindset, viewing challenges as opportunities to grow and improve. These organizations invest heavily in personal and professional development, providing resources and time for learning. They celebrate not only successes but also the lessons learned from failures. This approach creates a dynamic environment where innovation thrives and employees continually push the boundaries of what's possible. The result is a workforce that's adaptable, forward-thinking, and always ready for the next big challenge.

A prime example of this approach is Google, which has long been recognized for its innovative culture and commitment to employee growth. Google's famous "20% time" policy, which encourages employees to spend one-fifth of their work week on projects that interest them embodies the principles of curiosity and continuous learning. This policy has led to the development of numerous successful products, including Gmail and Google News.

To measure success in this area, many organizations track employee engagement scores, particularly in areas related to learning and growth opportunities. However, the effectiveness of this approach is heavily dependent on the methodology used and the subsequent actions taken. When implemented thoughtfully, high scores can indicate a workforce that's motivated, challenged, and committed to personal and organizational growth, reflecting the organization's success in nurturing ambition, curiosity, and a growth mindset. It's crucial to note that these scores alone are not definitive; they must be paired with robust follow-up strategies and concrete improvements to truly reflect and enhance organizational success in this domain.

Customer Focus in Everything They Do

At the heart of every great technology organization is an unwavering commitment to the customer. These organizations not only meet customer needs but also anticipate and exceed them. They maintain a deep understanding of their customers through regular engagement, feedback loops, and data analysis. Customer insights drive decision-making across all departments, from product development to marketing and support. Many use techniques such as design thinking to empathize with user needs and create innovative solutions. They use data to personalize experiences and anticipate customer needs. This customer-centric approach extends beyond product development to all aspects of the business.

Airbnb exemplifies this customer-focused approach in the tech industry. The company's success is largely attributed to its relentless focus on understanding and improving the user experience for both hosts and guests. Airbnb regularly conducts in-depth user research, including home visits and extended stays with hosts to gain firsthand insights into the challenges and opportunities in the short-term rental market. This research directly stimulates product development, leading to features like the "Superhost" program, which recognizes and rewards top-performing hosts, thereby improving the experience for guests.

To measure their success in this area, these companies employ a diverse set of metrics that capture various aspects of the customer journey and experience. These may include customer acquisition cost (CAC), customer lifetime value (CLV), user engagement metrics (such as daily active users or feature adoption rates), conversion rates, and churn rates. Product-specific usage metrics and customer effort scores (CES) can provide deeper insights into how well the product meets customer needs. By analyzing this comprehensive set of metrics, organizations can gain a more nuanced understanding of their customer focus and its impact on business success. This data-driven approach allows companies to adapt quickly to changing market demands and stay ahead of competitors by continuously refining their customer-centric strategies.

Relentless Focus on Delivering Business Value, Not Just Features

Great technology organizations understand that their ultimate goal is to deliver business value, not just features. They align every initiative with clear business outcomes, ensuring that their technology innovations contribute directly to the bottom line. These organizations embrace hypothesis-driven development, treating every new feature or change as an experiment to be validated. They formulate clear hypotheses about the expected business impact of their work and design experiments to test those hypotheses quickly and efficiently. This approach allows them to focus on delivering small increments of value frequently rather than big-bang releases. By continuously testing and learning, they can quickly validate ideas, minimize waste, and maximize impact.

Booking.com, the online travel agency, exemplifies this approach to delivering business value through technology. The company is renowned for its culture of experimentation and data-driven decision-making. For instance, when considering adding a new filter option for hotel searches, instead of simply implementing the feature based on assumptions, they might formulate a hypothesis such as "Adding a 'pet-friendly' filter will increase bookings for pet owners by 15%." They would then implement this feature for a subset of users, carefully measuring the impact on bookings and user engagement.

To quantify their success in delivering business value, they track a range of metrics. While they monitor the return on investment (ROI) of their technology initiatives, they also recognize the importance of balancing success rates with the volume and diversity of experiments conducted. Rather than solely pursuing a high success rate for their hypotheses, which could lead to overly conservative or biased testing, they track the number and variety of experiments run.

These metrics provide a more nuanced indication of how well the organization's technology efforts are translating into business success. They reflect not just the immediate wins, but also the organization's commitment to continuous learning and exploration. By maintaining this multifaceted focus on business value and adopting a robust hypothesis-driven approach, these organizations avoid the trap of pursuing technology for technology's sake or becoming too risk-averse in their experimentation. They leverage their technical capabilities to drive real, measurable improvements in business performance, ensuring that every development effort is tied to concrete business outcomes while contributing to an environment that encourages bold, innovative thinking.

Psychological Safety That Encourages Risk-Taking and Learning from Failures

In truly great technology organizations, psychological safety is a cornerstone of their culture. Psychological safety, a term coined by Harvard Business School professor, Amy Edmondson, refers to an individual's perception of the consequences of taking interpersonal risks in their work environment. In psychologically safe teams, members feel confident that they won't be embarrassed, rejected, or punished for voicing their ideas, questions, concerns, or mistakes.

The importance of psychological safety in the workplace has been underscored by extensive research, most notably, Google's Project Aristotle. This comprehensive study analyzed data from hundreds of Google's teams to understand what makes a team effective and found that psychological safety was the most critical factor in team success.

In organizations where psychological safety thrives, employees:

- Feel safe to take calculated risks and propose innovative ideas.
- Speak up about concerns or potential issues without fear of retribution.
- Are vocally self-critical, openly discussing their failures and learnings.
- Challenge the status quo, encouraging continuous improvement.

This safety net encourages innovation and creative problem-solving. When initiatives don't succeed as planned, they're viewed as crucial learning opportunities rather than mistakes to be penalized.

This approach aligns with the "fail fast, learn fast" mentality often associated with successful tech companies.

Leaders in these organizations play a crucial role in cultivating psychological safety. They model vulnerability by openly discussing unexpected outcomes and the lessons they've learned. This behavior normalizes failure as part of the learning process and encourages open dialogue and constructive feedback at all levels of the organization.

The benefits of psychological safety extend beyond innovation. Research has shown that it leads to more effective teamwork, increased employee engagement, and improved organizational learning.

While psychological safety can be difficult to measure directly, its effects are often reflected in metrics such as employee retention rates. Organizations can use specific psychological safety assessments or include questions in their employee engagement surveys to measure and improve this critical aspect of their culture. We discuss this topic in more depth in Chapter 14: How to Establish a High-performance Culture that Attracts Talent.

A Culture of Continuous Improvement

Great technology companies have continuous improvement baked into their DNA. They never rest on their achievements and are constantly looking for ways to enhance their processes, products, and people. This commitment to improvement can manifest in various ways, from small, incremental changes (akin to the Japanese concept of kaizen) to more significant innovations. They conduct regular retrospectives and post-mortems to learn from both successes and setbacks. These organizations encourage controlled experimentation, creating safe spaces for learning and growth. They may use techniques such as Wardley Mapping to continuously evolve their strategic positioning in the marketplace. Wardley Mapping will be discussed in greater detail in Chapter 3. This culture of improvement extends beyond technical practices to all aspects of the organization, including processes, culture, and strategy. Employees at all levels are empowered to suggest and implement improvements.

Toyota serves as an excellent example of a company with a deeply ingrained culture of continuous improvement that extends to its technology practices. Toyota's approach, often referred to as the Toyota Production System (TPS), has been widely studied and adapted in various industries, including tech. At the heart of Toyota's continuous improvement culture is the concept of "Kaizen," which encourages all employees, from factory workers to executives, to suggest and implement small, incremental improvements in their daily work.

To gauge their commitment to continuous improvement, these organizations may track various indicators, such as the number of implemented improvements (both small and large), employee engagement in improvement initiatives, or the impact of improvement efforts on key performance metrics. However, they are mindful of Goodhart's Law and avoid over-relying on any single metric. Instead, they use a balanced approach to measurement, combining quantitative data with qualitative assessments to get a holistic view of their improvement culture. This might include regular surveys, case studies of successful improvements, or assessments of how quickly the organization adapts to new challenges.

This multifaceted approach to continuous improvement not only leads to better products and more efficient operations but also creates a dynamic, engaging work environment that attracts and retains top talent. By nurturing a culture where every team member is encouraged to contribute to ongoing enhancement, these organizations remain agile and responsive in an ever-changing technological landscape.

Loosely Coupled Yet Highly-Aligned Organizational Structure

Successful technology organizations master the delicate balance between autonomy and alignment. They empower teams to make independent decisions within their domains, dramatically accelerating innovation and responsiveness, but this decentralized approach doesn't mean chaos. These organizations ensure that all teams are working toward clear, well-communicated strategic goals. They structure their teams to optimize the flow of change and minimize dependencies, often using models such as stream-aligned teams, enabling teams, and platform teams. To maintain cohesion, they define clear interfaces between teams and components that allow for independent evolution while maintaining system integrity. They also create internal platforms and common practices that allow team autonomy while ensuring consistency where it matters most.

Spotify provides an excellent example of a loosely coupled, yet highly-aligned organizational structure in the tech industry. The company's engineering culture, often referred to as the "Spotify Model," has been widely discussed and emulated in the tech world.

There are multiple ways to assess the degree of loose coupling in tech organizations beyond dependency ratios. Some organizations track deployment frequency per team, reasoning that more frequent independent deployments indicate looser coupling. Others monitor the Mean Time to Recovery (MTTR) from failures, as loosely-coupled systems often recover more quickly.

The adoption of event-driven architectures, where a higher percentage of inter-team communication happens through events rather than direct calls, can also indicate loose coupling. Some companies even assess team cognitive load through surveys, with lower cognitive load about other teams' work, suggesting looser coupling. By employing a combination of these metrics, organizations can gain a comprehensive view of their coupling status and identify areas for improvement.

Rapid Idea-to-Impact Cycle with High Throughput and Flow

In the digital age, speed is a competitive advantage. Great technology companies excel at minimizing the time from concept to production. They use agile methodologies and lean startup principles to quickly validate ideas and bring them to market. These organizations invest heavily in automation, using continuous integration/continuous delivery (CI/CD) pipelines and other tools to speed delivery and reduce manual errors. They optimize the flow of work throughout their value stream, identifying and eliminating bottlenecks that impede progress.

To measure their speed and efficiency, these organizations often turn to metrics established by the DevOps Research and Assessment (DORA) program, which has become an industry standard for evaluating software delivery performance. Among the key metrics DORA identifies, two are particularly crucial:

- Change Lead Time, which measures the time from the initial idea to the customer's successful use in production.
- Deployment Frequency, which tracks how often they successfully release to production.

Lower lead times and higher deployment frequencies indicate a more efficient and responsive development process. This focus on rapid idea-to-impact cycles and high throughput enables these organizations to respond quickly to market changes, customer feedback, and emerging opportunities. It creates a more satisfying work environment for employees, who can see the direct impact of their efforts and experience less frustration from process-related delays.

Netflix exemplifies the rapid idea-to-impact cycle in tech organizations. Their microservices architecture enables teams to deploy code to production thousands of times daily. Netflix's "chaos engineering" practices test system resilience, while their extensive A/B testing framework allows quick validation of new ideas with real users. This approach extends to content creation, where data-driven decisions show production, tailoring content to viewer preferences. By optimizing speed and flow throughout its value stream, Netflix maintains a highly responsive organization capable of swiftly adapting to changing market conditions and user needs.

The Accelerate State of DevOps Report 2023 reveals striking contrasts between elite and low-performing organizations in software delivery. Elite teams deploy on demand, implement changes in less than a day, maintain a 5% failure rate, and recover from problems in less than an hour. In sharp contrast, low performers deploy monthly at best, take weeks or months to make changes, suffer a 64% failure rate, and take up to six months to recover. These metrics underscore the huge efficiency gap between top and bottom performers. Interestingly, the report shows that elite and underperforming groups represent similar proportions of the industry at 18% and 17%, respectively, highlighting significant opportunities for improvement across many organizations.

REALITY TECH

Every source code commit was put directly into production by one of Matthias' previous employers. This resulted in over 100 releases per day, usually without stress, effort, or anyone noticing. This was made possible by fully automated testing, release processes, production environment, feature toggles, and strong monitoring. A lot of effort was necessary to achieve this. When he joined the company, they released once a month to production, and each release took five, six, or seven days depending on the quality of the source code and the test and production environments.

Uncompromising Commitment to Quality

For great technology companies, quality is non-negotiable and everyone's responsibility. They understand that cutting corners on quality leads to technical debt, customer dissatisfaction, and higher costs in the long run. These organizations have moved beyond the traditional model of relying on a dedicated QA team at the end of the development process. Instead, they've integrated QA into every step of their workflow and made it a core responsibility of every team member.

Atlassian, the Australian software company known for products like Jira and Confluence, exemplifies an uncompromising commitment to quality. The company has ingrained quality assurance into every stage of its development process, embracing the "shift left" approach. Atlassian's engineers practice test-driven development, writing tests before code to ensure functionality meets requirements from the outset. Their continuous integration pipeline automatically runs a suite of unit, integration, and end-to-end tests for every code change, catching issues early. The company's unique "ShipIt" days, where employees work on innovative projects, often result in quality improvements across their product line.

These organizations emphasize early and proactive quality measures throughout the development process. This approach, referred to in the industry as "shifting left," involves implementing robust testing and quality assurance from the very beginning of the development cycle and throughout. Developers, product managers, and operations personnel all play an active role in ensuring quality.

They use automated testing at multiple levels, integration, and end-to-end tests to catch problems early and often. Every team member is expected to write tests, perform code reviews, and participate in practices such as pair programming or mob programming. Continuous integration and deployment pipelines are set up to run these tests automatically, ensuring that quality checks are applied consistently.

These organizations also focus on non-functional requirements such as performance, security, and scalability as integral aspects of quality, with every team member considering these factors in their work. They continually refine their processes to improve quality and promote a culture where everyone feels accountable for the quality of the product.

To measure their success in maintaining high quality, these organizations track their Change Failure Rate, which measures the percentage of deployments that fail in production and optimizes for Mean Time To Recover. Lower rates of both metrics indicate higher quality and more stable releases. By maintaining this commitment to quality as a shared responsibility throughout the development process, these organizations build trust with their customers, reduce the cost of fixing problems in production, and create a solid foundation for rapid, confident innovation.

Adaptive and Resilient Cloud-Native Architecture

Forward-thinking technology organizations are embracing a cloud-native philosophy to enable greater speed, flexibility, scalability, and resiliency.

- They design their systems specifically for cloud environments, leveraging microservices, containerization, and serverless architectures.

- They treat infrastructure as a software problem, using infrastructure-as-code tools to version, test, and automate deployment.
- They build systems that automatically scale on demand, optimizing resource utilization and costs.
- They adapt their security practices to cloud environments, embracing concepts such as zero-trust architecture.

To measure their progress in cloud adoption, these organizations track the percentage of their systems that are cloud-native and elastically scalable. A higher percentage indicates a more flexible and scalable infrastructure. This cloud-native approach enables them to innovate faster, respond quickly to market changes, and operate more efficiently. It also allows them to focus more on their core business logic and less on infrastructure management. By taking full advantage of cloud capabilities, these organizations can achieve levels of agility, reliability, and global reach that were previously unattainable.

Data-Driven Decision Making

Great technology organizations are characterized by a relentless focus on using data and customer feedback to drive decision-making at all levels. This approach is embedded in every aspect of their operations, from product development to customer experience to internal processes.

At the core of data-driven decision making is a culture that values experimentation. These organizations encourage hypothesis-driven development, where teams formulate theories about user behavior or product performance and design experiments to test them. They implement A/B testing as a standard practice, allowing them to compare different versions of products or features with real users. This promotes a "fail fast" mentality where rapid, data-driven iterations are preferred over long development cycles based on assumptions.

LinkedIn, the professional networking platform, exemplifies data-driven decision making in the tech industry. The company leverages its vast trove of professional data to inform product development, user experience, and business strategy. LinkedIn's data science team employs sophisticated A/B testing methodologies to refine features and user interactions.

While intuition and experience play a role, great tech companies prioritize objective data supported by anecdotes over subjective opinions. They use advanced analytics to uncover patterns and trends that might not be apparent through casual observation. Product decisions are informed by user behavior data, ensuring that development efforts are closely aligned with actual user needs and preferences. Operational decisions are supported by performance metrics, enabling continuous optimization of processes and resource allocation.

These organizations apply the same data-driven approach to evaluating their performance. Key Performance Indicators (KPIs) are established for all major mechanisms and are monitored regularly. Teams use dashboards and real-time analytics to track progress and identify areas for improvement. The impact of changes and new features is quantified to objectively measure their success.

To enable this data-driven approach, great tech companies invest in a robust data infrastructure that ensures data quality, security, and accessibility. They implement tools and platforms that democratize data access, enabling teams across the organization to use data in their daily work. Training programs are put in place to build data literacy and analytical skills throughout the workforce.

By embracing data-driven decision making, these organizations can respond more quickly to market changes, continuously optimize their operations, and deliver products that truly meet user needs. This approach not only leads to better results but also nurtures a culture of objectivity and continuous improvement that is characteristic of great technology companies.

Tech and Business Intertwined

In the modern digital landscape, the greatest tech organizations have moved beyond viewing technology as merely supporting business or even being equivalent to business. They adopt an integrated business-tech perspective where technology and business are inextricably intertwined and mutually reinforced.

This perspective recognizes that technology isn't just a tool or a department, but a fundamental component of the organization's DNA. It shapes business strategy, drives innovation, and defines the company's value proposition. Simultaneously, business needs and market opportunities guide technological development and implementation.

In this integrated model:

- Strategic decisions involve both business and technology leaders from the outset.
- Teams are often organized around products or value streams rather than traditional functional silos.
- Technological innovation is seen as a key driver of new business opportunities and a competitive advantage.
- Data and analytics inform decision-making across all aspects of the organization.
- The boundaries between "tech" and "business" roles become increasingly blurred, with a focus on developing leaders and team members who understand both domains.

Common Misconceptions and Mistakes

Mistaking Activity for Value

Many organizations fall into the trap of equating more features with more value. This mindset leads to bloated products and wasted resources without necessarily improving key business metrics. To avoid this, focus on outcomes rather than outputs. Adopt hypothesis-driven development and regularly measure the impact of new features on business value (see the section titled "Relentless Focus on Delivering Business Value, Not Just Features" in Chapter 1).

Ask yourself: "How does this feature contribute to our core business objectives?" Before starting any new project, clearly define success criteria tied to business outcomes. Encourage teams to think critically about the potential impact of their work, and be willing to pivot or stop projects that don't add value. Remember, the goal isn't to be busy; it's to make a meaningful impact on your customers and your business.

Neglecting Psychological Safety

Leaders often underestimate the importance of creating a psychologically safe environment. Without it, innovation stagnates, problems go unreported, and learning opportunities are missed. To encourage psychological safety, leaders must model vulnerability and openness to feedback. Admit your own mistakes and share lessons learned. Encourage open dialogue and create regular opportunities for team members to voice concerns or ideas without fear of retribution. Celebrate instances where failure led to important insights. Train managers to respond constructively to bad news or mistakes. Remember, the goal is not to eliminate all mistakes but to create an environment where risks can be taken, mistakes can be learned from, and innovation can thrive as you cannot innovate if you don't accept you might be wrong.

Misunderstanding Cloud-Native Architecture

Many organizations believe that simply moving to the cloud makes them cloud-native. This misconception often leads to inefficient "lift and shift, cloud-first" migrations that don't improve the overall architecture or take advantage of the cloud. True cloud-native architecture involves embracing principles such as microservices, containerization, and serverless computing. Start by rearchitecting applications to take advantage of cloud capabilities, not just moving them. Invest in training your team on cloud-native concepts and technologies. Adopt infrastructure-as-code and automated deployment pipelines. Rethink your approach to security and compliance for cloud environments. Remember, becoming cloud-native is a journey that involves changes to your technology, processes, and culture. It's not just about where your applications run, but how they're built and operated.

Siloing Customer Focus

Many organizations make the mistake of siloing customer insights within specific departments, such as the product or marketing department. This leads to disjointed customer experiences and missed opportunities for innovation. To become truly customer-centric, make customer insights accessible to all departments and get out of your office buildings regularly. Encourage cross-functional collaboration on customer-centric initiatives. Include customer-centric goals in the objectives of every team, from the engineering team to finance personnel. Regularly share customer feedback and usage data across the organization. Consider rotating employees through customer-facing roles to build empathy. Create channels for every employee to submit customer-inspired ideas. Remember, in a truly customer-centric organization, everyone understands how their work impacts the customer experience regardless of their role or department.

Striking the Wrong Balance Between Autonomy & Alignment

Organizations often struggle to find the right balance between team autonomy and organizational alignment. Giving teams complete freedom without guardrails can lead to fragmented efforts, inconsistent experiences, and anarchy. Conversely, too much control can stifle innovation. To strike the right balance, provide a clear strategic direction and shared goals, while allowing teams to determine how to achieve them. Invest in internal platforms and practices that enable autonomy while providing the necessary consistency. Use clear objectives to align team efforts with organizational priorities. Promote a culture of transparency where teams regularly share their work and learnings. Remember, the goal is to create an environment where teams have the freedom to innovate within a framework that ensures their efforts contribute to the larger organizational mission.

TL;DR and Further Reading

Since this journey won't be done in a single step, the first approach might be to bring your people along on this journey and reflect together where you are right now. Most likely, you have already started one or more initiatives that have been mentioned in this chapter.

- High ambition, curiosity, and a growth mindset
- Psychological safety that encourages risk-taking and learning from failure
- A culture of continuous improvement
- Customer focus in everything you do

- Relentless focus on delivering business value, not just features
- A loosely coupled, yet highly-aligned organizational structure
- A rapid idea-to-impact cycle with high throughput and flow
- Uncompromising commitment to quality
- Adaptive and resilient cloud-native architecture
- Data-driven decision making

For a more in-depth look at this topic, these are some of our favorite books and websites:

- "Accelerate: The Science of Lean Software and DevOps," by Nicole Forsgren, Jez Humble, and Gene Kim
- "The Culture Code," by Daniel Coyle
- "Inspired: How to Create Tech Products Customers Love," by Marty Cagan
- "Project to Product," by Mik Kersten
- "Fearless Organization," by Amy Edmondson
- "Mindset," by Dr. Carol Dweck

2

HOW TO SET UP A TEAM

THE STRUCTURE and empowerment of teams are critical factors in a great tech organization's ability to innovate, adapt, and deliver value at scale. In today's dynamic digital ecosystem, traditional hierarchical structures and rigid role definitions often impede agility, stifle creativity, and ultimately hinder an organization's ability to respond quickly to market demands and technological changes.

This chapter explores the modern, cross-functional team model—a key ingredient in successful tech organizations that prioritize agility, product focus, and sustainable value creation. We'll present a blueprint for building high-performing teams that function as cohesive, autonomous units primed for success in today's complex technology landscape.

Our journey will begin by examining the limitations of traditional team structures and why they fail in great tech environments. We'll then dive into the essential components of an effective, great tech team—from its composition and responsibilities to its culture and operating principles. Throughout the chapter, we'll address common misconceptions, explore variations on the model, and offer practical implementation strategies. By the end, you'll have comprehensive guidance for transforming your teams into agile, product-focused powerhouses that consistently drive innovation and deliver exceptional results.

This chapter will provide you with the knowledge and tools to rethink your team structures and nurture an environment where autonomy, accountability, and continuous improvement thrive, ultimately leading to more resilient and adaptable tech organizations.

The Traditional Approach and Why It Falls Short

In many traditional IT organizations, the approach to setting up software development teams has long been rooted in project-based thinking and specialized resource allocation. While these methods aim to maximize efficiency and control, they often fall short in today's dynamic tech landscape, leading to fragmented teams, misaligned priorities, and reduced overall effectiveness.

One of the primary issues stems from the project-based view of the world. Teams are typically assembled temporarily for specific projects, disbanding just as they reach peak performance. This constant cycle of formation and dissolvement prevents teams from maintaining high productivity and cohesion. Moreover, team members often prioritize their home organizations' interests over project goals, resulting in fragmented responsibilities and misaligned objectives.

Another problematic aspect is the common practice of allocating individuals to multiple projects simultaneously. While this approach aims to maximize resource utilization, it often leads to counterproductive multitasking and context switching. The concept of partial Full-Time Equivalent (FTE) allocation, such as assigning

0.25 FTE to four different projects may seem efficient on paper, but in reality, it significantly hampers productivity, extends lead times, and increases the cognitive load on team members.

Furthermore, the traditional emphasis on specialization and individual efficiency often sabotages overall effectiveness. Large organizations tend to create numerous specialized roles that contribute little to actual software development, instead focusing on peripheral tasks like documentation or testing. This siloed approach, stimulated by the separation of frontend, backend, and database developers, creates inflexibility and dependency. It blurs responsibility, reduces project accountability, and often results in delays and bottlenecks as teams struggle to collaborate effectively toward a unified objective.

Collectively, these traditional practices create a disconnect between intentions and results in modern IT organizations. While aiming for control and efficiency, they instead create environments where teams struggle to adapt, innovate, and deliver value consistently. The fragmentation of responsibilities, coupled with constant disruptions to team dynamics, ultimately hinders the ability of organizations to respond effectively to rapidly changing tech landscapes and business needs.

As the limitations of these conventional methods become increasingly apparent, it's clear that a new approach is needed—one that prioritizes team cohesion, shared responsibility, and adaptability in the face of evolving tech challenges.

The General Blueprint for High-Performance Teams

Clear and Long-Term Responsibility for a Product

"Instilling a sense of ownership is crucial for driving innovation and growth. When employees feel like they have a stake in the company's success, they are more likely to bring their best ideas and efforts to the table." —Eric Ries[1]

In great tech organizations, software development teams have a clear and long-term responsibility for a product or part of a product. Each product is always and distinctly assigned to a team, ensuring that the team:

- has in-depth technical and business knowledge of the product and its users
- is accountable for the business success of the product
- takes care of functional and non-functional quality

The product scope of teams varies widely, from complete software applications to specific features and functions like search or log-in. Teams might own multiple products or multiple features of a product. In general, they are at different stages of their product lifecycle and are updated at different frequencies. This prevents a team from endlessly tweaking a product without adding any real value simply because it is the only product the team is responsible for.

These product teams own and oversee all technical aspects of the product, including user experience, business logic, data handling, and operations. Product teams collaborate to create a consistent

1. Eric Ries, in his book "The Lean Startup: How Today's Entrepreneurs Use Continuous Innovation to Create Radically Successful Businesses" (Crown Business, 2011)

and seamless user experience or business process, aligning with broader business processes or value chains.

A key to success in this setup is a compact, committed team structure where the entire team, not individuals, collectively owns the product's success. This requires management's trust and commitment in the team to prevent team members from being diverted to other projects or organizational areas. All products are collectively owned by a team regardless of their current stage—growth, decline, or maintenance—and this ownership is transparent to the entire organization.

As a best practice, a product catalog with a list of products, the responsible teams, key contacts, and their respective roles should be available to everyone in the organization. You want to make sure that questions about products, APIs, data testing scenarios, and bugs are easily addressable and solvable. Just an 'intranet search' might not be enough. In an organization with a couple hundred people, onshore and offshore, internal and external basics need to be easily accessible to everyone.

There are several main reasons why the responsibilities for products can change over time between software development teams in a product-driven organization:

- Strategic shifts: As the company's overall strategy evolves, certain products may become more or less important. This can lead to reassigning products to different teams to better align with new strategic priorities.
- Resource optimization: Over time, imbalances can develop where some teams are over- or under-utilized. Transferring product ownership can help balance workloads and ensure optimal use of development resources across teams.

- Team changes: Teams may gain or lose key personnel with specific expertise. This can necessitate shifting products to the teams best equipped to work on them from a skills and knowledge perspective.
- Product Lifecycle: As products mature and move through different stages (development, growth, maturity, decline), they may require different levels of investment and specialized skills. Moving a product to a different team can ensure it gets the appropriate focus for its current lifelead stage.
- Organizational restructuring: Larger reorganizations, such as merging or splitting business units can lead to rearranging product responsibilities among teams.

To effectively handle changes in product ownership, organizations should prioritize clear communication with all stakeholders, develop a structured transition plan, ensure comprehensive documentation, and manage the handover gradually with periods of shadowing and parallel working. It's important to recognize that while product responsibilities may occasionally change, these shifts should be handled carefully, with clear transitions.

The process often involves a few developers from the initial team to maintain consistency and ownership clarity. Having a proper plan in place to conduct the transition is important to avoid issues when bugs or similar problems arise. Developers who have been involved from the very beginning are usually keen to ensure their 'babies' are well taken care of and should be the ones judging the success of the handover period. Ideally, some development work and bug fixing should be conducted collaboratively between the 'old' and 'new' owners to understand how the product has been set up. Providing cross-team support from subject matter experts and closely monitoring post-transition metrics are also critical for a smooth transfer. In a constructive and productive work environment, helping each other out and staying in touch even after a handover should be positively recognized. Finally, conducting a retrospective to capture lessons learned helps optimize future transfers. By taking a proactive, structured approach that emphasizes knowledge sharing, collaboration, and a sense of shared ownership, organizations can successfully manage the complexities of transferring product responsibilities while minimizing disruptions to ongoing development work.

The Team Is Responsible for the Commercial Success of the Product

"Our highest priority is to satisfy the customer through early and continuous delivery of valuable software." [Agile Manifesto]

The team that owns a product is dedicated to ensuring that the product meets customer needs and organizational objectives, taking full ownership of its cost and impact to secure both immediate and long-term profitability. They consistently manage and optimize these aspects, ensuring the product's sustainable success.

Team members are not only aware of their software product's business and technical metrics but are also actively engaged in optimizing them. Take, for instance, the search team of an eCommerce site. Their responsibilities encompass a range of metrics: from the business's search results (e.g., number of searches without results, relevance of search results) to technical aspects such as load times and usability metrics such as auto-complete results to user conversion, bounce, and exit rates.

Some metrics are exclusive to a particular team while others are collaborative. In the given example, the conversion rate from site visits to sales involves coordination with other teams, like those handling product detail pages and checkout processes.

To maintain a customer-centric perspective, all relevant technical and business metrics are visualized in real-time, complete with set thresholds and alarms, ensuring immediate responsiveness and continual enhancement of the product's commercial success.

The Team Optimizes Effectiveness First, Efficiency Second

"You simply can't think efficiency with people. You think effectiveness with people and efficiency with things." —Stephen R. Covey[2]

In successful tech organizations, a key mental shift from traditional methods is the focus on effectiveness—the impact of activities—rather than just efficiency and optimal resource utilization. This shift influences organizational structure, processes, and culture. These successful organizations strike a balance between effectiveness and efficiency, always giving priority to effectiveness, i.e., the impact and benefit of their activities. They direct their teams toward impactful objectives and enhancing efficiency through streamlined processes, clear structures, targeted communication, and advanced tools.

For managers, this is a fundamental and ongoing consideration: What am I optimizing for...efficiency or effectiveness? Are the priorities set right?

Effectiveness should take precedence, with efficiency following in a way that doesn't undermine impact. This principle needs to be explicit and well-communicated. Both managers and teams should be open to critical feedback on this matter and be ready to implement necessary adjustments. These concepts are further explored in the chapters on "Innovation" and "Prioritization," providing detailed insights into balancing these crucial aspects.

---

2. — Stephen R. Covey, The 7 Habits of Highly Effective People: Powerful Lessons in Personal Change (web source)

Team Members Work Exclusively in a Team

"Talent wins games, but teamwork and intelligence wins championships." [attributed to Michael Jordan][3]

In a great tech organization, each team member dedicates their efforts entirely to a single team and its associated products. This approach eliminates the concept of individual contributors solely responsible for specific software parts, or team members dividing their time among various teams or projects. This reduces dependencies on other projects and stakeholders, speeds up throughput times, and increases the quality of the software systems because several developers are working on them, minimizing multitasking.

Implementing this exclusive team structure can be challenging, especially in organizations where historical practices have led to individuals becoming sole custodians of particular software knowledge. To mitigate this risk and prevent bottlenecks that slow down multiple teams, it's necessary to disseminate this specialized knowledge among colleagues. This dissemination is achieved through comprehensive training, thorough handovers, detailed documentation and, most importantly, through pair programming. It is an essential practice that we recommend a lot (see Chapter 11, "How to Ship Software Continuously in High Quality").

Make it an essential practice in your organization as well! This strategy ensures that knowledge is not siloed within individual team members, promoting a more agile and responsive team environment that aligns with the principles of modern, agile software development.

---

3. Michael Jordan, as quoted in the book "Michael Jordan Speaks: Lessons from the World's Greatest Champion" by Janet Lowe (Wiley, 1999)

These are long-term efforts, but they are already showing positive results in the short term. Invest the time...it is worth it.

However, there are valid exceptions. Team members may engage in activities beyond their primary team in the context of cross-team community collaborations or in defining overarching procedures and policies, as discussed in Chapter 12 concerning Cross-Cutting Concerns.

Team Members Are on the Team for the Long Haul

"Great teams are built on a foundation of stability, shared history, and trust that can only be developed over time." —Daniel Coyle[4]

For a software development team to cultivate strength and cohesion, long-term membership is essential. Ideally, team members should remain with the same team for at least a year. This is necessary for team members to fully understand, appreciate, and leverage each other's strengths across various situations and challenges.

Team dynamics are significantly impacted by changes in the team's composition. With each alteration, teams invariably navigate through Tuckman's stages of team building: Forming, Storming, Norming, Performing, and Adjourning.

4. "The Culture Code: The Secrets of Highly Successful Groups" by Daniel Coyle (Bantam Books, 2018)

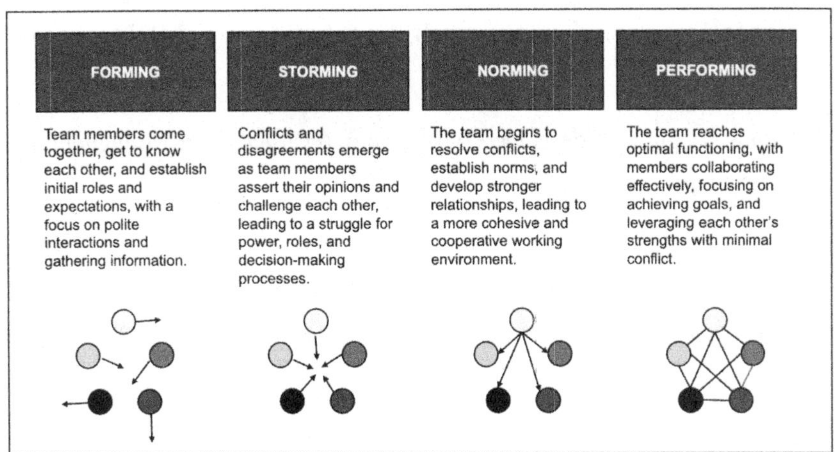

FORMING
Team members come together, get to know each other, and establish initial roles and expectations, with a focus on polite interactions and gathering information.
STORMING
Conflicts and disagreements emerge as team members assert their opinions and challenge each other, leading to a struggle for power, roles, and decision-making processes.
NORMING
The team begins to resolve conflicts, establish norms, and develop stronger relationships, leading to a more cohesive and cooperative working environment.
PERFORMING
The team reaches optimal functioning, with members collaborating effectively, focusing on achieving goals, and leveraging each other's strengths with minimal conflict.

Such transitions often lead to decreased productivity, longer lead times, diminished motivation, and compromised quality—all critical factors in measuring team effectiveness.

Prolonged tenure within a team allows members to develop a profound understanding of:

- customer needs
- the intricate business logic that drives their products
- work methodologies
- internal processes
- dependencies
- in-depth knowledge of the team's internal software design

Documentation, no matter how comprehensive, cannot replicate the depth of experience gained through sustained team involvement. Consequently, any decision to alter team compositions should be made consciously, with a focus on minimizing turnover to preserve team stability and performance.

A Cross-Functional Team with Members from All Necessary Functions

"Business people and developers must work together daily throughout the project." [Agile Manifesto]

Successful tech teams encompass all roles and skills needed to build, deliver, and operate from idea to deployment to reduce dependencies on persons outside of the teams, which usually lead to delays.

This includes not only technical roles but traditional business roles as well. The power of product teams lies in uniting business and technical roles collaboratively in one team.

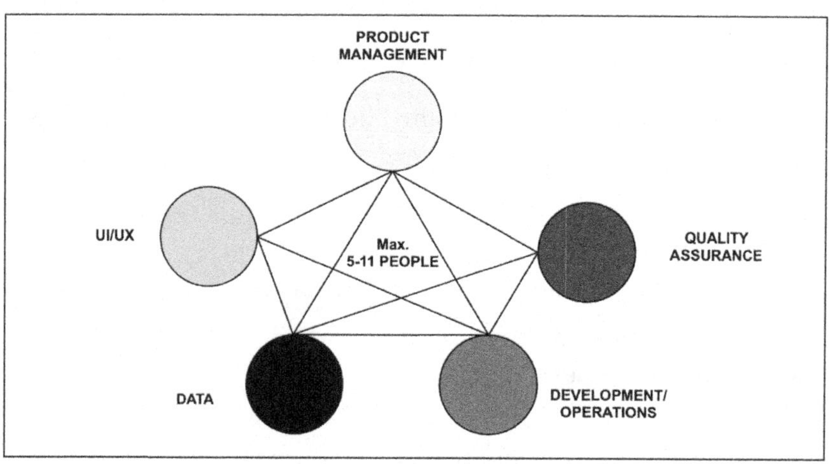

These roles and skills cover identifying, assessing, and describing customer needs, building software, delivering code, testing it, and running it. Typically, individuals with expertise in product management, UI/UX design, software development, quality assurance, and operations are included. A person with sufficient data skills complements the team. Depending on the company's processes, additional roles may be required.

Cross-functional teams often start with many specialized roles, which can lead to underutilization and ineffective prioritization. The solution is to allow team members to broaden their skills and roles so they can work together on the most critical tasks. For example, a front-end developer can learn back-end tasks, business analyst and product manager roles can be merged, and visual and UX designer roles can be consolidated. In highly effective organizations, developers also take on QA and operations responsibilities in a "you-build-it-you-run-it" model. Initially, team members have deep knowledge in one area and superficial skills in others, creating a "T-shaped" profile. As they gain experience, their expertise gets even broader and evolves into a 'V-' or 'M-shaped' skillset, indicating broader knowledge and skills across multiple domains, leading to a more integrated and efficient team structure.

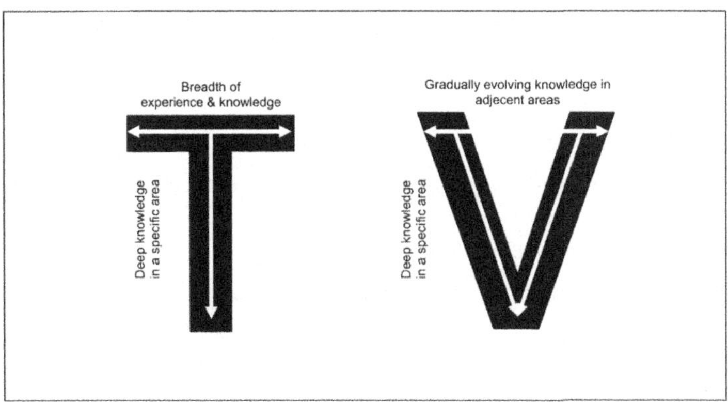

REALITY TECH

For one of Matthias' previous employers, the blueprint for a product team was: "8 +1 +1." This meant:

- eight engineers (the single technical role of individuals who develop, test, and run the software of the team)
- one product manager
- one UX designer

This represents a rather advanced setup that needs a lot of time and effort to develop the usually specialized people of the organization into a more T-shaped profile. Expect this to take years rather than months, but it is definitely worth it.

Small Enough to Be a Team, Big Enough to Be Effective

"The best teams are small enough to be agile and responsive, but large enough to bring diverse skills and perspectives to bear on complex problems."[5]

In successful software development organizations, the right team structure is crucial for peak performance, with team size playing a pivotal role in promoting efficiency, collaboration, and innovation.

However, there's no universally ideal team size; it varies from one team to another. A good rule of thumb is five to eleven people.

5. "Team of Teams: New Rules of Engagement for a Complex World" by General Stanley McChrystal, Tantum Collins, David Silverman, and Chris Fussell (Portfolio, 2015)

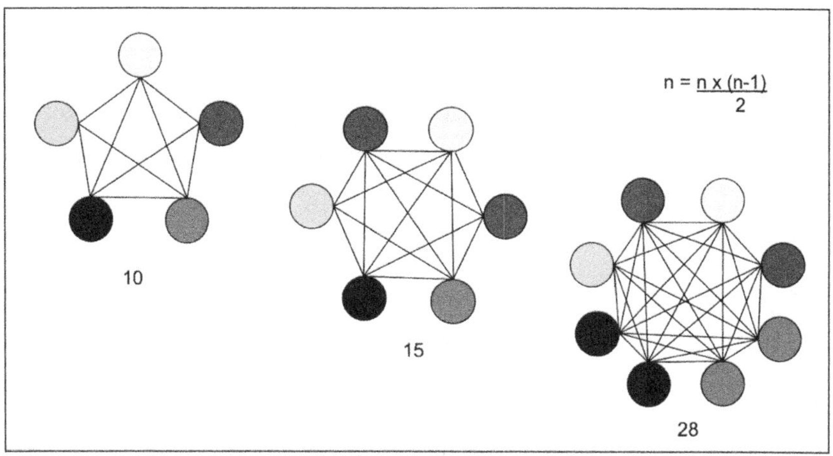

This range aligns with the concept of Dunbar's Number, a theory proposed by anthropologist Robin Dunbar. While originally suggesting that humans can maintain stable social relationships with about 150 people, Dunbar's work also identified smaller groupings. For close working relationships, the optimal number falls between five and 15 individuals. This range is thought to allow for effective communication, trust-building, and collaboration without overwhelming cognitive capacity or diluting personal connections.

Organizations often use heuristics to guide this decision. For instance, Amazon's approach is to form teams no larger than what two (American-sized) pizzas can feed, typically about eight people. Another common guideline is that teams "should be small enough to remain cohesive, yet large enough to be effective."

The size of the teams must be carefully monitored to avoid being too large or too small. Oversized teams tend to split into subgroups, each developing its own dynamics. This can lead to inefficiency, as these subgroups might not focus on the most critical tasks.

Conversely, teams that are too small may face operational challenges during absences, such as vacations or sickness, and may lack diversity, which can hinder long-term effectiveness. The key is finding a balance that ensures all team members are working on the most important tasks, maintaining the team's momentum and diversity.

Smaller teams tend to have more straightforward communication channels, which can lead to better collaboration and quicker decision-making.

The Team Organizes Itself (within the guidelines of the overall organization)

"The best architectures, requirements, and designs emerge from self-organizing teams." [Agile Manifesto]

In our experience, the teams that consistently outperformed were those empowered to organize and reorganize their work according to their unique needs without former permission because they were able to adapt to change. They operated very well without a manager consistently monitoring their activities and output on a daily or weekly basis.

Self-organized teams possess the capability, authority, and responsibility to decide on their work processes, tasks, and the best use of their collective skills. This autonomy, however, is exercised within the broader governance framework of the organization, aligning with essential guidelines like business and technology strategies, business priorities, and corporate culture. Importantly, these teams actively participate in defining these guidelines.

For self-organization to be successful, it requires trust from management and stakeholders, coupled with the team's transparency about their work methods and results, and openness to feedback.

Variations in team structure and methodologies are not only permitted but encouraged, as this diversity stimulates adaptability to immediate needs without cumbersome coordination and compromises. It also provides valuable learning opportunities for the organization to experiment with different approaches with minimal risk. We explain the aspect of team diversity in more detail in the next section.

In self-organized teams, leadership is fluid and situation-dependent, with any team member capable of assuming a leadership role based on the task at hand, the context, and their experience and skills. Clearly defining leadership distribution and decision-making processes is crucial for avoiding endless debates and indecision. Effective decision-making methods include the consensus model for significant, irreversible decisions and the majority model for more flexible, reversible decisions. For complex decisions, enlisting an external facilitator can be beneficial.

Regular retrospectives and feedback loops are vital for maintaining effective self-organization, with external feedback being a key component to consider.

Self-organized teams are not free radicals. How to establish guidelines for loosely coupled and self-organized teams from a technical, cultural, and business perspective is discussed in other chapters of this book.

The Right and Diverse Mix of Talent

"Diversity: the art of thinking independently together." — *Malcolm Forbes*[6]

Loosely coupled software development teams in large product development organizations benefit greatly from having the right diverse mix of talent. This concept goes beyond technical skills to include a wide range of experiences, backgrounds, and perspectives.

A truly diverse team brings together people with different:

- technical skills
- levels of experience
- domains of knowledge
- problem-solving approaches
- cultural backgrounds
- educational disciplines
- genders

This diversity creates a rich tapestry of skills and viewpoints that can significantly enhance team performance.

The importance of diversity cannot be overstated. When a team has a diverse mix of talents, it becomes more adept at solving complex problems. Different perspectives lead to more innovative solutions and better decisions. A diverse team is also more adaptable and able to pivot quickly when project requirements change or new technologies emerge.

A team that reflects the diversity of its user base is more likely to create products that resonate with a wide range of customers. The variety of viewpoints can spark creativity and prevent the team

---

6. Malcolm Forbes, as quoted in "Wisdom for a Young CEO: Incredible Letters and Inspiring Advice from Today's Business Leaders" by Douglas Barry (Running Press, 2004)

from falling into the trap of groupthink. Team members with complementary skills can learn from each other, filling knowledge gaps and continuously improving the team's overall capabilities.

Achieving this ideal mix of talent requires a conscious effort.

- Intentional hiring: Actively seek candidates with diverse backgrounds and skill sets.
- Promote inclusivity: Create an inclusive work environment where all team members feel valued and heard.
- Cross-functional collaboration: Encourage collaboration across teams, domains, and disciplines.
- Continuous learning: Provide opportunities for team members to learn new skills and technologies.
- Rotate team members: Periodically rotate team members to encourage knowledge sharing and fresh perspectives.
- Mentoring programs: Pair junior and senior team members to facilitate knowledge transfer and diverse viewpoints.
- Diversity and inclusion training: Provide training to help team members understand the value of diversity and how to work effectively in diverse teams.
- Balanced team composition: Consciously consider a mix of skills, experiences, and backgrounds when building teams.
- Open communication: Create an environment where team members feel comfortable sharing their unique perspectives.

If a team faces skills or diversity issues, it's important to address them proactively. If there's a skills gap, consider providing targeted training or bringing in outside expertise. This could include workshops, online courses, or pairing less experienced team members with mentors who can guide their skill development.

With diversity issues, it's important to first acknowledge the problem. Have honest discussions with the team about the benefits of diversity and how it can improve their work. Look for ways to bring in new perspectives, perhaps by collaborating with other teams or departments or by seeking input from a more diverse group of stakeholders.

If the lack of diversity is due to hiring practices, work with HR to revise recruitment strategies. This may include expanding candidate sources, rewriting job descriptions to be more inclusive, or implementing blind resume reviews to reduce unconscious bias.

REALITY TECH

An insightful lesson in creating diversity of mind as opposed to diversity based on "other factors" came from a team Sophie has extensively collaborated with: The existing team decided rather than simply hiring individuals who technically fit and easily meshed with the existing team, they implemented a "team recruiting process." This process involved candidates being interviewed by different people, including people who were explicitly not on the existing team, stimulating an objective view and challenging the team's dynamics. Despite the pressure to expedite hiring, the team consistently brought on board top performers and extraordinary talent, positively impacting the product in unique ways.

During periods of rapid organizational growth, companies often prioritize rapid hiring over careful team composition. However, our experience shows that teams deliberately built with diversity and exceptional talent in mind consistently outperform teams assembled based on availability. These thoughtfully assembled teams demonstrate greater innovation, engagement, and long-term productivity. While we recognize that real-world hiring practices don't always align with this ideal, we believe that actively thinking about and optimizing team composition is a critical responsibility of effective leadership.

The Team Runs What It Builds

"The traditional model is that you take your software to the wall that separates development and operations, and throw it over and then forget about it. Not at Amazon. You build it, you run it. This brings developers into contact with the day-to-day operation of their software." — Werner Vogels, 2006

"The team runs what it builds," more commonly known as "You build it, you run it" (YBIYRI), is a core principle of modern software development and operations. This principle means that the same team responsible for building a software product or service is also responsible for deploying, operating, and maintaining it in production environments. It's a key aspect of DevOps culture, breaking down the traditional separation between development and operations teams. The team takes full ownership of its product throughout its lifecycle.

This approach offers several key benefits. It increases accountability by making developers directly responsible for the performance and reliability of their code in production. This leads to higher-quality code and more robust systems because developers are incentivized to build with operational concerns in mind. It also accelerates the feedback loop, allowing teams to quickly learn from real-world usage and iterate accordingly. Teams gain a deeper understanding of their product in action, leading to more informed decisions and improvements. In addition, this model often results in faster deployment cycles and more efficient problem resolution because the team has comprehensive knowledge of the system.

There are several key steps to implementing this principle:

- Cross-training: Developers must learn operations skills and operations personnel must understand development processes.
- Shared ownership: Create a culture where the entire team feels accountable for both development and operations.
- Automate extensively: Implement robust CI/CD pipelines and infrastructure-as-code practices.
- On-call rotations: Have developers participate in on-call rotations to handle production issues.
- Monitoring and visibility: Implement comprehensive monitoring tools that give developers visibility into production performance.
- Blameless post-mortems: Encourage learning from mistakes without pointing fingers.
- Empower decision-making: Empower teams to make decisions about their product's infrastructure and operations.

Platforms and cloud technologies play a critical role in making this approach feasible and efficient. Cloud platforms provide a scalable, flexible infrastructure that teams can manage programmatically, eliminating much of the underlying complexity. Containerization technologies, such as Docker, and orchestration platforms, such as Kubernetes, enable consistent deployment across environments. Infrastructure-as-Code tools allow teams to manage their infrastructure alongside their application code while managed services from cloud providers can handle many operational tasks.

Cloud-native observability and monitoring tools give teams deep insight into the performance and health of their applications. Serverless technologies take abstraction even further, allowing teams to focus almost exclusively on application logic rather than infrastructure management.

For teams that follow the YBIYRI mode, cognitive load must be properly managed. We explain cognitive load in a later section of this chapter.

The Team Takes Care of Security and Data Protection

Security and data protection are core responsibilities of software development teams. Their responsibilities include adopting a security-first mindset, conducting regular threat modeling, adhering to secure coding practices, and integrating security testing into the development process. Teams are also responsible for managing vulnerabilities, ensuring compliance, implementing appropriate access controls, protecting sensitive data, participating in incident response, and managing third-party components.

To implement these responsibilities effectively, software development teams should:

- Implement Security as Code (SaC).
- Designate a security champion to liaise with the central security platform team (which we describe in more detail in Chapter 12).
- Maintain a dedicated security backlog.
- Incorporate security requirements into their feature development.
- Integrate automated security checks into their CI/CD pipeline.
- Implement security review gates.
- Provide regular security training.
- Track security metrics.
- Maintain up-to-date security.

Security as Code (SaC) is an approach that applies software engineering principles to cybersecurity, treating security configurations and policies as code. This methodology integrates security directly into the development and operations processes, allowing for automated, version-controlled, and repeatable security implementations. SaC enables teams to define, manage, and enforce security measures programmatically across cloud environments and application infrastructures. By codifying security practices, organizations can achieve more consistent, scalable, and auditable security postures. This approach aligns security with DevOps practices, encouraging collaboration between development, operations, and security teams. Ultimately, SaC helps organizations respond more quickly to threats, reduce human error, and maintain compliance in rapidly evolving technology landscapes.

By following these guidelines, product teams can effectively manage their security responsibilities while safely leveraging cloud technologies. This approach ensures that security is integrated throughout the development lifecycle, balances team autonomy with organizational security standards, and promotes a culture of continuous security improvement.

The Team Regularly Reflects and Improves on Its Outcome, Skills, Culture, Relationships, and Mechanism

"At regular intervals, the team reflects on how to become more effective, then tunes and adjusts its behavior accordingly." [Agile Manifesto]

In great tech organizations, especially those where teams run what they build, the practice of regular reflection and improvement is critical. This principle involves a team's continuous evaluation and improvement of its results, skills, culture, relationships, and operating mechanisms.

This approach is essential because the technology industry is in a constant state of change, with evolving technologies, changing market demands, and emerging best practices. Teams that don't adapt risk falling behind or becoming inefficient. Regular reflection prevents complacency, stimulates innovation, and ensures alignment with organizational goals and user needs.

The benefits of this practice are many. It leads to:

- Continuous improvements in team performance and product quality.
- Team cohesion and job satisfaction tend to increase because problems are addressed proactively.
- The team becomes more adaptable, responding effectively to changes in technology or business needs.
- The process often sparks innovative solutions and helps identify potential problems before they escalate.

Implementing this practice involves several key activities. Teams should schedule regular retrospectives, perhaps biweekly or monthly, to discuss successes, challenges, and areas for improvement. Using different retrospective formats keeps the process interesting. It's important to track action items from these sessions and review progress. Regular competency assessments help identify areas for team and individual growth.

Teams should regularly review and update their work agreements and best practices. Establishing stakeholder feedback mechanisms provides valuable insight into team performance and product quality. Conducting regular technical debt reviews and setting aside time to address them is also critical.

In an agile setup with self-organizing teams, managers play a supportive rather than directive role. They facilitate the reflection process without dominating it, ensure that teams have the resources they need, and help remove organizational barriers. Managers provide a broader perspective on how team improvements align with organizational goals, offer coaching and mentoring, and encourage psychological safety for honest feedback. They also connect the team to other parts of the organization and advocate for the team's needs at higher levels.

When teams or divisions struggle with self-improvement, it's important to investigate the root causes. These may include a lack of time, skills, motivation, or understanding of the importance. Providing additional training or bringing in external facilitators can help jumpstart the process. Sharing success stories from other teams can illustrate the benefits. In some cases, temporarily increasing management involvement can guide the process until it becomes self-sustaining.

Setting specific, measurable improvement goals can create focus and motivation. Implementing cross-team reviews or peer feedback provides valuable outside perspectives. If interpersonal issues impede effective reflection, team composition may need to be reconsidered. Aligning improvement activities with performance reviews can reinforce their importance.

Regular team reflection is important, but it's useless if the issues aren't solved. When teams address problems, they make progress, take ownership, develop new skills, build trust, and improve. To make this effective, teams should prioritize, set deadlines, allocate, and follow up. Celebrating and learning are also key. Leaders help by removing obstacles and providing resources. This makes reflection useful for improving the team. It also makes the team more dynamic and innovative.

The Team Is Culturally and Strategically Aligned with the Rest of the Organization

Each team must be culturally and strategically aligned with the rest of the organization. This means that the cultural values and norms of the organization are widely accepted and promoted.

While team autonomy is critical in agile organizations, it must be balanced with organizational alignment. This is important because of:

- Coherent product development: Alignment ensures that autonomous teams are working toward common organizational goals rather than pursuing disparate ones.
- Efficient resource allocation: When teams are aligned, the organization can more effectively allocate resources based on overall strategic priorities.
- Consistent user experience: Alignment helps maintain a consistent user experience across different products or features developed by different teams.
- Reduced duplication of effort: Aligned teams are more aware of what others are doing, reducing the likelihood of redundant work.
- Faster decision-making: When teams understand the broader context, they can make decisions faster and more confidently without having to run back and forth with management.
- Improved collaboration: Alignment creates a common language and understanding, facilitating better cross-team collaboration when needed.
- Stronger culture: Alignment reinforces company values and culture across teams, creating a more cohesive work environment.

By implementing these practices, organizations can maintain a balance between team autonomy and organizational alignment. Teams retain the freedom to make decisions in their own areas while ensuring that their efforts contribute cohesively to the overall organizational strategy and culture. An easy way to do this is to integrate cultural values into the regular people-development process.

REALITY TECH

As a best practice, we want to highlight one of Sophie's approaches: One of the core values was to be 'collaborative,' so we asked people to give themselves 360 feedback on how they were living up to this value. This included not only feedback from the team but perhaps also from stakeholders or sometimes even from suppliers. A simple, yet effective idea that can be implemented without any budget or major initiatives.

In addition, the overall strategy of the product organization is periodically put into perspective for the entire organization. The strategy update highlights successes and areas that need to be focused on or improved. Long-, medium-, and short-term goals are transparent to the entire organization, and every team knows exactly what their contribution is to those goals. The overall strategy must be laid out so that the teams can operationalize it. Nothing is worse than a team guessing what is expected of them.

Ideally, in larger planning sessions where multiple teams come together, time is spent getting everyone to understand the strategy and getting the teams to translate those strategies into actionable items. For example, a long-term goal might be to increase sales by x%. This is obviously not just a task for the product team to optimize the checkout process, but it has the whole chain of events, including moving more people from the top of the funnel to the bottom of the funnel by creating attractive and new product offers.

Functional People Managers Are Not Part of the Team

"The manager's function is not to make people work, but to make it possible for people to work." — Tom DeMarco

Chapter 2: How to Set Up a Team describes how self-organized teams have the ability, authority, and responsibility to decide on their work processes, tasks, and the best use of their collective skills. Nonetheless, the role of people managers is still necessary. These people managers focus on hiring, coaching, mentoring, and career and organizational development. They provide support, guidance, and resources needed by the team. Their primary focus is on the professional and personal development of team members.

People managers in agile setups also pay close attention to team dynamics, ensuring that the team functions effectively as a unit. They may intervene if there are issues affecting team performance or cohesion.

These people managers have deep, hands-on experience in a job family and manage only team members in that job family. It is only through this experience that they can effectively develop the team members of a discipline. As a result, team members report to different people managers.

In self-organized teams, people managers typically lead individuals across multiple teams. For example, an engineering manager might manage twelve engineers spread across two or more teams while a UX manager might manage eight UX designers spread across eight different teams. The ideal management span ranges from six to twelve direct reports depending on the manager's experience, the needs of the team members, and the specific circumstances of the organization.

We discourage having all team members report to a single team manager. While this approach may be beneficial for team dynamics, it can limit opportunities for specialized professional development. Instead, we prioritize functional or disciplinary reporting lines to promote the development of people we believe are critical to long-term success and innovation.

Importantly, these functional or disciplinary people managers are not embedded within the product teams. This separation creates non-hierarchical self-organized teams where all members interact on an equal footing regardless of seniority or role. This structure is important for creating an environment where each team member feels empowered to speak up, promoting true autonomy and encouraging diverse perspectives.

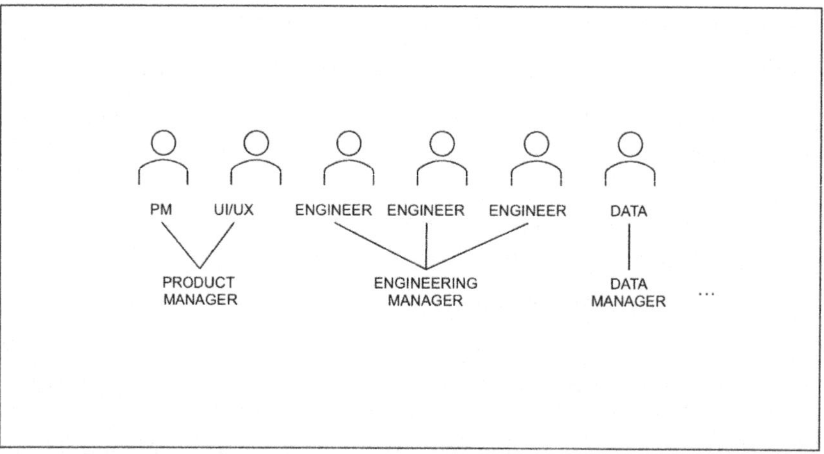

Team members are assigned to specific functional areas such as product management, engineering, QA, operations, or UX. While we try to minimize the number of these functional divisions for simplicity, they serve an important purpose. For example, UX designers belong to the UX function for professional development and standards, but their primary affiliation and day-to-day work is with their cross-functional product team.

This dual affiliation provides several benefits:

- Career development: Functional managers can focus on long-term skill development and career progression within their discipline.
- Best practices: Functional groups can share best practices and maintain consistency across product teams.
- Resource flexibility: This structure makes it easier to reallocate resources between teams as project needs change.
- Performance Management: Provides a more holistic view of an individual's performance, combining input from both the functional manager and the product team.
- Conflict resolution: Functional managers can serve as neutral parties in resolving conflicts within product teams.
- Organizational alignment: They can help translate broader organizational strategies into specific functional areas across multiple teams.

While team members are autonomous in their day-to-day work and decision-making within their product teams, they can turn to their functional managers for career guidance, performance feedback, and resolution of issues that go beyond the scope of their immediate team. This balance is designed to provide the benefits of specialization and career development while maintaining the agility and autonomy of self-organized teams.

We will dive into this topic in Chapter 15: How to Lead and Manage Within a Tech Organization.

Valid Variants for Different Situations

Adapt Your Teams to Different Contexts

When building a great tech organization, it's crucial to recognize that the principles of great teams apply beyond just software development. While many associate cross-functional, agile teams with coding, this model can be equally effective for teams managing SaaS solutions, COTS applications, or even specific features within these systems.

The key is to adapt the team structure and mindset to the specific context of your product or service. A team responsible for a complex SAP implementation, for instance, may not write custom code daily, but they still benefit from the same core characteristics: clear product ownership, cross-functionality, and a focus on business outcomes.

Consider a team managing critical SaaS software for your organization. They might not be building the software from scratch, but they are:

- Responsible for the software's success and alignment with business goals
- Configuring and customizing the solution to meet the organization's specific needs
- Ensuring seamless integration with other systems
- Managing updates, security, and performance
- Driving user adoption and continuously improving processes

These teams require the same mix of skills, autonomy, and long-term focus as traditional development teams. They need to understand the business domain deeply, collaborate across functions, and take ownership of their product's success.

The goal is to create empowered, accountable teams that can drive innovation and deliver value regardless of whether they're building custom software, managing SaaS solutions, or optimizing COTS applications. By adapting the team model to different contexts while maintaining core principles, organizations can build a truly responsive and effective tech organization.

Dynamic Mission and Liquid Teams for Certain Situations

In general, we recommend steady teams that have existed for a long time and whose team members change rarely. Under certain conditions, however, it can make sense to choose other team constellations. Jurgen Appelo's unfix model describes three other constellations very well:

- Dynamic Teams: These teams are long-lived, but team members change regularly. In our experience, this is a valid setup for platform teams. For platform teams, we recommend that for up to one-third of the platform, engineers rotate into product teams each quarter to consume their products and free up seats for product team engineers to co-create the next version of platform services.
- Mission Teams: These are short-lived teams to accomplish a specific mission. The team membership is stable for this short time. This can be useful when team members from multiple teams need to work together to launch a software product in a new market.
- Liquid Teams: These are short-lived teams where team members come and go. This might be the case to solve a larger incident or outage.

In-House Teams as a Best Practice

Building an in-house software development capability has become a best practice for many organizations that recognize software as a future pillar of their business. Our experience is based primarily on having a large in-house team capable of handling the entire product development chain independently. This setup gives you many advantages:

- Cultural Alignment: In-house developers share the company's values and goals, cultivating a stronger commitment to long-term success.
- Improved Communication: Direct, real-time communication with in-house teams leads to faster decision-making and fewer misunderstandings.
- Deeper Product Knowledge: In-house teams have a better understanding of the company's products, allowing for more tailored and effective solutions.
- Greater Flexibility: In-house developers can quickly adapt to changing business needs, ensuring faster iterations and more agile responses.
- Higher Quality Control: Companies have more oversight of coding standards and product quality, leading to better outcomes.
- Cost Efficiency: Although hiring in-house has a higher upfront cost, it avoids ongoing outsourcing fees and retains full ownership of the code.
- Enhanced Security: In-house teams provide better control over sensitive data, reducing risks associated with outsourcing.
- Team Cohesion: In-house teams develop stronger working relationships and a sense of ownership, improving collaboration and morale.
- Career Development: Companies can invest in their developers' growth, leading to higher retention and a more skilled workforce.

Collaboration with third parties remains relevant and can be advantageous in certain cases. For example, to ramp up and share knowledge, to balance capacity constraints, or simply to challenge your teams from time to time and gain new insights, having mixed teams or parts of them remaining in day-to-day business. Maintaining a balance between internal and external teams is key to ensuring that internal teams continue to add value and own the entire development process.

Virtual/Remote and Hybrid Teams

Co-located teams excel in tight cohesion and rapid, direct communication, facilitating swift problem-solving, effective brainstorming, and quicker decision-making. The adoption of remote and hybrid team setups has become widespread, extending beyond the pandemic. Virtual teams operate from different geographic locations while hybrid teams seamlessly blend office and remote work.

Diverse team configurations offer numerous advantages: a larger talent pool with remote work options, potentially competitive day rates, and remote work becoming a baseline preference post-pandemic. Yet, ensuring the performance of non-co-located teams presents challenges, such as maintaining effective communication across time zones, strengthening team cohesion without face-to-face interactions, managing work/life balance in home-office settings, ensuring equitable participation in hybrid meetings, and mitigating the potential for isolation or disconnection among remote team members.

Foundational elements are crucial for success. Language plays a key role in interaction; establishing accessible language courses and conducting interviews in the agreed language are vital. Consistent use of the same language in documentation and meetings enhances inclusivity, a cornerstone of high-performing teams.

In various team setups, regular in-person meetings are essential for enriching team identity, strengthening relationships, and enhancing morale. Leaders should maintain an open dialogue about expectations on being onsite, considering the challenges of a daily commute.

For teams spanning multiple locations, routine meetings or virtual setups facilitate quick communication and enhance project success. While travel costs are often cut in tough times, safeguarding a budget for onsite collaboration is vital for team success.

Lastly, ensuring uninterrupted work, especially in remote settings is essential. Creating quiet zones or allowing remote work without disturbance supports productivity, particularly for developers sensitive to noisy office environments.

DevOps and SRE as an Alternative to You-Build-It-You-Run-It

"You build it, you run it" (YBIYRI) is currently the most advanced variant of DevOps, but it is difficult to achieve. This might overwhelm some organizations that are still at the beginning, especially when your IT operations are still in their organizational silo manually managing on-premise data centers (or something in-between). The technical, cultural, and organizational changes required for YBIYRI are daunting for many organizations.

One valid variation that already brings many benefits in terms of lead time, throughput, quality, and motivation is true DevOps, which is challenging enough. We are talking about DevOps in the traditional sense, where software development and IT operations departments work together efficiently in a spirit of partnership and appreciation.

In short, the most important thing is that both parties understand that they have a common goal: to create value for the customer and that they can only be successful if they work together.

To achieve this, the causes of historical conflict must be addressed. These are primarily poor-quality software releases on the development side; unstable, unavailable, and disparate test and production environments on the operations side; and a lack of direct communication.

We explain the necessary practices for reliable, fast, and reproducible software deliveries in Chapter 9 - How to Deliver Twice As Fast.

Google's Site Reliability Model, which is Google's specific implementation of DevOps practices could be a proven and well-documented approach for you as well.

A Tech Lead Helps the Team Become Technically Self-Sufficient

"On the best teams, different individuals provide occasional leadership, taking charge in areas where they have particular strengths. No one is the permanent leader, because that person would then cease to be a peer and the team interaction would begin to break down." — Tom DeMarco, Peopleware: Productive Projects and Teams

In well-established teams, a formal tech lead who makes technical decisions isn't necessary. These teams self-organize and make decisions collectively through consensus or majority vote.

However, in scenarios where new technologies or architectures are being adopted (like microservices, event-driven systems, data mesh, or cloud-native services), having a tech lead is beneficial. This individual who holds a senior role not only possesses deep technical knowledge but also provides leadership.

- They steer the team's technical direction
- They mentor members

- They tackle complex issues
- They work in tandem with various team roles

While leading, they also actively contribute to coding and maintaining high quality in the project. Crucial to their role is effective communication and ensuring the team's efforts align with project objectives.

The long-term aim for a tech lead is to gradually become redundant, equipping the team to independently make decisions. As an interim step, a tech coach can be introduced to guide the team in making sound technical choices, bridging the gap between a formal tech lead and a fully self-organized team.

Common Misconceptions and Mistakes

Mismanaging Cognitive Load

Cognitive load refers to the amount of mental effort being used in a person's working memory. In the context of teams that build and run their code (YBIYRI), cognitive load can become a significant challenge due to the breadth of responsibilities team members are expected to handle. There are two sides to mismanaging cognitive load:

- Overloading: Some organizations push too much responsibility onto their teams without proper support or resources. This can lead to burnout, decreased productivity, and lower-quality work. Team members might struggle to keep up with both development and operational tasks, leading to stress and potential system failures.
- Underutilizing: On the flip side, some organizations might use cognitive load as an excuse to avoid necessary changes or to maintain outdated structures. They might resist

giving teams full ownership of their systems, citing concerns about overwhelming them. This can lead to missed opportunities for innovation and growth.

To effectively manage cognitive load in software development teams, organizations should focus on a balanced approach.

- Regularly assess team cognitive load through health checks and adjust responsibilities accordingly.
- Set realistic expectations and encourage cross-team collaboration to share expertise.
- Provide regular breaks and focus time to manage cognitive load.
- Maintain strong feedback loops between teams and management to address issues quickly.

The goal is to challenge teams to grow while providing the necessary resources, striking the right balance that allows teams to handle complex systems efficiently without becoming overwhelmed.

Overload Due to Incident Management & Support Activities

For YBIYRI teams, managing incidents outside of regular business hours is a significant challenge that impacts work-life balance, fairness, and compensation. The most effective mitigation strategy is to make stability, availability, and performance the top team priorities, giving teams the freedom to decide how much effort to put into hardening their applications. This approach, combined with cloud technologies that massively reduce operational overhead and increase the resilience of applications, can significantly reduce after-hours incidents.

Other best practices to reduce overwork include rotating on-call responsibilities, establishing clear escalation procedures, developing incident playbooks, and conducting post-incident reviews. Automated monitoring and well-defined severity levels help manage response times effectively.

Fair solutions balance the needs of employees and employers. For employees, this may include additional compensation, time off, flexible work schedules, and mental health support. Employers should establish clear policies, invest in automation, and provide cross-training opportunities. Regular policy reviews and ongoing dialog between management and teams are critical for adapting to evolving needs.

The goal is to ensure system reliability and customer satisfaction while respecting the well-being of team members, leveraging cloud technologies and automation to minimize out-of-hours disruptions.

Too Much Team Autonomy Reduces the Performance of the Entire Organization

"To achieve autonomy, not anarchy, you need a model that makes autonomy work." —Gregor Hohpe[7]

Autonomy and loose coupling is the secret sauce to increasing performance and speed in organizations. The more autonomy a team has, the shorter the lead times, and as the performance of individual teams increases, so does the performance of the entire organization. This is only true up to a point, after which the performance of the teams continues to increase, but the performance of the organization as a whole, especially from the point of view of the end customer, declines.

---

7. Gregor Hohpe—former AWS Enterprise Strategist: https://aws.amazon.com/executive-insights/content/the-customer-centric-cio/

An example of too much autonomy is when teams are free to choose their technology stack, especially their programming language. This has massive implications for the collaboration model and code-sharing model of the teams. If two teams use the same programming language, several of these models are possible (e.g., pull request or even collective code ownership) with different degrees of coupling. If they use different programming languages, there is only one high-coupling collaboration model. One team must ask the other to make the necessary adjustments.

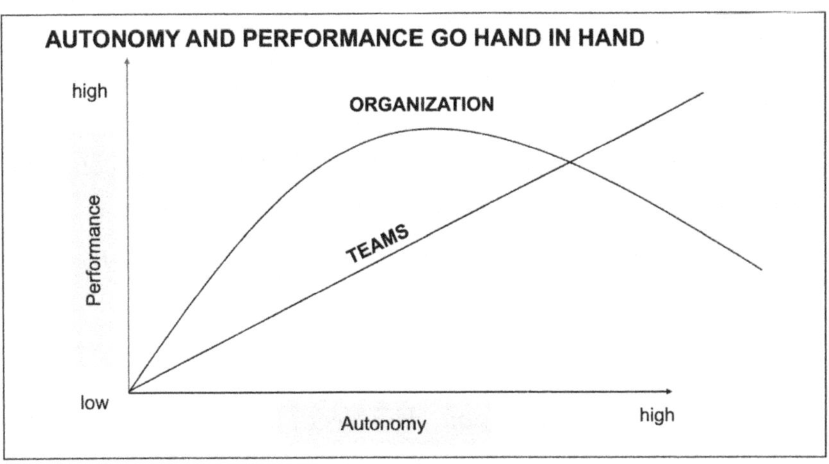

High-performing teams thrive on the principles of self-organization and empowerment, which are closely tied to team autonomy. While this approach may appear to grant teams boundless freedom, there's a risk of teams becoming detached from organizational objectives and pursuing their own agendas. Thus, it's crucial to establish and communicate a framework for collaborative work effectively.

A mere email with guidelines won't suffice. For instance, engineers may be eager to experiment with new coding languages or tools. While exploration is encouraged, adherence to overarching technical guidelines is essential. Individual preferences may overlook potential issues such as licensing concerns or resource scarcity. Balancing these trade-offs requires clear communication between the team and the organization.

In some cases, organizations allow teams to choose their technology stack. This approach can lead to scalability challenges; hence, clear and communicated guidelines are imperative. An open feedback culture enhances the adaptation and improvement of these guidelines, benefiting the entire organization.

Guidelines shouldn't be dictated by central entities but developed by respected experts within the organization. They encompass various aspects like culture, technology, design, and business practices. Merely relying on teams to figure things out independently isn't sufficient; leadership plays a pivotal role in aligning teams with the broader organizational objectives.

Too Many Compromises

Building high-performing teams is the foundation of any successful great technology organization. However, many well-intentioned attempts to become such an organization have failed due to a variety of trade-offs.

Examples abound, such as maintaining traditional reporting lines despite implementing cross-functional teams, individuals juggling multiple initiatives simultaneously, excessive documentation that inhibits team autonomy, and outsourcing critical development work to third parties.

Transitioning to a great engineering organization is not a simple reorganization; it's a comprehensive and time-intensive process that requires reevaluating roles, processes, and tasks. This holistic endeavor requires significant time for discovery, rethinking, and realignment, often spanning months or even years. It's critical to approach this transformation with patience, commitment, and a willingness to challenge existing norms.

To successfully navigate this complex transformation, organizations should take a phased approach. Start by clearly articulating the vision for the great tech organization and securing buy-in from key stakeholders. Then, identify pilot teams or projects to implement changes on a smaller scale, allowing for learning and adaptation before a broader rollout. Invest heavily in change management, providing training and support to help people adapt to new ways of working. Evaluate progress regularly, celebrate small wins, and address challenges promptly. Create feedback loops to gather insights from all levels of the organization, and be prepared to iterate on your approach. Most importantly, leadership must consistently model the desired behaviors and mindset and demonstrate an unwavering commitment to the transformation, even in the face of setbacks. Remember, the goal is not perfection, but continuous improvement toward becoming a great technology organization.

Unhealthy Ratio of Builders to Non-Builders

The larger the organization, the more roles seem necessary to complete a work package from idea to impact. However, in traditional organizations, the majority of these roles are not actively involved in the ongoing development of the product, especially the software. In some organizations, we've observed that only 20% of the team members were software developers while the rest had descriptive, testing, or advisory roles.

The Agile Manifesto principle that "working software is the primary measure of progress" emphasizes that software developers who build the actual software are the core team members. While all roles and skills contribute valuable expertise to the product development process, it's the developers who create the tangible, working product that delivers value to users. Other roles perform necessary and supportive work, but the developer's role is central to the team's primary output.

It's important to maintain a healthy balance between developers and support roles while reducing the number of non-software artifacts in the organization. In the context of a lean organization, excessive non-software artifacts are often considered waste and can indicate fundamental weaknesses that need to be addressed. For example, business analysts and architects may produce numerous documents describing the intended functionality, architecture, and design of the software. While some documentation is necessary, an overabundance of these artifacts without corresponding working software can slow the development process and potentially lead to a misalignment between the documented intent and the actual product.

In a great tech organization, the focus should be on producing working software, not extensive documentation. This doesn't mean eliminating all documentation, but rather ensuring that it directly supports the development process and doesn't become an end in itself. The goal is to strike a balance where support functions enhance the ability of developers to produce high-quality software efficiently rather than adding bureaucratic overhead.

Getting People Management Wrong

A critical, often overlooked aspect of this transformation is clearly defining the role of leaders. There are several common pitfalls in this area. Some organizations mistakenly have managers double as agile coaches or scrum masters, creating potential conflicts of interest and undermining team self-organization. Conversely, others go to the extreme of making managers pure people managers with unrealistic spans of control, sometimes overseeing 50 to 80 people. This approach often results in superficial management and disconnection from the daily challenges of the team.

Another misstep is to eliminate people managers altogether in an attempt to be "fully agile." This can leave team members without the career guidance and professional development support they need. Equally problematic is when managers remain too operationally involved and struggle to step back from their previous hands-on roles. This can inhibit team autonomy and stifle leadership development within the team.

The key is to strike a balance. Managers should provide strategic guidance, support team members' growth and career development, and facilitate rather than control the team's work. They must create an environment of psychological safety where teams feel comfortable speaking up, experimenting, and acquiring new skills. This requires a conscious effort to cultivate trust and openness within the organization.

In summary, effective people management in a great tech organization involves more than just managing the change process. It requires clearly defining the role of leaders, providing appropriate support structures, and creating an environment that nurtures continuous learning and adaptation. This delicate balance requires constant attention and adjustment throughout the transformation journey. We explain the role of managers in more detail in Chapter 13.

Individual Goals and Rewards Encourage the Wrong Behavior

While well-intentioned, individual goals and rewards in a team environment can often have unintended negative consequences. When team members are incentivized based on personal achievements, it can create a competitive environment that undermines collaboration and overall team success. This approach can encourage individuals to prioritize their own goals over the collective goals of the team or organization.

In a great tech organization, the focus should be on individual development goals for every team member without any monetary compensation. Team performance should be measured based on speed, value, and quality. Yearly bonuses can be arranged based on overall business performance. This approach enables the team to put personal ambitions aside and focus on the overall achievement of the business.

TL;DR and Further Reading

As a first step, looking at your current people and understanding where their workload is currently allocated can give many insights into the effectiveness of your organization. Try to focus on one team and focus their work entirely on that product. You can encourage your team to look at their roles from different perspectives without necessarily adding more resources right away (e.g., try to put the QA hat on, try to put the data hat on, etc.).

- Clear and long-term responsibility for a product
- The team is responsible for the commercial success of the product
- The team optimizes effectiveness first and efficiency second
- Team members work exclusively in a team
- Team members are on the team for the long haul
- A cross-functional team with members from all necessary functions
- Small enough to be a team, big enough to be effective
- The team organizes itself within the guidelines of the overall organization
- The right and diverse mix of talent

- The team runs what it builds
- The team takes care of security and data protection
- The team regularly reflects and improves on its outcome, skills, culture, and relationships and mechanism
- The team is culturally and strategically aligned with the rest of the organization
- Functional people managers are not part of the team

For a more in-depth look at this topic, these are some of our favorite books and websites:

- "Management 3.0: Leading Agile Developers, Developing Agile Leaders," by Jurgen Appelo
- "Succeeding with Agile," by Mike Cohn
- "The Five Dysfunctions of a Team: A Leadership Fable," 20th Anniversary Edition by Patrick M. Lencioni
- "Agile Retrospectives: Making Good Teams Great," by Esther Derby, Diana Larsen

3

HOW TO SET FOCUS AND DIRECTION

IN GREAT TECH ORGANIZATIONS, achieving alignment and focus across loosely coupled teams is a critical challenge that can make or break success. Without a clear, shared direction, even the most talented teams can find themselves working at cross-purposes, leading to wasted resources, missed opportunities, and a lack of cohesive impact. This chapter addresses the vital question of how to set focus and direction in a way that empowers autonomous teams while ensuring they collectively drive toward common goals.

Our approach balances organizational cohesion with the flexibility required in today's fast-paced tech landscape, using tools like compelling missions, Wardley maps, and adaptive strategy formulation.

The chapter begins by examining traditional top-down approaches to strategy and their limitations in great tech environments. We then introduce a comprehensive framework for setting direction in loosely coupled organizations, including techniques for crafting resonant purposes, defining high-stakes challenges, and establishing North Star metrics. Along the way, we'll debunk common misconceptions about strategy in agile contexts, address potential pitfalls, and explore variations of the model to suit different organizational needs.

By the end of this chapter, you'll be equipped with practical tools and insights to facilitate alignment, drive focus, and cultivate a strategic mindset across your entire tech organization, ensuring that autonomy and alignment work in harmony to propel your company forward.

The Traditional Approach and Why It Falls Short

In many traditional IT organizations, the approach to setting focus and direction for software development teams often falls short of facilitating true strategic alignment. This traditional method frequently leads to disconnection and inefficiency.

One primary issue is the misalignment of purpose. Companies often lose sight of their true mission, reducing their goals to purely financial metrics. This shift toward "making money" as the primary objective waters down the organization's original purpose, leaving employees struggling to identify with company goals and losing sight of customer needs. Similarly, outsourcing strategy development to external consultants can create a significant gap between vision statements and the day-to-day reality experienced by employees. This disconnection can lead to decreased engagement and a lack of authentic inspiration within the workforce.

Another problematic aspect is the tendency to create overly broad, all-encompassing strategy statements. While intended to demonstrate inclusivity and ethical responsibility, these wide-reaching visions often fail to provide clear direction. They can blur an organization's unique strengths and challenges, weakening strategic focus and making it difficult for employees to see how their work contributes to overarching goals. This lack of specificness not only hinders effective resource deployment and innovation but also reduces these critical statements to mere rhetoric, failing to distinguish the company in a competitive landscape.

Furthermore, the traditional approach often relies on intensive planning and research to reduce uncertainties. While this seems logical, it can lead to rigid strategies that are slow to adapt to rapidly changing market conditions. This inflexibility can result in missed opportunities and compromised competitiveness in an environment where agility and responsiveness are crucial.

Collectively, these traditional practices create a significant disconnect between strategy and execution in traditional IT organizations. The result is often a workforce that views strategic goals as abstract concepts rather than actionable principles, leading to reduced engagement and effectiveness. As technology and markets continue to evolve at an unprecedented pace, it's clear that a new approach is needed—one that can bridge the gap between high-level strategy and day-to-day operations in software development teams.

The General Blueprint

Align and Focus the Technology Organization with a Compelling Purpose and Mission

"When you're surrounded by people who share a passionate commitment around a common purpose, anything is possible." — Howard Schultz, Starbucks

In loosely coupled software development organizations, a clear purpose and mission are essential for alignment and focus. They provide a unifying direction that guides decision-making, promotes unity of direction, and enhances motivation across teams. This shared guidance allows for autonomy while ensuring that all efforts contribute to common goals, balancing flexibility with cohesion.

A purpose is the fundamental reason an organization exists. It articulates why the company, domain, or team does what it does, beyond making money or achieving specific goals. A purpose answers the question, "Why do we exist?" It's aspirational, enduring, and gets to the heart of what the organization stands for. A well-defined purpose inspires and guides decision-making at all levels, providing a sense of meaning and direction that transcends individual projects or goals.

An example purpose statement for a sports apparel company might be: "To lead the future of athletics, technology, and sustainability in the sportswear industry."

A mission is a clear, actionable statement that defines what an organization, domain, or team does to achieve its purpose. It outlines the primary goals and approaches to creating value for stakeholders. A mission answers the questions, "What are we doing?" and "How are we doing it?" It's more specific and practical than the purpose, often including a timeframe or measurable goals. A good mission statement provides clarity about the organization's focus, its target audience, and the unique value it seeks to deliver.

An example mission statement for the tech organization of a sports apparel company might be: "We build advanced technologies that transform the way athletes engage with our products, from smart apparel to immersive retail experiences, while optimizing our supply chain for sustainability and efficiency."

In essence, the purpose provides the "why," while the mission provides the "what" and "how." Together, they provide a powerful framework for guiding the strategy and operations of an organization or team.

The process of defining a tech organization's purpose and mission begins with a comprehensive understanding of the company's overarching business strategy. Tech leaders work closely with business executives to interpret how the business strategy should inform and shape the tech organization's focus. Through workshops and interviews, they gather input from various stakeholders to ensure the tech strategy is a direct extension of the business strategy. Initial drafts of purpose and mission statements for the tech organization are created, always with the question in mind: "How does this serve our overall business objectives?"

These drafts are refined through iterative feedback, consistently validating that they are not merely aligned with, but fundamentally driven by the broader organizational goals. The statements are then presented to senior leadership for approval and tested with employees before being widely communicated and integrated into strategic planning and operations.

This collaborative process, with its emphasis on open communication, ensures that the tech organization's guiding principles are not just compatible with, but directly derived from the company's strategic direction. Regular reviews maintain this intrinsic connection as the organization evolves, promoting a tech strategy that is always in service of the company's broader business strategy.

Effective purpose and mission statements for aligning domains and loosely coupled teams share key characteristics.

- They are clear, concise, and inspiring, avoiding jargon in favor of accessible language that motivates and energizes.
- Good purpose and mission statements are relevant and specific to the teams' work, yet flexible enough to be applied across contexts.

- They provide actionable guidance for day-to-day decisions while remaining forward-looking, focusing on long-term impact.
- Importantly, these statements should be measurable so that teams can track progress and success.
- The best purpose and mission statements are inclusive and resonate with all team members regardless of role or location.
- They highlight the unique value of the domain's contribution, differentiating it while connecting it to the broader organizational purpose.

This balance—aligned and distinct—is key to their effectiveness in a loosely coupled environment.

By creating and communicating such purpose and mission statements, leaders can create a sense of shared identity and direction. This approach empowers teams to make independent decisions that consistently advance organizational goals, nurturing an environment where autonomy and alignment coexist productively in modern software development organizations.

Use High-Stakes Challenges to Define and Develop Your Strategy

At the core of any successful strategy on the organizational level is a thorough description and analysis of the organization's high-stakes challenge—a single obstacle that must be overcome to ensure long-term growth and relevance to customers.

The basic idea is that by identifying and focusing on this high-stakes challenge, organizations can align their efforts, resources, and strategies to tackle the most crucial issue that will determine their future success on a strategic level. This approach helps prioritize initiatives and create a clear direction for the entire organization.

Overcoming high-stakes challenges is crucial to organizations. They are often complex and carry significant risks and consequences. Therefore, it is vital to meticulously analyze these problems, investigating their root causes with a hypothesis-driven approach. To identify high-stakes challenges, organizations must analyze industry trends and disruptions, assess internal capabilities and weaknesses, gather input from stakeholders across the organization, evaluate the competitive landscape and market dynamics, consider regulatory and technological changes, and examine financial and operational risks. This comprehensive approach ensures that all potential major challenges are considered.

When describing high-stakes challenges, it's important to articulate the challenge in simple, understandable terms, explain its potential impact on the organization, outline the timeframe for addressing it, identify key stakeholders and affected departments, highlight the consequences of not addressing the challenge, and quantify potential outcomes where possible. This clear description helps create a shared understanding across the organization.

As an example, traditional banks face a critical high-stakes challenge: *modernizing legacy systems and processes to deliver competitive digital banking services while maintaining security and regulatory compliance*. This challenge is exacerbated by neo-banks such as Nubank, Monzo, and Revolut as well as digitally-advanced traditional banks such as Capital One and BBVA.

To remain competitive, traditional banks will need to:

- Make significant investments in IT infrastructure and cybersecurity
- Overhaul decades-old core banking systems
- Cultivate a culture of agility and innovation
- Rethink branch networks and digital customer engagement strategies
- Manage the risk of system failures or security breaches during the transition

Strategies to address this challenge include incrementally modernizing core banking systems, partnering with or acquiring fintech companies, creating internal innovation labs or digital-only subsidiaries, leveraging AI and machine learning to improve services and risk management, and emphasizing trustworthiness, security, and comprehensive service offerings as competitive advantages.

Address different parts of the problem separately. A thorough diagnosis clarifies the problem, enabling strategic choices and options. Based on this diagnosis, develop a strategy as an approach for addressing the challenge. This strategy:

- sets the direction for the organization
- provides criteria for decision-making
- focuses efforts and resources on the most critical areas
- streamlines the decision-making process during strategy execution

Defining a strategy based on high-stakes challenges involves prioritizing challenges based on urgency and potential impact; setting clear, measurable objectives for addressing each challenge; identifying required resources and capabilities; developing action plans with specific initiatives and timelines; assigning responsibilities and creating accountability structures; and establishing metrics to track progress and success.

This structured approach ensures that the strategy is directly tied to addressing the most critical issues facing the organization. We describe how to execute a strategy coherently in Chapter 7 - How to Execute Your Strategy for Maximum Impact and Flexibility.

Breaking down this single high-stakes organizational challenge into domain-specific challenges is a valid and effective approach. It balances alignment with autonomy, improves scalability, and allows each domain to focus on specific aspects of the overall organizational challenge.

Applying this concept to a loosely coupled, domain-driven tech organization requires clear communication of the high-stakes challenges across all domains. Each domain should be allowed to interpret how the challenges relate to their specific areas and develop localized strategies that align with the overall challenge. Cross-domain collaboration should be facilitated to address challenges holistically.

Different parts of an organization contribute differently to overcoming this high-stakes challenge. Each area, and in the context of this book, the tech area, describes its contribution and its strategy for overcoming the challenges.

The responsibility for high-stakes challenges and driving them forward is typically distributed across different levels of the organization, with clear ownership at each level.

Here's a breakdown of responsibilities at the organizational level:

- The CEO or chief strategy officer is ultimately responsible for identifying and articulating the overarching high-stakes challenge for the entire organization. They ensure that this challenge is aligned with the company's vision, mission, and long-term goals.
- The executive leadership team (C-suite) collectively owns the responsibility for addressing the high-stakes challenge. They work together to develop the overall strategy and ensure that resources are allocated appropriately across the organization.
- A dedicated strategy team or office often assists the C-suite in analyzing, documenting, and communicating the high-stakes challenge and related strategies.

At the domain level:

- Domain leaders (e.g., VPs, directors, or department heads) are responsible for interpreting the organizational high-stakes challenge in the context of their specific domain. They identify how their domain can contribute to addressing the challenge.
- These domain leaders are also responsible for articulating domain-specific challenges that align with and support the overarching organizational challenge. They drive strategy execution within their domain.
- Cross-functional teams may be formed within each domain to address specific aspects of the challenge, with clear ownership assigned to team leaders or single-threaded leaders.

As the world evolves, so do your high-stakes challenges, influenced by external factors such as technological, cultural, political, and ethical shifts. Additionally, consider your competitors—both traditional ones and new—along with non-traditional ones with innovative capabilities and approaches, such as digital-native, mobile-first, cloud-native, and generative AI-native companies.

Watch for weak signals that might become trends, incorporate trends into your strategy description, and think in scenarios. Ask yourself, "What do we do if this or that happens?"

In analyzing this challenge, you will inevitably encounter internal resistance. Employees and managers fear that their past performance will not be appreciated, that they will be misunderstood, or that actual gaps in results, skills, and readiness will be revealed.

Fundamentally, this analysis must be forward-looking and fearless. The organization must also address deficiencies regardless of individual sensitivities. We describe how to drive change in Chapter 13.

Describe Your High-Stakes Challenges and Your Strategy in Clear and Concise Briefing Documents

Your people need to know and understand the high-stakes challenges and the strategy, which means they need to be clear, concise, and to the point. We recommend not using Powerpoint presentations.

They leave too much room for interpretation. Powerpoint presentations often oversimplify complex strategies. This format can encourage bullet-point thinking, obscure critical relationships between ideas, and fail to provide necessary context and depth. Instead, well-crafted documents allow for more nuanced explanations, deeper analysis, and clearer articulation of complex strategies and challenges.

Documents provide a more comprehensive and flexible medium for describing high-stakes challenges and strategies. They allow for detailed narratives, in-depth analysis, and the inclusion of supporting data and examples.

To write effective briefing documents, use clear, concise language, organize information logically, include visual aids where appropriate, and ensure each document stands alone as a complete reference. For versioning and management, implement a robust document management system with version control, clear naming conventions, and a defined review and approval process.

Use collaborative tools that track changes and comments, and establish a regular review cycle to keep documents up-to-date. This approach ensures that strategic information is thoroughly communicated, easily accessible, and consistently maintained across the organization.

These documents must be accessible to employees, even if there is a risk that they will be made public or fall into the hands of competitors. The important and difficult thing is not to have a strategy, but to be able to execute it. The strategy document describes:

- how you will proceed and what you will focus on
- what you won't do and what you won't focus on
- the role of specific teams and domains in executing the strategy

While documents serve as the primary medium for detailed strategy communication, Powerpoint presentations can play a complementary role in visualizing key aspects of the strategy and high-stakes challenges.

These visual aids can be effective in executive summaries, board presentations, or all-hands meetings where a quick, high-level overview is needed. When used judiciously, Powerpoint can help reinforce the main points of the strategy, make abstract concepts more tangible, and facilitate discussions in group settings.

However, it's crucial to ensure that these presentations are always backed by more comprehensive briefing documents, serving as visual supplements rather than standalone strategy communications.

A Single North Star Metric Provides Strategic Direction

Your clear and concise strategy document should result in a single North Star metric that indicates whether the organization is making progress toward solving the high-stakes challenge.

This single metric guides all of the organization's strategic activities. It is the ultimate measure of whether strategy execution activities are having an impact. Because it is a single metric, it helps the organization focus and prioritize.

This clarity allows individual parts of the organization to make decisions more quickly and in a more decentralized manner while promoting the alignment of all activities with the strategy.

A good North Star metric is:

- Actionable: Teams can directly influence it through their work.
- Understandable: Everyone in the organization can understand its meaning and importance.
- Reflects customer value: It represents the value customers receive from the product or service.
- Predictive of long-term success: Improvements in this metric correlate with overall business growth.

- Not easily manipulated: It can't be artificially inflated without actually improving the business.

It is therefore essential that the North Star metric is a leading metric that, unlike lagging metrics, indicates very early on whether and to what extent activities are having an impact. Lagging metrics, especially monetary and absolute metrics such as sales and profit, are unsuitable as North Star metrics.

However, in practice, many organizations struggle to identify perfect leading indicators and may use metrics that have both leading and lagging characteristics. The key is to choose a metric that is as forward-looking as possible while still being closely tied to the core value the business provides.

Relative metrics that represent both customer value and shareholder value are very appropriate. A potential leading North Star metric for a sports apparel company could be the Active Customer Engagement Score (ACES): It measures the depth and frequency of customer interactions across all channels (physical and digital) on a rolling 30-day basis. It is good because it is a leading indicator of customer satisfaction, brand loyalty, and long-term revenue potential.

ACES is highly actionable across multiple teams—product development can create features that drive engagement, marketing can create campaigns that drive interaction, engineering teams can optimize digital platforms for increased usage, and retail operations can improve in-store experiences to complement digital engagement. By focusing on ACES, the company aligns its entire organization to create a truly engaging omnichannel experience that drives sustainable business growth.

Another relevant and very interesting but lagging North Star metric is Active Customer Lifetime Value (ACLV). This metric combines customer retention, purchase frequency, and average order value into a single measure. It reflects the long-term value created for both the customer and the company.

It is good because it's actionable across departments (product, marketing, sales), it's understandable, it reflects customer value, it predicts long-term success, and it's difficult to manipulate without truly improving customer experience and product quality. Changes in ACLV often take time to manifest because they incorporate long-term factors such as customer life and repeat purchase behavior.

The North Star metric is described in detail in your strategy document.

- Why it was chosen
- Why other metrics were not chosen
- How it is defined
- How it is measured
- How it relates to customer value and business success
- Its baseline performance and growth targets
- Its influencing input metrics

In large organizations, individual business units that have their own profit and loss statements may have different North Star metrics. For domains within the organization, the organizational North Star metric should be translated by the domain leaders into domain-specific metrics that contribute to the overall goal.

This process involves analyzing how each domain's activities impact the organizational North Star and identifying the most relevant metric that reflects that contribution. While these domain-specific metrics should be linked to the organizational North Star, they must be directly actionable within the domain's sphere of influence. We caution against over-engineering the relationships between metrics across different levels of the organization.

While it's important to understand how metrics relate to each other, attempting to create the perfect cascade of perfectly aligned and comparable metrics can be counterproductive.

Strategies and their implementation often involve uncertainties and complexities that resist such rigid structuring. Instead of spending excessive time trying to establish and maintain a complex hierarchy of interdependent metrics, focus on ensuring each level's metrics are meaningful, actionable, and broadly aligned with the overall strategy.

This approach allows for more flexibility and adaptability as the strategy evolves and as different parts of the organization learn and adjust their contributions to the overall goals.

Responsibility for the North Star metric typically lies with the:

- Organizational level: The CEO or a designated C-suite executive (e.g., Chief Strategy Officer) owns the overall metric.
- Domain level: Domain leaders are responsible for understanding how their area contributes to the North Star and for defining and tracking domain-specific metrics that align with and influence the overall North Star.

In a loosely coupled organization, dependency management between domains should strike a balance between alignment and autonomy. While domains should be aware of how their metrics and activities impact others, strict dependency management can lead to bureaucracy and slow decision-making.

Instead, focus on clear communication channels, regular cross-domain synchronization, and transparent reporting of domain-specific metrics. This approach allows domains to operate independently while remaining aligned with the overall strategy.

North Star metrics should remain stable over a longer period, from a few months to a few years, but can and should be adjusted if the strategy changes.

Wardley Maps Help You Understand Your Strategic Context and Options

Wardley maps are a strategic tool developed by Simon Wardley to help organizations visualize their business environment, components, and dependencies. They provide a unique perspective on strategy by combining the concepts of value chain mapping with the evolution of components over time. They also help organizations understand their current position, anticipate future changes, and make more informed strategic decisions.

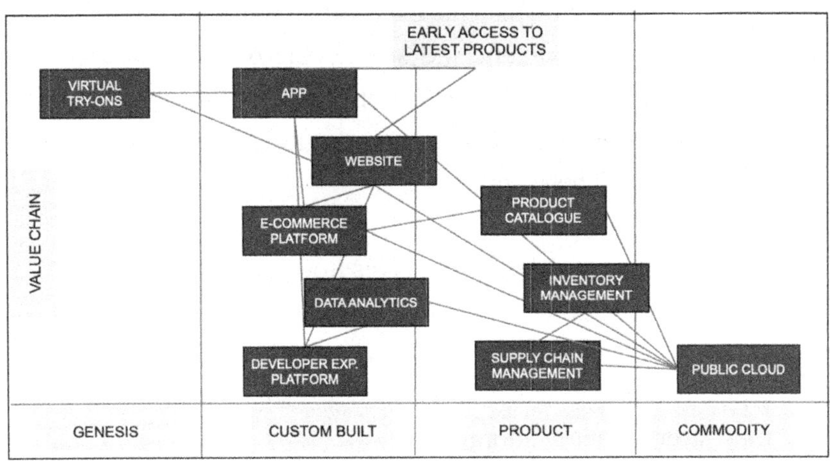

Wardley maps are composed of multiple layers:

- Customer Needs: The top of the map starts with customer needs, defining what users or customers want from the services or products offered. In this case, 'Early Access to latest Products.'
- Value chain: Below the customer needs, on the vertical dimension of the map, it outlines a chain of components or activities needed to meet those needs, arranged from left to right. This visualizes how different elements contribute directly or indirectly to satisfying customer needs.
- Evolution: One of the distinctive features of a Wardley map is its emphasis on the evolution of components. Each element in the value chain is plotted on the horizontal axis on the map according to its stage of maturity—from genesis (novel, emerging technologies) to custom, product (and rental), and commodity (or utility)—showing its development and adoption curve over time.

The evolution layer is what makes Wardley maps so interesting to us for strategy development and structuring our product development organization. The four stages of maturity describe the evolution of components, products, or services from inception to commoditization. These stages are:

- Genesis: This initial stage involves novel, innovative ideas or technologies that are newly created. Products or services in the genesis stage are highly uncertain, experimental, and typically not well understood outside a small group of innovators or early adopters.
- Custom Built: As ideas begin to prove their value, they move into the custom-built stage. Here, solutions are developed to address specific problems or needs. They are

more refined than they are in the genesis stage, but still require custom development, making them relatively expensive and limited in distribution.

- Product (and rental): In this stage, offerings become more standardized and packaged as products that can be mass-produced and widely distributed. The focus shifts from customization to achieving economies of scale that make the technology or service more accessible and affordable to a broader audience.
- Commodity (or Utility): The final stage is when a product or service is fully commoditized, often delivered as a utility. At this point, it is widely available and highly standardized, and the focus is on price and reliability rather than differentiation. Commoditization reflects a mature market where the offering is essential and ubiquitous, similar to utilities such as electricity and water.

By categorizing your current components into these four areas, you can identify and correct common strategic mistakes. We typically see two mistakes:

- Some components are too far to the left. They are too customized. Products and solutions available on the market are not used and resources are wasted. For example, we see in many IT organizations that far too many resources and budgets in the product and commodity areas are wasted on the manual operation of applications and infrastructure that could be much better used for innovation through the use of automated, cloud-native solutions. Many organizations still maintain custom content delivery infrastructure, overlooking the efficiency and global reach of established Content Delivery Network (CDN) services like AWS CloudFront.

- Some components are too far to the right. Companies use products and off-the-shelf solutions in areas where they can create competitive differentiation and value for their customers through custom-built solutions or new innovations. Many businesses settle for generic, template-based mobile apps, missing opportunities to create distinctive user experiences and brand engagement through custom-developed applications.

Creating a Wardley map is a complex process that requires practice and a deep understanding of both the mapping technique and the business context. While a complete guide is beyond the scope of this book, here's an expanded overview of the process:

- Identify the user need or business goal.
- Clearly define the specific user need or business objective you're mapping
- Ensure it's concrete and actionable
- Map the value chain.
- List all components needed to meet the user's needs
- Arrange components vertically based on their visibility to the user
- Top: User-facing components
- Bottom: Foundational components
- Position components on the evolution axis.
- Place each component horizontally based on its evolutionary stage
- Genesis: Novel, uncertain
- Custom-Built: Tailored solutions
- Product: Standardized offerings
- Commodity: Ubiquitous, utility-like
- Draw dependencies.
- Connect components with arrows to show dependencies

- Consider both direct and indirect dependencies
- Add movement.
- Indicate expected changes in component positions over time
- Use arrows to show anticipated evolution
- Identify opportunities and threats.
- Analyze the map for strategic insights
- Look for clusters, gaps, and inefficiencies
- Iterate and refine.
- Review and adjust the map with stakeholders
- Ensure it accurately represents your understanding of the landscape

This overview provides a starting point, but mastering Wardley mapping requires deeper study and practice. For a comprehensive guide, I highly recommend Simon Wardley's book, *Finding a Path* (available online for free) or attending workshops specializing in this technique. These resources will provide the depth needed to fully leverage this powerful strategic tool.

Wardley maps show not only where components are currently located, but also where they could be in the long term. They are the first key indicators for transformation, migration, and innovation initiatives.

Nested Wardley maps provide a multi-layered view of an organization's strategic landscape, combining the high-level organizational perspective with detailed domain-specific insights. At the organizational level, a high-level Wardley map outlines the organization's broad value chain, key components, and evolutionary stages. This map serves as a strategic blueprint, guiding overall direction and priorities.

Below that, each domain creates its own Wardley map, providing a more granular view of its specific area of responsibility. These domain-level maps align with the organizational map but delve deeper into domain-specific components, dependencies, and evolutionary stages. To maintain coherence across domains and organizational levels, regular cross-functional reviews ensure alignment between maps.

Components that appear in multiple domain maps are identified and their representations are synchronized. The organizational-level map is updated periodically to reflect significant changes or patterns emerging from the domain maps. This nested approach allows for both strategic alignment and domain autonomy, providing a comprehensive yet flexible framework for decision-making in a loosely coupled, domain-driven organization. It facilitates better communication between domains, highlights interdependencies, and ensures that domain-specific strategies contribute effectively to overarching organizational goals.

Responsibility for the Wardley maps typically lies with a designated C-suite executive on the organizational level and the domain leaders on the domain level.

Briefing and Back Briefing to Ensure Effective Strategy Communication

In product organizations, we aim for loosely coupled teams and organizational units that are all aligned with the strategy. To achieve this, the strategy must be communicated in a way that is understood and considered reasonable and feasible by all relevant parties. It is important to understand that this communication is two-way, with both parties agreeing and creating clarity.

The concept of briefing and back briefing is an effective process for this. In the briefing, the leader of an organization or domain clearly articulates the strategy and all necessary information to the subordinate management team or even all domain or team members in written and verbal ways. This ensures everyone understands their roles and responsibilities.

The subordinate team may ask questions to seek clarification and ensure they grasp the briefing thoroughly. Once the briefing is complete, the team engages in back briefing, where they recap and confirm their understanding of the strategy. Each member of the subordinate leadership team shares their interpretation of the briefing, outlining their understanding of the goals and how they plan to contribute to achieving them.

The briefing includes:

- A clear statement of intent
- A definition of the desired outcomes
- An outline of the boundaries within which the initiative will be conducted
- An explanation of the context in which it will be carried out
- An identification of the key tasks to be completed
- An allocation of the necessary resources
- And feedback mechanisms

The back briefing includes:

- Summarizing the key points of the briefing
- Interpreting the goals and objectives
- Ensuring alignment among team members
- Seeking clarification
- Expressing commitment to the tasks
- Providing feedback

- And gaining consensus before proceeding with the work

It is a crucial feedback loop that verifies alignment and understanding among leadership teams and their staff. It allows for the identification of any misunderstandings or discrepancies early on, enabling prompt resolution and preventing misalignment during execution. Through this iterative process of briefing and back briefing, teams enhance their collective understanding, alignment, and commitment to the domain goals.

Cultivate Strategy Through Continuous Dialogue and Adaptation

Regularly explaining, discussing, challenging, reviewing, and aligning strategy across the organization is important for effective strategy execution, especially in dynamic business environments. This practice ensures that the strategy remains relevant, builds understanding and buy-in, uncovers diverse perspectives, maintains alignment, and facilitates adaptation to changing circumstances.

The process includes several activities at varying frequencies.

- Quarterly strategy review meetings at the organizational level.
- Monthly domain-level reviews: Each domain should review its strategic progress monthly.
- Annual deep dives: Conduct a comprehensive strategy review and possibly reset annually.
- Open forums: Create spaces for employees at all levels to ask questions and provide input.
- Strategy communication channels: Maintain ongoing communication about strategy through newsletters, intranets, or dedicated strategy platforms.

- Cross-domain workshops: Organize semi-annual cross-domain strategy alignment workshops.

Strategy review meetings are essential for assessing progress and adapting to change. They require a variety of inputs, including quantitative data and qualitative information like domain updates and competitive intelligence.

Customer feedback gathered through direct interaction or "getting out of the building" provides critical insights as well. This includes customer anecdotes that reveal unexpected product uses or changing market needs. Employee feedback, especially from front-line employees, provides unique perspectives on customer needs and operational challenges. External viewpoints from industry analysts, partners, or academic research help challenge internal assumptions and provide fresh perspectives on strategy.

To do this effectively, organizations should establish a clear rhythm for strategy discussions at all levels. It's critical to promote a culture where challenging the strategy is seen as constructive. Documenting and sharing key points from strategy discussions ensures broader understanding, while always linking the strategy to concrete actions and results keeps it grounded in reality.

This approach helps maintain a living, breathing strategy that adapts to changing circumstances while keeping everyone aligned and engaged. It's especially important in loosely coupled, domain-driven organizations where autonomy must be balanced with overall strategic coherence. By making strategy review and alignment a regular, inclusive process, organizations can more effectively manage complexity and change and ensure that strategic intent is translated into coordinated action at all levels.

Be Stubborn on the Vision but Flexible on the Details

"Be stubborn on the vision but flexible on the details." —Jeff Bezos

Jeff Bezos' advice encapsulates a powerful principle in the context of purpose and strategy. This philosophy emphasizes the importance of having a clear, long-term vision that guides the overall direction and purpose of an organization while being open to adapting the specific tactics, methods, and approaches used to achieve that vision.

The vision represents the ultimate goal or desired future state of the organization. It's the beacon that keeps everyone aligned and moving in the same direction. By being stubborn on the vision, leaders commit to their overarching goals and never lose sight of what they are trying to accomplish, even when faced with challenges, setbacks, or opportunities that might tempt them to deviate from their core objectives.

Flexibility on the details recognizes that the path to achieving a vision is often unpredictable and may require adjustments based on new information, changing circumstances, or feedback from the marketplace and internal processes. This means being open to experimentation, learning from failure, and iterating on strategies. It involves a willingness to change tactics and operations in pursuit of the vision.

Leaders need to emphasize this flexibility consciously, frequently, and explicitly. This is the only way to create a culture in which people feel safe to question current plans, suggest alternatives, and try things out. This approach nurtures a culture of innovation, resilience, and continuous improvement. We will dive deeper into how to establish the right culture in Chapter 14 - How to Establish a High-performance Culture that Attracts Talent.

Valid Variants for Different Situations

Defining a Destination Instead of a Direction

A destination-oriented North Star metric can be valid and beneficial in most scenarios. In others, setting a fixed destination rather than a direction allows an organization to navigate the complexities of the business environment with agility and adaptability.

It's particularly effective in turnaround situations, startup growth phases, regulatory-driven environments, or when targeting specific market share goals. This approach is also useful for meeting funding-related goals, driving product launches, or managing crises. The key benefit is that it provides absolute clarity on what success looks like, which can greatly motivate teams and align efforts across the organization.

Destination-oriented North Star metrics can be powerful tools in various business scenarios. Consider a struggling retail chain aiming to improve profitability. By setting a clear goal to achieve a 5% operating profit margin within 18 months, the entire organization gains a tangible target to work toward, allowing for diverse strategies while maintaining a fixed objective.

Similarly, a B2B SaaS startup in its growth phase might set a North Star metric of reaching 100,000 active paid users within 24 months. This laser-focused goal directs all company efforts toward user acquisition and retention, providing a clear benchmark for success in the critical early stages of the business. In both cases, these metrics offer absolute clarity on what the organization's success looks like, motivating teams and aligning efforts across different departments and functions.

However, organizations should be prepared to reevaluate and adjust their goals as circumstances change. Once achieved, a new goal may need to be set or a transition made to a more directional approach.

The choice between a directional or destination-oriented North Star metric should be based on the organization's current context, goals, and challenges. Some may even use a hybrid approach, combining an overarching directional metric with specific, destination-oriented sub-metrics or milestones. Ultimately, the North Star metric should provide clear direction, facilitate alignment, and drive behaviors that lead to long-term success.

Extreme Urgency or Crisis Situations

In times of acute crisis or imminent threat, the comprehensive strategic approach we've discussed may be too slow and cumbersome. Crises require rapid, decisive action focused on immediate survival or threat mitigation.

Instead of long-term planning and extensive stakeholder engagement, leadership must quickly assess the situation, identify critical actions, and mobilize resources. The focus shifts from long-term strategic positioning to short-term stability and damage control.

Communication becomes more directive, decision-making is more centralized, and the time frame for action is compressed. While elements of strategic thinking remain important, the priority is to respond quickly and effectively to get through the immediate crisis.

Very Small or Early-Stage Startups

For early-stage startups or small organizations, our detailed strategy approach can be overwhelming and potentially counterproductive. These organizations typically operate in a high-uncertainty environment, seeking product-market fit and early traction.

Their focus is on rapid experimentation, learning, and iteration based on a strong vision rather than long-term planning. A more appropriate approach for startups involves lean methodologies that emphasize hypothesis testing, minimum viable products, and rapid pivots based on market feedback.

The strategy process for startups should be light, flexible, and focused on immediate growth opportunities. Instead of comprehensive Wardley maps or extensive strategy documentation, startups benefit from simple, adaptable frameworks such as the Business Model Canvas or Lean Canvas. We dive deeper into the Business Model Canvas in Chapter 8 - How to Innovate and Deliver Business Value, Not Just Features.

Highly Volatile or Unpredictable Markets

In highly volatile or unpredictable markets, the long-term planning aspects of our strategic approach can quickly become obsolete. These environments, characterized by rapid technological change, changing consumer behavior, or unstable economic conditions require a more agile and adaptive strategic approach.

Instead of detailed long-term plans, organizations in these markets benefit from scenario planning, real-time market sensing, and the ability to quickly reallocate resources. The focus shifts from fixed strategic positions to building organizational capabilities for rapid adaptation. Strategy in these contexts becomes more about setting guiding principles and developing strategic options rather than defining specific long-term goals or actions.

Common Misconceptions and Mistakes

We Are Agile! We Don't Plan for the Long Term

The belief among some agile teams that planning is unnecessary because they are "agile" represents a common misconception about the nature of agility in the context of strategy.

Agility does not mean the absence of planning; rather, it emphasizes adaptive planning, evolutionary development, early delivery, and continuous improvement, all of which require a thoughtful approach to planning that is responsive to change. Agile methods emphasize the importance of having a clear vision and goals to guide decision-making and prioritize work.

This misconception comes from a misunderstanding of agility as purely spontaneous or improvisational, overlooking that effective agile practices are grounded in strategic goals that drive iterative development. By dismissing the need for planning, agile teams risk losing direction, coherence, and the ability to align their efforts with the organization's overarching strategic goals, undermining their potential to deliver value effectively and efficiently.

We Are Autonomous! No Top-Down Strategy, Please

When agile teams reject top-down strategy and demand autonomy, they put organizational coherence and strategic alignment at risk. While agility and autonomy are valuable for innovation and responsiveness, rejecting top-down strategy altogether can lead to fragmented efforts and misaligned goals across the organization.

Without a unifying strategic direction, teams may pursue goals that diverge from the company's overarching priorities, potentially wasting resources and diluting the organization's competitive advantage. This lack of alignment can hinder long-term planning and execution, undermining the company's ability to achieve its overall mission and vision. Balancing autonomy with strategic alignment is critical for maintaining focused and effective progress.

Confusing Planning with Strategy

Organizations often confuse detailed planning with strategic thinking. Planning is important, but it's not a strategy. True strategy involves making critical decisions about what to do and, more importantly, what not to do. It's about setting a clear direction and making tough trade-offs.

Many companies create extensive plans, forecasts, and budgets and think they've created a strategy, but these are merely tools for executing the strategy, not the strategy itself. A true strategy articulates a coherent set of actions designed to create a sustainable competitive advantage. It's about the "why" and "what" before the "how," focusing on key decisions that shape and position the entire organization.

Overemphasis on Quantitative Data

In our data-driven world, organizations often over-rely on quantitative metrics when formulating strategy. While numbers are crucial, this approach can lead to neglecting vital qualitative insights.

Quantitative data tells you "what" is happening, but qualitative data explains "why" it's happening. Customer anecdotes, market observations, and frontline employee feedback provide context and depth that numbers alone can't capture. Overemphasis on quantitative data can result in missing emerging trends, misunderstanding customer needs, or overlooking competitive threats.

Balancing quantitative analysis with rich, qualitative insights, especially those gained from direct customer interactions or "getting out of the building" leads to more robust, nuanced strategies.

TL;DR and Further Reading

To get started, you may want to start with a simple question: ask your people what they think the mission of their tech organization is—you will probably get different views. Try to understand where this comes from and start from there. The idea of judging right away seems close, but try to understand the motivation and listen to your organization. Remember to stay humble.

- Align and focus the technology organization with a compelling purpose and mission
- Use high-stakes challenges to define and develop your strategy
- Describe your high-stakes challenges and your strategy in clear and concise briefing documents
- A single North Star metric provides strategic direction
- Wardley maps help you understand your strategic context and options
- Cultivate strategy through continuous dialogue and adaptation
- Be stubborn on the vision but flexible on the details

For a more in-depth look at this topic, these are some of our favorite books and websites:

- *Good Strategy Bad Strategy:* The Difference and Why It Matters, by Richard Rumelt
- *The Art of Action:* How Leaders Close the Gaps Between Plans, Actions, and Results, by Stephen Bungay, Andrew Hunt, et al.
- Amplitude's "North Star Playbook" (link)
- Learn Wardley Mapping https://learnwardleymapping.com/

4

HOW TO GROUP TEAMS AROUND BUSINESS DOMAINS

AS TECH ORGANIZATIONS SCALE, they often struggle with complex interdependencies that slow down innovation and impede agility. This chapter addresses the critical challenge of structuring teams to optimize for speed, autonomy, and alignment with business goals.

The way we group our teams can dramatically impact an organization's ability to deliver value rapidly and adapt to changing market conditions. Poorly structured organizations often suffer from communication bottlenecks, duplicated efforts, and a disconnect between technical work and business outcomes. By contrast, effective team grouping can lead to faster delivery, improved product quality, and greater responsiveness to customer needs.

We'll explore a modern approach to organizational design that leverages business domains and value streams as the primary criteria for team structure. This method, rooted in Domain-Driven Design and the Inverse Conway Maneuver, aims to create loosely coupled, highly-aligned teams that can operate with maximum efficiency and effectiveness.

The chapter begins by describing the traditional approach and its limitations in today's fast-paced environment. We then introduce a comprehensive framework for identifying business domains, creating high-level domain architectures, and aligning team structures accordingly. Along the way, we'll address common misconceptions about organizational design, discuss potential pitfalls, and explore variations to suit different organizational contexts. We'll also touch on the importance of flexible communication models and code-sharing practices that respect domain boundaries.

By the end of this chapter, you'll have a practical toolkit for reimagining your organizational structure to facilitate innovation, reduce dependencies, and optimize lead times. This knowledge is crucial for tech leaders seeking to build organizations that can thrive in an increasingly complex and competitive landscape.

The Traditional Approach and Why It Falls Short

Historically, organizations have structured their IT departments along conventional lines, often with contradicting effects on agility and innovation. This approach, rooted in outdated perceptions of technology's role in business, has led to significant challenges in the modern, fast-paced digital landscape.

One major issue is the organization of teams based on reporting hierarchies, functional departments, and technology skill sets. While this structure may seem logical from a management perspective, it creates silos that impede cross-functional collaboration. These barriers slow decision-making processes and hinder innovation, ultimately reducing the organization's ability to respond quickly to market changes and customer needs.

Another problematic aspect is the perception of software development as a commodity, leading to widespread outsourcing. This view often stems from the misunderstanding of technology's strategic value and a focus on short-term cost reduction. While outsourcing may appear financially attractive, it can result in a loss of control over critical IT capabilities, reduced innovation potential, and increased dependency on external vendors whose priorities may not align with the business's goals.

The financial treatment of IT investments further complicates matters. Organizations have varied in their approach, some capitalizing development costs as long-term investments, others expensing ongoing IT operations. This mixed approach can obscure the true strategic value of technology investments and lead to misguided decision-making.

Collectively, these traditional practices create a disconnect between IT capabilities and business needs. Organizations find themselves ill-equipped to leverage technology for competitive advantage, struggling with reduced agility, compromised innovation, and an inability to create unique value propositions in a rapidly evolving digital marketplace.

As these shortcomings become increasingly apparent, it's clear that a new approach is needed to align IT structures with modern business realities and unlock the full potential of technology in driving organizational success.

The General Blueprint and Approach

Group Your Teams Around Business Domains and Value Streams

In this book, we want to share our experiences on how to build a great technology organization at scale—which is not easy. From our perspective, technology and business are deeply intertwined, forming an integrated ecosystem. In this context, business domains and value streams become the fundamental elements for designing such an organization.

A Business Domain is a distinct area of expertise and knowledge within an organization that represents a core aspect of its business model and value proposition. A sports apparel company might have business domains such as footwear, apparel, and digital products.

A Value Stream is the end-to-end sequence of activities that deliver a product or service to a customer, focusing on the flow of value creation. A sports apparel company in this aspect might have value streams such as retail operations for both physical and online stores, or supply chain management from raw materials to delivery.

Business domains and value streams are complementary in organizational design. Domains represent vertical slices of expertise while value streams cut horizontally across these domains. Together, they create a matrix that helps organizations balance specialized knowledge with end-to-end value delivery, ensuring both depth of expertise and customer-focused outcomes.

This approach recognizes that in modern organizations, business strategy and technological innovation are inseparable. It enables faster decision-making, more efficient resource allocation, and greater agility in responding to market changes. By structuring around these integrated business-tech domains and value streams, organizations can leverage emerging technologies for business growth while maintaining a strong focus on core business objectives and customer needs.

The approach we propose optimizes for:

- Alignment with business goals: The organizational structure ensures that software development teams are directly aligned with specific business objectives, leading to more focused and relevant software solutions.

- A tailored technology approach: Each domain or value stream can adopt a technology approach that best suits its specific needs, within the bounds of organizational standards.
- Improved communication: Teams organized around domains have a deeper understanding of their specific area, facilitating better communication with business stakeholders and within the domain itself.
- Autonomy and ownership: Domain-focused teams can make decisions more quickly and take full ownership of their products or services, creating a sense of responsibility and entrepreneurship.
- Scalability: As the business grows, new domains or value streams can be added without disrupting existing structures, allowing for flexible organizational expansion.
- Faster time-to-market: With teams focused on specific value streams and equipped with tailored technology, they can deliver features and improvements more rapidly, responding quickly to market demands.
- Better resource allocation: Resources are allocated based on business priorities, ensuring that high-value areas receive appropriate attention and investment.
- Enhanced innovation: The deep domain expertise and technological autonomy create an environment where innovative solutions can emerge, tailored to the specific challenges of each domain or value stream.

Identify Your Business Domains and Value Streams with Wardley Maps

To identify business domains and value streams, we recommend a comprehensive approach that combines several powerful methodologies. These include Wardley mapping, Domain-Driven Design (DDD), and Event Storming.

Let's break this down into steps:

- Review and refine strategic maps. We start with Wardley maps—a technique for visualizing the structure of a business or service. These maps show the components of your business, from user needs to the underlying technologies, positioned according to their evolution and value. If you've created these maps during strategy development (as discussed in Chapter 3 - How to Set Focus and Direction), review them to ensure they accurately reflect your current business landscape.
- Identify strategic domains. Analyze your maps to identify potential strategic domains. These are areas of your business that provide significant value or differentiation. Look for clusters of components, especially those that are unique to your business or are in the early stages of development. These often indicate areas of high strategic importance.
- Align with business capabilities. Next, connect these strategic domains to your business capabilities. A business capability is something your organization does to deliver value (like "product development" or "customer service"). Evaluate how mature these capabilities are and how important they are to your strategy.
- Conduct Domain Discovery Workshops. Organize workshops with key stakeholders to explore each strategic

domain in depth. Use techniques from Domain-Driven Design, an approach that focuses on the core complexity of your business.

In these workshops:

- Develop a common language: Agree on terms and concepts that everyone in the domain will use consistently.
- Identify core concepts: What are the fundamental ideas in this domain?
- Define boundaries: Where does this domain start and end? This helps us identify what DDD calls "bounded contexts" —coherent areas of functionality with clear interfaces to other parts of the system.
- Map value streams. Finally, map out your value streams. A value stream is the end-to-end sequence of activities that deliver value to your customers. Use the insights from your Wardley maps and domain discovery to identify these streams and how they flow through your strategic domains.

By following this process, you'll gain a clear picture of your business domains and value streams, grounded in your strategic goals and business realities. This understanding forms the foundation for designing your organizational structure and technology systems.

This domain-analysis process involves a wide range of participants from across the organization, each of whom plays a critical role in its success. Executive Leadership is responsible for initiating the process, providing strategic direction, and making final decisions about organizational structure. The strategy team typically leads the Wardley mapping process and helps identify strategic areas. Domain experts, who are subject matter experts from various parts of the organization, participate in domain discovery workshops and help define bounded contexts.

IT leadership is involved in aligning technical capabilities with business domains and designing system architectures that support loose coupling. HR and organizational design specialists help translate domain insights into practical organizational structures and support the change management process. Team leaders and middle management participate in domain discovery and help implement the new organizational structure.

Developers and engineers participate in event-storming sessions and help refine domain models, while business analysts help map business capabilities and refine value streams. The change management team supports the transition to the new organizational structure and helps nurture a culture of continuous adaptation.

This process requires broad participation from across the organization to be successful. It's not a top-down imposition of structure, but rather a collaborative effort to discover and design an organization that can effectively deliver value in a complex, evolving environment. The inclusion of diverse perspectives and expertise ensures that the resulting organizational design is informed, practical, and aligned with both business goals and technical realities.

By combining Wardley mapping and DDD, you can gain a holistic understanding of the business landscape, identify the key domains and value streams, and align the organizational structure accordingly. This approach helps create autonomous, cross-functional teams that are aligned with the business domains and can effectively deliver value to customers.

Remember that this process is iterative and ongoing. As the organization evolves and new insights emerge, the identified domains and value streams should be revisited and refined.

Align Organization with Architecture: Leveraging the Inverse Conway Maneuver

"[O]rganizations which design systems are constrained to produce designs which are copies of the communication structures of these organizations." — Melvin E. Conway

Conway's Law states that organizations design systems that mirror their communication structures, reflecting the architectural patterns of their internal social structures. However, this internal social structure is often based on criteria that make no sense for a software architecture, such as teams based on functional expertise, reporting lines, human sensitivities, career paths, budgets, mergers and acquisitions, or even office politics.

That's what we don't want; architecture that looks like the organization. We want the organization to adapt to the needs and structure of the domain, the value stream, and the architecture. Therefore, we model the business domain, the value streams, and the high-level architecture first. Only in the second step do we model the organizational structure.

This approach is called the Inverse Conway Maneuver. It is an approach in which organizations, especially their communication and organizational structures, are designed to reflect the target architecture they have in mind for their systems. In other words, the organization is structured exactly as the long-term target architecture should be.

By applying the Inverse Conway Maneuver, organizations aim to facilitate the development of systems that are well-integrated and aligned with their business goals. In the context of identifying business domains and value streams, the Inverse Conway Maneuver plays an essential role by advocating an organizational structure that naturally supports the flow of these value streams and the autonomy of these business domains. By organizing teams around business domains and value streams, the organization encourages communication patterns and collaboration that are consistent with the desired system architecture.

Implementing the Inverse Conway Maneuver requires thoughtful organizational design and a clear understanding of the company's strategic priorities, greatly aided by tools such as Wardley maps. These maps can help visualize the organization's landscape, identify critical areas and value streams, and then guide restructuring efforts to support desired outcomes, ensuring that the organizational structure supports efficient, value-driven development processes.

Each Sub-Domain Is Owned and Operated by a Team

Following the Inverse Conway Maneuver and Domain-Driven Design approach, each subdomain within the larger business domain is owned and operated by a dedicated cross-functional team. As discussed in Chapter 2 - How to Set Up a Team, these teams do not necessarily have to be software development teams. They can be responsible for commercial off-the-shelf (COTS) or software-as-a-service (SaaS) applications, or even just parts of them.

The number of subdomains is a fairly accurate indicator of the number of teams required. However, because different products, and therefore subdomains, have different product life cycles, and some products may not require ongoing attention, the actual number of teams is usually less than the number of subdomains.

A subdomain team views the subdomain as its product and embodies a deep sense of ownership and responsibility for its end-to-end delivery, including planning, design, implementation, testing, deployment, and maintenance. This ownership extends beyond mere technical responsibility; it encompasses the business and commercial success of the subdomain as well. The team is responsible for ensuring that its "product" effectively meets the needs and expectations of its users and stakeholders and contributes positively to the overall goals of the organization.

Having dedicated teams responsible for each subdomain promotes a deeper understanding of the business domain, faster decision-making, and improved collaboration with stakeholders. This ownership model enables teams to be more responsive to changing business needs and promotes a culture of continuous improvement.

However, it is important to recognize that having dedicated teams for each sub-domain can be resource-intensive and may require careful prioritization and allocation of resources based on business value and strategic importance. Effective communication and coordination mechanisms must be in place to ensure alignment and collaboration between subdomain teams. We describe this in more detail in Chapter 7 - How to Execute Your Strategy for Maximum Impact and Flexibility. To illustrate this concept, consider an e-commerce company with subdomains such as product catalog, shopping cart, payment processing, and order fulfillment. Each of these subdomains would have a dedicated team responsible for its entire lifecycle, from understanding the business requirements to delivering and maintaining the corresponding software components.

By nurturing a culture of accountability and innovation, the subdomain ownership model empowers teams to invest directly in the success of their domain, driving them to continuously improve and align their efforts with the strategic goals of the organization. This approach is a key enabler of organizational agility, enabling the company to quickly adapt to market changes and more effectively deliver value to its customers.

Within this domain-driven organizational structure, teams can be of four different team types, as described in detail by Matthew Skelton and Manuel Pais in their book, *Team Topologies: Organizing Business and Technology Teams for Fast Flow.* These four team types are:

- Stream-aligned team: aligned to a flow of work from (usually) a segment of the business domain. Those teams focus on delivering value along a flow of work that directly serves a specific business stream, such as a product line or a customer journey.
- Enabling team: helps a stream-aligned team overcome obstacles. They also detect missing capabilities. They provide expertise, tools, and practices for a limited time, focusing on upskilling and enabling autonomy rather than delivering direct contributions to product codebases. Agile Coaches are a good example.
- Complicated Subsystem team: where significant mathematics/calculation/technical expertise is needed. These teams are tasked with developing and managing these intricate components, ensuring they meet the broader system's needs while operating efficiently. Their work supports stream-aligned teams by providing robust, specialized solutions that integrate seamlessly into the overall architecture.
- Platform team: a grouping of other team types that provide a compelling internal product to accelerate delivery by stream-aligned teams.

The teams responsible for the subdomains are either stream-aligned teams or complicated subsystem teams.

The Domains Are Jointly Led by a Cross-Functional Leadership Team

In Domain-Driven Design, a dedicated leadership team at the domain level plays a critical role, especially in larger, fast-moving, and highly uncertain domains. While smaller organizations or domains with stable and clear technical and business activities might rely on subdomain collaboration, a cross-functional domain-level leadership team brings significant benefits to more complex environments.

This team's primary responsibilities include:

- Overseeing the strategic direction and integrity of the domain.
- Ensuring alignment with overarching business goals.
- Defining technical guardrails at both macro and domain levels.
- Managing interactions between subdomains.
- Providing strategic guidance without getting involved in day-to-day operations.
- Facilitating effective collaboration across subdomains.

The diversity of this leadership team, with representatives from various functions, brings a holistic perspective to decision-making and strategy development. This multifaceted expertise enables the team to identify opportunities, mitigate risks, and ensure that the domain's products or services meet the needs of all stakeholders.

By focusing on setting the overall direction and framework for the domain, this leadership team creates an environment where subdomains can operate effectively within a cohesive strategic vision. The domain-level leadership team should comprise key roles essential for the commercial and technical success of the domain's software product.

At its core, this cross-functional team typically includes:

- A Product Leader: Representing the product management perspective and ensuring alignment with overall product strategy.
- A Business Domain Expert: Providing a deep understanding of the business context and requirements.
- A Technology Leader: Overseeing technical direction and ensuring alignment with broader IT strategy.

These individuals can represent each other's interests and perspectives. Depending on the domain's scope and mission, especially if it operates as a separate business unit, the leadership team may be expanded to include:

- A Marketing Leader: Ensuring market alignment and effective product positioning.
- A Sales Leader: Providing insights on customer needs and go-to-market strategies.
- A Hardware Leader: In organizations with combined hardware and software offerings to ensure integration and alignment.

The functional leaders of the subdomain teams, as discussed in "Building Cross-Functional Teams for Agility and Innovation," report to this domain-level leadership team.

It is important to emphasize that the domain-level leadership team leads in a highly situational and collaborative manner, balancing short- and long-term local and domain-wide issues. The team must strike a delicate balance between empowering subdomains to make local decisions and ensuring that those decisions are consistent with the overall interests of the domain. As a general rule, the leadership team should not micromanage or interfere with the day-to-day decisions of subdomains. However, there may be situations where subdomain decisions conflict with the broader goals of the domain, requiring the leadership team to step in and provide guidance or exercise its veto power. Examples of such situations might include decisions related to technical standards, resource allocation, or strategic partnerships.

In addition to providing strategic guidance, the domain-level leadership team plays a critical role in facilitating collaboration and knowledge sharing among subdomains. By establishing formal and informal communication channels, such as regular cross-domain meetings, communities of practice, or shared documentation, the leadership team can promote the exchange of best practices, lessons learned, and innovative ideas. This collaborative approach helps break down silos, leverage collective expertise, and drive continuous improvement across the domain.

As the domain evolves and matures, the composition and focus of the domain-level leadership team may need to adapt. Periodic reassessment of the team's effectiveness and adjustments to its structure and priorities are necessary to ensure that it remains aligned with the domain's goals and challenges.

The role of managers is discussed in more detail in Chapter 13, the effective implementation of strategy in Chapter 7, and innovation in Chapter 8.

The Right People at the Right Time at the Right Place to Strengthen Outcome, Culture, and Cohesion

"The business we're in is more sociological than technological, more dependent on workers' abilities to communicate with each other than their abilities to communicate with machines." — Tom DeMarco, Peopleware: Productive Projects and Teams

So far, we have mainly talked about logical structuring, which looks very much like a drawing board exercise and follows the logic and needs of the business. However, we must not make the mistake of forgetting the human factor in the socio-technical system.

Organizations are made up of people, and they and their interactions are usually the most important strategic competitive advantage an organization can have. Having the right people in the right place at the right time makes all the difference. Therefore, you need to create workspaces that bring the right people together at the right time and enable and support the three essential types of work:

- Focused individual work.
- Creative group work.
- Random socializing.

Each employee should be able to do focused individual work where he or she is best able to do so without interruption whether it is in a one- or two-person office, at home, in a coffee shop, or on an island in a rocking chair.

Organizations should have workspaces in their offices that do not resemble a call center but instead allow for truly focused work. The benefits in terms of quality, lead time, and employee motivation can be easily demonstrated in A/B tests and expressed in monetary terms such as costs of delay.

Creative group work is when all team members get together and develop or plan things together. This is best done physically in a large workshop room with plenty of space for standing and sitting group work whether on chairs, armchairs, beanbags, or sofas. The focus is on sharing, communicating, and visualizing. Traditional meeting rooms with cramped seating are less suitable. No virtual workshop, no matter how good, can replace this kind of group work.

A lot of valuable interaction happens by chance in the corridor, in the coffee kitchen, or in the canteen. It can be about specific projects, the company in general, or just getting to know each other. Modern offices are designed to encourage these chance encounters and invite people to linger.

At the domain and subdomain level, it is important to carefully plan and coordinate the times for these three types of work, especially when it makes sense for everyone to be physically together to collaborate creatively, and when it makes sense to work with as little disruption as possible. It is up to managers to ensure that their employees can truly work without interruption.

Embracing Different Ways of Working Across Domains and Subdomains

As mentioned in Chapter 3 concerning Wardley maps, domains and sub-domains can have their specific ways of working. Simon Wardley's work highlights the importance of using different methodologies—such as Agile, Lean, and Six Sigma—in different parts of the business.

Agile methodologies, like Scrum and Kanban, are well-suited for domains that require rapid iteration, flexibility, and responsiveness to changing requirements. Lean principles, on the other hand, focus on eliminating waste and optimizing processes, making them ideal for domains with stable, predictable workflows. Six Sigma is a data-driven approach that aims to reduce defects and improve quality, making it valuable for domains where precision and consistency are critical. Additionally, frameworks like Design Thinking can be applied in domains that require innovative problem-solving and a strong emphasis on user-centric solutions.

This diversity of approaches is vital because each part of an organization faces unique challenges and operates in different contexts at different times. Tailoring working methods to these specific conditions allows teams to optimize their effectiveness, innovation, and efficiency. While established methodologies provide a solid foundation, teams should be encouraged to adapt and tailor these approaches to their specific context and needs. This flexibility enables teams to address unique challenges, leverage the strengths of their domain or sub-domain, and continuously improve their processes.

However, managing multiple methodologies across an organization can be complex, which requires careful coordination and governance. It is essential to establish clear guidelines, communication channels, and knowledge-sharing mechanisms. Leadership plays a crucial role in nurturing a culture that embraces and supports diverse ways of working. By providing the necessary autonomy, resources, and support, leaders can empower teams to adopt and adapt methodologies that best suit their needs.

Embracing different ways of working can lead to increased agility, innovation, and responsiveness to changing market conditions. This approach allows organizations to leverage the strengths of each methodology and facilitate a dynamic and resilient operating model. By enabling teams to work in ways that optimize their effectiveness, organizations can reduce time to market, improve product quality, and enhance customer satisfaction.

While methodologies may vary, it is critical to ensure that all teams are aligned with the overarching culture, strategy, and organizational principles and guardrails. Establishing clear communication channels and maintaining alignment ensures that all teams are working toward common goals and objectives, enabling a coherent yet flexible operating model that supports the organization's strategic goals.

By embracing different ways of working across domains and subdomains, organizations can create a flexible and adaptive environment capable of responding to changing market demands and internal challenges.

Define Communication and Code Sharing Models Based on Subdomain and Value Stream Boundaries

"Communication is a sign of dysfunction. It means people aren't working together in a close, organic way. We should be trying to figure out ways for teams to communicate less with each other, not more." —Jeff Bezos

Effectively managing communication is vital for reducing dependencies and coupling between teams and domains. Poorly managed communication can lead to tight coupling, confusion, and delays, hindering the overall efficiency and agility of the organization. On the other hand, well-managed communication promotes autonomy, clarity, and seamless collaboration.

Different communication models are needed within and between organizational units, such as teams, subdomains, and domains. The level of interaction and the nature of dependencies between these units dictate the appropriate communication models in terms of frequency, bandwidth, and mode.

Frequency, mode (synchronous or asynchronous), and bandwidth are critical aspects of communication at different organizational levels. Within a team or subdomain, high-frequency, high-bandwidth synchronous communication (e.g., daily stand-ups, pair programming) is common and facilitates close collaboration and rapid problem-solving. This allows for immediate feedback and is useful for solving complex problems. However, it can also lead to interruptions and dependencies if not managed carefully.

Between teams or domains, lower-frequency, asynchronous communication such as documentation and the use of APIs might be more appropriate to maintain autonomy and reduce coupling. Asynchronous communication is flexible and allows participants to respond at their convenience, promoting thoughtful decision-making. However, it may not be appropriate for time-sensitive or highly collaborative tasks.

The Team Topologies framework introduces interaction models that are critical for managing communication and dependencies between these domains. It advocates clear, defined modes of interaction, such as:

- Collaboration involving teams working closely together to solve complex problems, and is often preferred for intra-domain (within the same domain or subdomain) interactions to facilitate innovation and team cohesion.
- X-as-a-Service enabling teams to use services provided by others without direct collaboration, allowing them to maintain autonomy.
- Facilitation involving one team helping another to adopt or improve practices, which can be effective for inter-domain (between different domains or subdomains) interactions.
- Consumption involving one team using the results of another with minimal interaction to streamline the flow of information and minimize friction.

By adopting these interaction models, organizations can effectively manage cross-domain interactions, ensuring that each team remains focused on its core responsibilities while still benefiting from the expertise and services of other teams. This structured approach to communication and interaction enables teams to collaborate effectively while maintaining their autonomy and focus.

Organizations should continually evaluate and adjust their communication models based on factors such as the level of interaction, the nature of dependencies, and the complexity of the tasks involved.

Valid Variants for Different Situations

Single Domain Leader

In organizations where the mixed management team model for a domain is not possible, the domain can be managed by a single person. However, this person should have a business background and fully manage the domain in terms of its commercial success. All other functions such as software development, UX, design, etc. report to this person.

In the case of a single domain leader, he or she should think primarily in business terms and have P&L responsibility for the domain.

Common Misconceptions and Mistakes

Static Organizational Structure with Infrequent but Massive Changes

The design of domains and their subdomains is never perfect but evolves with the participation of a limited number of people who make decisions based on a specific situation and with limited information. Some of these decisions are likely trade-offs between conflicting goals.

The context, assumptions, customer needs, strategies, and business processes change, and the domain structure should change accordingly. We often see organizations wait too long to adapt their domain structure for a variety of reasons. In an attempt to make up for this, they try to implement too many changes at once, often overwhelming people and making it difficult to measure impact and success.

We recommend frequent, local adjustments where impact and success can be measured locally and adjusted if necessary.

Creating a Primarily Technical Organization

A common mistake in domain setup is the creation of domains composed solely of technical teams, with minimal or part-time representation from business departments. This approach leads to domains operating in a silo, with requirements handed down as feature requests rather than collaborative projects.

Consequently, the measurement of domain success tends to lean toward completion metrics instead of economic key figures, undermining the potential for cross-functional synergy and the alignment of technical efforts with business goals. One reason is a lack of integration between the IT and business strategies.

This approach often stems from a traditional view of IT as a service provider rather than a strategic partner, leading to silos where technical teams operate independently from business units. The challenge is to bridge this gap and promote a culture where technology and business collaboratively drive innovation and value creation.

Neglecting the Human Aspect of Organizational Design

Neglecting the human and socio-technical aspects of organizational design, focusing only on headcount, skills, and reporting lines, is a mistake because it overlooks the importance of collaboration, motivation, and job satisfaction among employees.

This approach can lead to a lack of engagement, reduced innovation, and inefficiencies due to poor communication and alignment. Ultimately, it can hinder an organization's ability to adapt and thrive in a competitive landscape, affecting its overall performance and success.

TL;DR and Further Reading

Business domains and value streams are the main criteria for defining the organizational structure; therefore, it is worthwhile to take the time and be precise about what your domains could look like. Draft a high-level idea about your business domains and value streams.

Based on that, you can follow the next steps:

- Create High-Level Domain Architectures with Domain-Driven Design
- Align organization with architecture: leveraging the Inverse Conway Maneuver
- Each sub-domain is owned and operated by a team

- The domains are jointly led by a cross-functional leadership team
- Embrace different ways of working across domains and subdomains
- Define communication and code sharing models based on (sub)domain and value stream boundaries

For a more in-depth look at this topic, these are some of our favorite books and websites:

- *Adaptive Systems with Domain-Driven Design, Wardley Mapping, and Team Topologies: Architecture for Flow,* by Susanne Kaiser

5

HOW TO EMPOWER ENGINEERING TEAMS WITH EFFICIENT AND STRESS-FREE PLATFORMS

AS TECH ORGANIZATIONS SCALE, engineering teams often struggle with inefficient toolchains and complex infrastructure, hindering their ability to deliver value quickly and reliably. This chapter addresses the critical challenge of empowering engineering teams with efficient and stress-free platforms.

Effective platforms can dramatically impact an organization's productivity, innovation speed, and overall engineering happiness. Without them, teams waste time on repetitive tasks, struggle with inconsistent environments, and face increased security risks. Conversely, well-designed platforms enable teams to focus on their core missions, accelerate development, and maintain high standards of reliability and security.

We'll explore an approach to platform development that treats internal tooling as products, emphasizing user-driven scope, self-service capabilities, and continuous improvement through internal A/B testing. The chapter begins by examining the traditional approaches to tooling and infrastructure. We then introduce a framework for building and evolving internal platforms, including strategies for proving platform value, integrating security as a service, and accelerating development through Inner Source practices.

By the end of this chapter, you'll have a practical blueprint for creating platforms that significantly enhance your engineering teams' efficiency and satisfaction.

The Traditional Approach and Why It Falls Short

Traditional IT organizations often struggle to empower engineering teams with efficient and stress-free platforms despite their best intentions. This approach, rooted in established practices, fails to meet the demands of great tech environments in several critical ways.

Central support units in these organizations typically prioritize governance and compliance over productivity and innovation. While this focus aims to minimize risks and errors, it creates a conservative "play not to lose" mindset. Consequently, strict adherence to rules hinders agility and responsiveness, leaving organizations ill-equipped to compete in rapidly changing markets.

Another significant issue lies in how solutions are developed and implemented. Central support teams frequently create tools without adequate customer participation, resulting in a mismatch between the solutions provided and the actual needs of internal users. This disconnect leads to resistance to adoption and reduced effectiveness. Moreover, the tendency to over-engineer solutions or succumb to scope creep further exacerbates the problem, leading to extended delivery times and unnecessary features.

When selecting off-the-shelf products, traditional IT organizations often fall into the trap of choosing solutions that meet requirements on paper but fail to address real-world needs. This misalignment occurs because decision-makers may lack hands-on building experience or a deep understanding of the tasks these tools are meant to support. As a result, theoretically sound choices often prove impractical in day-to-day operations.

These traditional practices collectively create a significant gap between intentions and outcomes, hindering the organization's ability to build and maintain efficient, user-friendly platforms. To truly empower engineering teams and nurture innovation, a new approach is needed.

The General Blueprint

Platforms Provide Simple, Efficient, and Stress-free Toolchains for Engineering Teams

The mission of internal platforms is to provide simple, efficient, and stress-free tools and services for engineering teams to deliver business value effectively. Developer experience platforms, a specific type of internal platform, offer a comprehensive suite of tools and services that support the creation and maintenance of both transactional and analytical applications.

These platforms typically include a wide range of products and services, such as:

- Software development tools (e.g., integrated development environments (IDEs), version control systems)
- Testing and quality assurance tools (e.g., automated testing frameworks, bug tracking systems)
- Continuous integration and continuous delivery (CI/CD) pipelines (e.g., Jenkins, GitLab CI/CD)
- Monitoring and logging solutions (e.g., Prometheus, ELK stack)

- Containerization and orchestration platforms (e.g., Docker, Kubernetes)
- Service and data discovery tools (e.g., service registries, API gateways)
- Analytics and business intelligence platforms (e.g., Tableau, PowerBI)
- Security measures (e.g., identity and access management, vulnerability scanners)
- Collaboration tools (e.g., Slack, Jira)
- Billing and backup services

In some organizations, developer experience platforms also provide hosting services to deploy and run applications, further streamlining the development process. By centralizing tools and processes, internal platforms minimize the friction and stress developers often face with disjointed or manual systems. This allows teams to focus more on creating value through their code rather than battling with infrastructure and toolchain issues.

Centralization also promotes collaboration, knowledge sharing, and consistency across teams, reducing duplication of effort and facilitating the adoption of best practices. As a result, developers can enjoy a more efficient, enjoyable, and productive development experience.

In addition to providing tools and services, platform teams offer consulting, support, and training to help engineering teams effectively utilize the platform and continuously improve their development practices. They also provide metrics and reports on the usage, benefits, and costs of their tools and services, enabling data-driven decision-making and demonstrating the value of the platform to stakeholders.

Organizations may have different platforms catering to specific audiences and application areas, such as:

- Developer Experience Platform for Transactional Applications:
- This platform focuses on supporting the development of transactional applications and provides tools such as CI/CD pipelines, development environments, testing frameworks, monitoring, billing, backup, and account management.
- Developer Experience Platform for Data Applications:
- This platform is tailored for teams building and operating analytical and AI/ML data applications, often in a data mesh architecture. It offers tools like data catalogs, ETL (Extract, Transform, Load) tools, data pipelines, development environments, CI/CD pipelines, and monitoring solutions.
- Complex Subsystem Platforms:
- This platform is designed for teams with only internal customers, building centralized, critical systems with complex business logic, which supports the development and maintenance of shared services and components used by other teams.

To ensure seamless integration and interoperability, these platforms must work together harmoniously, especially when multiple platforms are used within an organization. Platform teams should focus on strategies for ensuring data and workflow compatibility between different platforms and tools.

Implementing internal platforms can come with challenges, such as resistance to change, skill gaps, or legacy system integration. To address these challenges and ensure successful adoption, platform teams should work closely with engineering teams, provide adequate training and support, and gradually migrate existing systems and processes to the new platform.

Platform Teams Are Internal Product Development Teams

Platform teams operate as internal product development teams focused on creating and maintaining the tools and services used by their primary customers: the internal engineering teams, including developers, data scientists, and other technical roles. These teams are characterized by small size, diversity, cross-functionality, and self-organization, encapsulating all the necessary roles to effectively design, build, and maintain platform products.

To truly understand and address the needs of their internal customers, platform teams should adopt a user-centric approach. This involves actively engaging with engineering teams to gather feedback, understand pain points, and validate solutions. By prioritizing user experience and usability, platform teams can ensure that the tools and services they provide are intuitive, well-documented, and easy to adopt.

The role of the platform product owner is critical in driving the success of the platform. They are responsible for defining the platform roadmap, prioritizing features, and managing stakeholder expectations. The product owner should have a deep understanding of the socio-technical landscape of developer tools, often based on their own experience as a user of the platform. They should also possess strong ideation, communication, facilitation, and delivery management skills. Collaborating closely with internal customers, the product owner ensures that the platform's direction aligns with their needs and the overall organizational goals.

An optimal platform team size ranges from five to 10 members, although this may vary slightly depending on specific needs. The team typically includes a product owner and several software developers who have worked on domain teams for an extended period. For a platform team to be truly effective, it's crucial to include members with diverse operational and development backgrounds. Ideally, developers should be versatile and able to work across their team's technology stack while also specializing in certain areas—often referred to as T- or V-shaped developers due to their broad yet deep skill sets.

Testing responsibilities within platform teams can vary. In some environments, developers take on testing responsibilities for their creations. Alternatively, a dedicated QA engineer may be added to the team to focus on test automation. However, empowering developers to test their products is recommended to increase team flexibility and effectiveness. If a dedicated QA engineer is involved, integrating them into the platform team rather than placing them in a separate QA group ensures that they are deeply connected to a specific platform segment, facilitating independence and long-term accountability.

Platform teams should operate with an agile mindset, continuously gathering feedback from their internal customers and iterating on their products based on that feedback. By using metrics, user surveys, and other data-driven approaches, platform teams can measure the success and impact of their products and identify areas for improvement.

One of the key challenges platform teams face is balancing standardization and flexibility. While providing standardized, consistent tools and services is important, it's equally crucial to allow for flexibility to accommodate the unique needs of different internal customers. Platform teams can manage this balance by offering extensible platforms, providing customization options, or supporting integration with third-party tools.

Open communication and collaboration are essential for platform teams to succeed. They should nurture close collaboration with their internal customers, as well as with other platform teams and stakeholders across the organization. Platform teams play a vital role in promoting best practices, sharing knowledge, and facilitating cross-team collaboration to drive overall engineering effectiveness.

As a general guideline, platform development should represent approximately 10% to 20% of a company's total product development effort. However, this benchmark may vary based on factors such as the organization's size, maturity, and specific needs. Organizations should assess their platform development needs and adjust resource allocation accordingly, ensuring that platform teams have sufficient capacity to deliver value to their internal customers.

Proving the Value of Platforms with Internal A/B Testing

To determine whether your platform is delivering value, you need to measure its effectiveness, usability, and impact on your business using well-defined, measurable metrics that align with the platform's goals and the organization's strategic objectives.

Key indicators to track include:

- User Satisfaction: Measure through feedback sessions, surveys, and usage patterns. Monitor metrics like Net Promoter Score (NPS), Customer Satisfaction Score (CSAT), or User Engagement Score.
- Operational Efficiency: Compare time and resources spent on tasks before and after implementing the platform. Track lead time or the number of manual steps eliminated.
- Quality and Reliability: Monitor uptime percentage, mean time to recovery (MTTR), or defect density. Continuously measure and track performance over time.

- Scalability: Assess the platform's ability to handle growth and increased loads without compromising performance. Track response time under load, maximum concurrent users supported, or resource utilization efficiency.
- Alignment with Strategic Business Goals: Evaluate the platform's impact on broader business objectives, such as accelerating product development, improving customer satisfaction, or driving revenue growth.

To rigorously evaluate new services, use A/B testing. Roll out a new service to a small group of domain teams while a control group operates without the service. Monitor and analyze key performance indicators (KPIs) such as deployment frequency, incident rates, time to market, and developer satisfaction scores for both groups.

A/B testing helps isolate the impact of specific platform changes and enables data-driven decision-making. Define clear success criteria and select appropriate sample sizes for A/B tests while recognizing potential limitations.

Effectively communicate the platform's value to stakeholders by creating compelling narratives and visualizations that showcase the platform's impact and align with the organization's goals and priorities.

By establishing clear metrics, continuously measuring performance, and leveraging A/B testing, platform teams can demonstrate the tangible value their platform delivers to the organization. This data-driven approach ensures that decisions are based on objective evidence, validates the effectiveness of new services, and acts as a feedback loop for continuous improvement.

The Users of the Platform Drive Its Scope and Backlog

Many platforms do not live up to their claims and do not deliver the promised benefits to their users. We have used the following effective strategies to address common challenges in driving the adoption of platform services:

- Involve experienced engineers from the domain teams in the decision-making processes related to platform strategy, backlog, and prioritization. It's important not only to listen to their input but also to empower them to make decisions about what gets built and when. This approach will ensure that the platform evolves in a direction that truly meets users' needs and priorities.
- Facilitate the rotation of engineers between the platform team and domain teams. This strategy serves a dual purpose: engineers destined to use the platform contribute directly to its development, ensuring that it meets their needs. At the same time, platform engineers gain first-hand experience with the challenges and needs of user teams, often referred to as "eating their own dog food." The ideal duration for such rotations ranges from a few weeks to a maximum of a quarter, balancing fresh perspectives with continuity.
- Don't build a product until there is a commitment from user teams that they will use it. Generalizations should be delayed until there's a clear demand to avoid the pitfalls of speculative design and excessive embellishment known as "gilding the lily." Starting with a prototype for a single team can provide valuable insights and create a tailored solution that truly addresses specific needs. The product can then be transitioned to platform-level ownership and generalized

for broader use once at least two other teams commit to adopting it.

By integrating these strategies, platform teams can significantly increase the adoption rate of their services and ensure that they create value that resonates throughout the organization.

Improve the Acceptance Rate of Platform Services through Job Rotation

Job rotation is a powerful strategy for improving the acceptance and adoption of internal platform services within an organization. By regularly rotating engineers between platforms and product teams, typically every quarter, organizations can promote a culture of collaboration, knowledge sharing, and continuous improvement.

When platform engineers join product teams, they gain valuable insight into the real-world needs and challenges faced by users of their services. This first-hand experience allows them to understand the context in which their services are used, identify pain points, and gather critical feedback. Armed with this knowledge, they can return to the platform team and use these insights to develop and refine platform offerings, ensuring that services are tailored to the specific needs of product teams.

Conversely, when product team engineers rotate to the platform team, they bring their domain expertise and deep understanding of product requirements. They can work with the platform team to co-create and shape the next version of platform services, ensuring that the tools and services are optimized for their specific use cases. This collaborative approach builds trust, ownership, and buy-in among product teams because they have a direct impact on the development of the tools and services they rely on.

To maximize the benefits of job rotation, it's important to establish clear goals, duration, and expectations for each rotation. The duration should be long enough, typically a quarter or more, for engineers to fully immerse themselves in their new roles, gain a deep understanding of the challenges and opportunities, and make meaningful contributions. Providing adequate onboarding, support, and resources is critical to helping rotating engineers quickly adapt to their new responsibilities and hit the ground running.

A key aspect of successful job rotation is creating a structured knowledge transfer process. As engineers rotate between teams, it's important to ensure that the knowledge and insights gained during the rotation are effectively captured, documented, and shared with both the platform and product teams. Regular knowledge-sharing sessions, retrospectives, and documentation efforts can facilitate this transfer of expertise and ensure that the benefits of the rotation are sustained and built upon over time.

Security as a Platform That Provides Tools and Guidance

Security platform teams play a critical role in modern organizations. These teams serve as the cornerstone of an organization's security strategy, bridging the gap between high-level security policy and practical implementation across different software development teams and domains.

The primary responsibility of a security platform team is to create, maintain, and evolve a robust security infrastructure that supports the entire organization. This includes developing and managing centralized security services, tools, and frameworks that can be easily integrated and used by individual software development teams.

Key responsibilities of the Security Platform team include:

- Security Architecture: Design and implement a scalable, enterprise-wide security architecture that aligns with business goals and regulatory requirements.
- Tool Development and Integration: Build custom security tools and integrate third-party solutions to create a comprehensive security ecosystem.
- Automation and DevSecOps: Develop automated security checks, scans, and controls that can be seamlessly integrated into CI/CD pipelines, enabling a true DevSecOps approach.
- Security as Code (SaC): Implement and maintain security as code practices that enable version-controlled, repeatable, and auditable security configurations.
- Compliance and Governance: Establish frameworks and tools to ensure ongoing compliance with relevant standards and regulations across the enterprise.
- Threat Intelligence: Collect, analyze, and disseminate threat intelligence to inform security strategy and incident response.
- Incident Response Coordination: Develop incident response plans and coordinate cross-team efforts during security incidents.
- Security Education: Provide ongoing security training and resources to enhance the security capabilities of all teams within the organization.
- Innovation and Research: Stay abreast of emerging security technologies and threats, and innovate to address evolving security challenges.

By centralizing these functions, the security platform teams enable software development teams to focus on their core objectives while maintaining a strong security posture. They provide a foundation of security best practices, tools, and knowledge that can be leveraged across the organization, ensuring consistency and efficiency in security implementation.

In addition, security platform teams play a critical role in nurturing a culture of security awareness and shared responsibility. By making security more accessible and integrated into daily operations, they help transform security from a bottleneck to an enabler of innovation and rapid development. To do this, they collaborate regularly with the security champions of the software development teams.

In essence, security platform teams are the force multipliers of an organization's security efforts, enabling scalable, consistent, and effective security practices across diverse and dynamic technology landscapes.

Accelerate Platform Development with Inner Source

Inner Source is the application of open source principles and practices to internal software development within an organization, enabling collaboration, transparency, and code reuse across different teams and departments. The Inner Source model leverages the collective expertise of an organization by enabling product team developers to contribute directly to internal platforms.

This approach makes sense on several levels: it leverages the diverse expertise of day-to-day development experience, accelerates problem resolution, increases platform adoption, and facilitates knowledge sharing across teams. As organizations grow, this model allows platforms to scale more effectively by distributing development efforts and ensuring alignment with real business needs.

Implementing an Inner Source model requires a structured approach. Key steps include:

- Open access to repositories: Host platform code in internal Git repositories accessible to all developers. Implement a clear folder structure and documentation to aid navigation.
- Contribution guidelines: Create comprehensive guidelines for coding standards, testing requirements, and PR processes. Provide templates for issues, feature requests, and pull requests.
- Onboarding process: Develop an onboarding process for new contributors. Offer regular workshops or office hours to help product team developers get started.
- Mentorship program: Assign platform team members to mentor product team contributors. Provide code reviews with constructive feedback to help improve contributions.
- Recognition and incentives: Implement a system for recognizing and rewarding valuable contributions. Consider including platform contributions in performance reviews.
- Continuous integration/deployment: Implement robust CI/CD pipelines to ensure that all contributions are thoroughly tested. Provide contributors with rapid feedback on the status of their contributions.

While the benefits are significant, this model isn't without its challenges. Maintaining code quality and architectural integrity with diverse contributors can be difficult. There's also a risk of misaligned priorities, with product teams potentially focusing on short-term fixes over the long-term health of the platform.

Ownership and maintenance of contributed features can become unclear, and product teams may struggle to allocate time for platform work. Knowledge gaps about platform internals and the potential for scope creep are additional concerns.

Overcoming these challenges requires careful management. Rigorous code review processes, clear architectural guidelines, and long-term ownership policies are critical. Executive support and clear communication of benefits can help overcome cultural resistance. By carefully navigating these potential pitfalls, organizations can create a more collaborative, efficient, and innovative environment for platform development. This approach not only improves the platform itself but also contributes to a more skilled and engaged engineering workforce, ultimately advancing the organization's technical capabilities.

Valid Variants for Different Situations

A One-Size-Fits-All Setup

In organizations where domains share similar technologies, methodologies, and tools, a unified and centralized platform can provide comprehensive support across the organization. This centralized approach ensures that all domains have access to a consistent set of tools and practices, facilitating smoother collaboration and integration across teams.

By leveraging common technologies and ways of working, the central platform enables efficient use of resources, reduces the learning curve for new team members, and minimizes duplication of effort. It also streamlines the maintenance and updating of tools since changes only need to be implemented once on the central platform rather than across multiple, disparate systems. This not only improves operational efficiency but also nurtures a more cohesive technology culture within the organization.

A Domain-Specific Setup

In organizations where domains use significantly different technology stacks, methodologies, and tools, a domain-specific platform setup may be essential. For example, one domain might use commercial off-the-shelf (COTS) software such as SAP, requiring a platform that supports traditional enterprise resource planning systems.

Meanwhile, another domain might be developing a cutting-edge, cloud-native microservices architecture, requiring a platform with modern, scalable cloud infrastructure and DevOps capabilities. A third domain might be maintaining a legacy monolithic system on-premises, requiring a platform that provides stability and security for legacy architectures.

While each domain benefits from a customized platform that addresses its unique needs, there can also be a generic platform that provides cross-enterprise tools and services, such as identity management, cross-domain collaboration tools, and centralized logging and monitoring. This hybrid approach balances the need for specialization with the benefits of shared services, enabling efficiency and innovation across diverse technology landscapes.

A Community-Driven Setup

In some organizations, domain teams are tasked with the dual responsibility of building and maintaining specific platform services in addition to their primary responsibility of delivering business products. This "users are builders" model has the advantage of ensuring that platform services are closely aligned with the actual needs of their users, potentially increasing adoption and satisfaction. However, this approach presents significant challenges.

Conflicts with domain team product owners often arise as team capacity is diverted from business products to platform service maintenance, impacting the team's ability to meet business goals. In addition, the development and enhancement lead for platform services tends to be longer.

Because domain teams can only devote a limited portion of their resources to platform services, progress is slower compared to a dedicated platform team approach. This can delay critical updates and enhancements, impacting the overall responsiveness and evolution of the platform infrastructure.

REALITY TECH

Matthias introduced this model at one of his previous employers, believing that the best internal tools are built by the users themselves. However, this was not the case (there). The tools were what the users wanted, but the implementation took a long time because the 20% capacity per team meant that the internal tools were only worked on on Fridays, and yet the product managers were complaining about this capacity that they could not use. After eight months, an engineering manager pulled him aside and said: "It was a nice idea, but it's not working. Let's create dedicated platform teams." He did this but with other (solvable) problems. Matthias knows companies where this platform model works.

Common Misconceptions and Mistakes

Building the Platform without Real User Involvement

Building an internal development platform without real user involvement is a critical misstep that organizations can make, resulting in solutions that are not aligned with real needs. When business teams are not part of the design, build, and feedback process, the platform can end up with features that lack relevance, usability issues, or workflows that do not align with day-to-day practices.

This disconnect leads to low adoption rates, frustration among potential users, and ultimately a failure to achieve the platform's intended benefits of increased efficiency and productivity. Engaging, involving, and collaborating with real users throughout the development process is essential for creating a platform that truly supports and enhances the developer experience.

Gold Plating the Platform Services

Gold plating platform services, or overengineering, involves adding unnecessary features or complexity to internal developer platforms beyond what users need. This tendency can make the platform cumbersome, difficult to navigate, and intimidating to users, detracting from its core purpose of streamlining and simplifying development processes.

Overly complicated platforms require more resources to maintain and can lead to longer onboarding times, reducing overall productivity. Finding the right balance between functionality and simplicity is critical. By focusing on essential features and involving users in the development process, organizations can avoid the pitfalls of gold-plating and create more efficient, user-friendly platforms.

Lack of Proper Governance and Guidelines

The lack of proper governance and policies around internal developer platforms can lead to significant challenges. Without a clear framework for how the platform should be used, who has access to what resources, and the standards for security and compliance, organizations can find themselves dealing with inconsistent practices, security vulnerabilities, and inefficient use of resources.

This lack of direction not only hinders the effectiveness of the platform but can also create friction between teams and hinder the platform's ability to scale. Establishing robust governance and clear, accessible policies is essential for ensuring the platform serves its intended purpose and supports seamless collaboration and innovation across the organization.

Reinventing the Wheel

A common mistake some organizations make when developing internal developer platforms is reinventing the wheel by building in-house solutions that are already available as commercial off-the-shelf (COTS), software as a service (SaaS), or cloud-native tools.

This approach can result in unnecessary allocation of resources, including time and budget to develop, maintain, and update technologies that could be more efficiently sourced from external providers. Such duplication not only diverts focus from core business objectives but also delays the availability of tools to developers. Leveraging available technologies can accelerate development leads, leverage industry best practices, and provide scalability and support that may be difficult to replicate in-house.

Neglecting Training and Support

Neglecting training and support in the rollout of internal developer platforms is a critical mistake that can severely impede their success and adoption. Without proper training, users may struggle to navigate the platform, leverage its full capabilities, or integrate it effectively into their workflows, leading to frustration and reduced productivity.

Similarly, inadequate support mechanisms can leave users feeling stranded when they encounter issues, further diminishing their trust and willingness to use the platform. Investing in comprehensive training programs and setting up robust support systems is essential not only for smooth onboarding but also for ensuring ongoing user engagement and satisfaction, ultimately maximizing the platform's value and impact across the organization.

TL;DR and Further Reading

Establishing a platform team that acts as a 'technical' service provider is something to aspire to become a great tech organization. In our case, it is an absolute must. You can start with a small set of tools that create the highest value. Appoint two to three people to work on a small toolset that can mark the beginning, and start from there.

Platforms provide simple, efficient, and stress-free toolchains for engineering teams.

- Platform teams are internal product development teams
- They prove the value of platforms with internal A/B testing
- The users of the platform drive its scope and backlog
- Security as a platform provides tools and guidance
- Accelerate platform development with Inner Source

For a more in-depth look at this topic, this is one of our favorite books:

- *Platform Strategy—Innovation Through Harmonization,* by Gregor Hohpe

6

HOW TO DISTRIBUTE DATA MANAGEMENT ACROSS DOMAINS WITH DATA MESH

IN TODAY'S DATA-DRIVEN WORLD, effective data management is critical for great tech organizations to maintain a competitive edge. However, as organizations scale, traditional centralized data architectures often become bottlenecks, hindering agility and innovation. An organization's ability to make informed decisions, develop innovative products, and respond quickly to market changes can be significantly impacted by how it manages its data.

We therefore introduce Data Mesh, a paradigm shift in data management that aligns with modern, domain-oriented organizational structures. This approach treats data as a product, distributing ownership and responsibility across domains while providing a self-service platform for seamless data access and governance.

This chapter will guide you through the evolution of data management, from centralized data warehouses to the distributed Data Mesh architecture. We'll explore the core principles of Data Mesh, debunk common misconceptions, and provide practical strategies for implementation. Along the way, we'll address potential challenges and discuss how to adapt the Data Mesh concept to different organizational contexts.

By the end of this chapter, you'll have a comprehensive understanding of how to use Data Mesh to unlock the full potential of your organization's data assets and drive innovation and agility throughout your technology ecosystem.

The Traditional Approach and Why It Falls Short

Traditional IT organizations have long grappled with data management, often employing centralized approaches that fall short in today's dynamic business landscape. These conventional methods, born from the need for specialized skills in data-related fields, have inadvertently created a host of challenges that hinder organizational agility and innovation.

At the heart of these issues lies the monolithic, centralized data infrastructure. This approach often results in data silos and restricted access. Different departments find themselves isolated, unable to share crucial information effectively. The centralization of data management leads to bottlenecks, with teams relying heavily on a core data group for analysis and insights. This not only slows decision-making processes but also limits the organization's ability to respond swiftly to market changes. Moreover, the central team may lack the nuanced understanding of specific business domains, potentially leading to misinterpretations and suboptimal strategies.

Another significant drawback is the separation of analytics from business domains. By centralizing analytical capabilities, organizations inadvertently disconnect data processing from both the data producers and consumers. This separation results in generic solutions that do not address the unique challenges within each business area. It stifles innovation and experimentation, as domain experts are distanced from the tools and data they need to drive insights. The autonomy of business units is compromised, forcing them to rely on centralized resources rather than developing tailored analyses that could propel their specific objectives forward.

Compounding these issues is a pervasive underinvestment in data literacy across organizations. While tools like Microsoft Excel are ubiquitous, their potential remains largely untapped due to limited user ability. This lack of data literacy manifests in various ways: employees struggle to extract actionable insights, there's a general mistrust in data-driven decision-making, and data-related initiatives often face resistance.

Simultaneously, many data teams fall into the trap of technology obsession, focusing more on building sophisticated infrastructures than on delivering tangible business value. This misalignment of priorities leads to increased costs, project delays, and a disconnect between technological capabilities and business goals.

The collective impact of these traditional practices is a data management approach that hampers rather than helps modern IT organizations. The disconnect between the intended efficiency of centralization and the resulting inflexibility highlights the urgent need for a paradigm shift in how organizations approach data management and analytics. As we look to address these shortcomings, it becomes clear that a new, more distributed, and business-aligned approach to data management is necessary.

The General Blueprint

Producers and Consumers of Data Take Ownership of It

The data mesh concept offers an alternative to the traditional centralized approach of data lakes and data warehouses where data is handled by a dedicated central data team leading to limited collaboration between teams.

With data mesh, the sub-domain teams that generate, process, and use data with their transactional applications are also responsible for the analytical use of this data. This leads to distributed ownership and management of this data by the domain-specific teams that know the underlying business transactions and their data best —on the producer and consumer side of data.

Producers are sub-domain teams that build and run transactional applications, like the team that builds e-commerce checkout pages, the team that maintains the application for manufacturing operations, or the team that creates data as part of their business operations, i.e., the marketing campaign team or the financial services team. All of them are generating transactional, operational, and analytical data specific to their domains that might be consumed by other teams.

Consumers are sub-domain teams such as marketing analytics teams, business intelligence teams, data science teams, and customer support teams that leverage this data for diverse purposes, ranging from optimizing marketing strategies and generating reports to developing predictive models and enhancing customer satisfaction.

This distributed ownership model of the data mesh concept has several advantages:

- It encourages a sense of accountability and ownership among domain teams, encouraging them to prioritize data quality, reliability, usability, and value.
- It promotes greater collaboration and alignment across business domains as teams work together to create insights, actions, and value from data. They also

collaborate to define data standards, protocols, and interfaces.
- It enables faster decision-making and innovation by giving teams direct control over the data they need, reducing reliance on centralized data teams, and streamlining data access and use.

Overall, by decentralizing data ownership, data mesh empowers teams to use data more effectively, driving business value and agility across the organization.

Data Is Treated as a Product That Delivers Business Value

In the context of the data mesh, a "data product" refers to a self-contained unit of analytical data designed to address specific business needs or use cases within an organization. It includes not only the raw data itself, but also its metadata, the source code required to prepare and deliver it, infrastructure configurations, and necessary documentation.

In addition, data products are treated as independent entities like microservices that provide interfaces or APIs for easy access and consumption by other teams or applications.

Specific examples of data products on the producer side include:

- AI-driven recommendation engines
- APIs that expose sales transaction data
- machine learning models that predict equipment failures

On the consumer side, examples of data products include:

- reporting tools for generating sales performance reports
- real-time dashboards that track customer engagement metrics

- and data visualization tools for exploring trends in customer feedback

A key aspect of a data product includes clear ownership by domain-specific teams. A sub-domain team might own none, a single, or many data products, but a data product is always owned by a dedicated team.

This might be a producing or consuming sub-domain team. This ensures that the data products are tailored to the specific needs of the respective business areas and that it is clear which team is responsible for the benefits, quality, maintenance, support, and troubleshooting.

Data products are created only when there is a specific need and at least one team that wants to use that data product. Speculative design should be avoided at all costs. There should be constant monitoring of whether a data product is being used. Many data products are created on suspicion but are never used. Such products should be shut down or paused. If necessary, they should be marked as depreciated, and if they are not used for an extended period, they should be completely deleted.

In a data mesh framework, producers and consumers have the flexibility to choose the technology, tools, and architectures that best suit their specific context and domain. This approach recognizes that different teams may have unique data processing and analysis requirements and preferences. By empowering teams to choose their preferred technology stack, they can leverage familiar tools and methodologies that align with their domain technology stack, expertise, and goals.

This flexibility facilitates innovation and efficiency, as teams can adopt solutions that optimize performance and meet their specific needs without being constrained by a centralized, one-size-fits-all approach dictated by a centralized data team.

Data Producers and Consumers Get More Resources and Skills

As producers and consumers who originally built and ran transactional systems such as e-commerce stores, ERP systems, or as marketing tools take on more responsibilities for building and operating data products within the data mesh, they have to acquire additional skills and become even more T-shaped engineers.

This means deepening their existing expertise in their respective domains from the aspect of analytical use cases while also gaining proficiency in areas such as data engineering and data science. This is certainly not the most efficient way, but it is the most effective one. With these expanded skill sets, the team becomes more cross-functional and can build the transactional aspect of a use case (maybe in the form of a microservice) and the respective analytical part as a data product. The team as a whole can better understand the end-to-end process of their use cases, including the data product development and deployment, contributing to more effective collaboration and innovation within the organization.

To support these efforts, it may be necessary to add additional data engineers or data scientists to the team who can provide specialized expertise and guidance on how to effectively implement data products. This can be either temporary if the subdomain team is inexperienced with data or if an elaborate or complicated data product is to be created, or it can be permanent, increasing the team size which may also have negative impacts on the team. You must be careful that the additional people don't make the teams too big. Our advice is to reduce the scope of the subdomain team, if possible, so that the team is still responsible for both transactional and data products instead of dividing the large team into a dedicated transactional and a dedicated data team (which, after all, is a valid variant).

It is often suggested that there be another product owner on the team for the data products. We do not recommend this because there is too much risk of creating two informal teams within the team. This is not desirable. Each team has only one product owner, and their scope of responsibility is extended.

A Self-Service Data Platform Supports the Data Producers and Consumers

The additional responsibility for data products places a significant burden on subdomain teams, increasing cognitive load and complexity. To mitigate these challenges and empower teams to independently manage their data products, a data mesh platform with dedicated platform teams is introduced.

This platform provides a suite of self-service tools, consulting services, guidance, and governance to streamline operations and help subdomain teams effectively manage data products.

The data mesh platform offers a range of tools to support the creation, management, and consumption of data products:

- Data Catalog: A centralized repository for discovering, understanding, and accessing data products, including metadata management, data lineage, and data quality metrics.
- Data Governance and Security: Ensuring data privacy, security, and compliance with regulations such as GDPR and HIPAA.
- Data Integration and Transformation: Enabling data producers to ingest, transform, and enrich data from various sources.

- Data Infrastructure and Storage: Providing scalable and reliable infrastructure for storing and processing data products.
- Data Testing and Quality: Ensuring the reliability and accuracy of data products through automated testing and quality checks.
- Data Visualization and Business Intelligence: Empowering data consumers to explore, analyze, and derive insights from data products.

By establishing and enforcing standards for data quality, metadata, and interfaces, the data mesh platform ensures consistency and interoperability across data products. The data mesh platform serves as an enabler rather than a producer of data products, providing comprehensive resources and expertise to help teams navigate complexity, make informed decisions, and ensure alignment with business objectives.

Through clear governance protocols and expert guidance, the platform empowers teams to focus on their core responsibilities while facilitating seamless data management practices across the organization.

Adopting a data mesh platform may present challenges, such as resistance to change or learning curves. However, these can be overcome through targeted training programs and change management initiatives. As the organization grows and business needs evolve, the data mesh platform scales to support an increasing number of data products, ensuring long-term sustainability and value.

By embracing a data mesh platform and leveraging the right tools, organizations can efficiently build, deploy, and manage data products while maintaining consistency, security, and governance across their data landscape.

Governance Is Decided in a Federal Approach by Producers, Consumers, and the Platform

Data mesh decentralizes data ownership, empowering domain-specific teams with agility, scalability, and innovation in analytics. Distributing data processing closer to its sources increases effectiveness, responsiveness, and alignment with business needs.

However, alignment is required at the domain and organizational levels. Data mesh introduces a federated governance model in which clear data governance policies, standards, technologies, and processes are jointly defined and enforced by producers, consumers, and the data mesh platform. This approach ensures that while domain teams have autonomy over their data products, there is still alignment with overarching organizational goals and policies. It balances decentralized decision-making and ownership while maintaining consistency, interoperability, and compliance across the organization.

In this federated approach within a data mesh, each domain is responsible for defining and enforcing its own data governance policies, standards, and processes. This means that producers and consumers within each domain work together to establish rules and best practices tailored to their specific needs and objectives.

These policies can include data quality standards, data access policies, metadata management practices, and security protocols. The data mesh platform facilitates coordination and communication across domains to ensure that governance practices are consistent and compatible across the enterprise. The platform can provide tools for sharing governance artifacts, monitoring compliance, and resolving conflicts or discrepancies.

In situations where domains can't reach a consensus or decision, it's important to have a mechanism in place to resolve conflicts or make final determinations. Typically, this responsibility falls to higher-level leadership or governance bodies within the organization, such as a data governance council or steering committee. These bodies are composed of representatives from different domains and departments to ensure that decisions are made with input from multiple perspectives.

In addition, the data mesh platform team plays a role in facilitating discussions and providing expert advice to inform these decisions. Ultimately, the goal is to make decisions that align with organizational goals while balancing the needs and priorities of each domain.

Valid Variants for Different Situations

A Combination of a Distributed Data Mesh and a Central Data Lake as a Hybrid Data Landscape

We expect that many large organizations will adopt a hybrid approach. Parts of the organization will use the distributed data mesh approach while others will use the traditional, centralized approach of a data lake with a central data team. This is perfectly fine and even a benefit of the distributed nature of the data mesh.

This hybrid model leverages existing investments in centralized infrastructures and teams, reduces the risks associated with wholesale migration to a new approach, and ensures the continuity of critical data operations. It also allows for a gradual transition to data mesh by piloting the approach in specific domains before scaling it across the organization.

By facilitating knowledge sharing of best practices among teams operating under different models, the hybrid approach promotes flexibility and adaptability to changing business needs. This pragmatic approach enables organizations to realize the benefits of data federation while navigating the complexities of large organizational structures.

Dedicated Data Teams at the Domain Level

Having dedicated data teams at the domain level is a valid variation or immediate step that results in reduced cognitive load within the subdomain teams because they don't have to worry about their data products.

This setup also minimizes the need for extensive re-skilling, as subdomain teams can keep expertise in their particular area of focus. It also allows for a clear separation of concerns. However, there are drawbacks to this approach, such as increased communication overhead and dependencies within the domain, which can lead to longer data product development lead times. Furthermore, while these issues are mitigated compared to centralized data teams, they still exist at a smaller scale, potentially limiting the organization's agility and responsiveness.

A Central Technical Data Lake-Operated Organization Like a Distributed Data Mesh

In this approach, while all data products are technically implemented in a central data lake, the execution is distributed across domain teams. Each domain team is responsible for building and managing the data products relevant to its domain within the centralized data lake infrastructure.

This setup allows for a unified technical architecture and centralized data governance while still leveraging the domain-specific knowledge and context of each team. Domain teams can access and manipulate data within the central data lake according to their needs and requirements, ensuring alignment with business objectives and domain-specific use cases. By decentralizing execution while maintaining a centralized infrastructure, organizations can balance agility, scalability, and data governance.

A significant drawback is the potential for increased complexity in coordination and communication among domain teams. With each team responsible for its data products within the central infrastructure, there can be challenges in managing dependencies and ensuring consistency across different domains. This can lead to longer lead times for implementing new features or changes, as well as potential conflicts or duplication of data management efforts.

In addition, relying on a centralized data lake for all data products introduces a single point of failure and can limit the flexibility to adopt specialized technologies or tools tailored to specific domain needs. Overall, while this approach offers benefits in terms of leveraging domain expertise and centralizing governance, it requires careful management to mitigate potential drawbacks related to coordination and flexibility.

Dedicated Data Product Owner

It might be necessary to introduce a new role in those subdomain teams: a Data Product Owner who works alongside the traditional Product Owner role. This additional position is introduced to address the specific responsibilities related to managing data products within the domain team.

While the Product Owner typically focuses on the overall development and management of a product, the Data Product Owner specializes in handling data-related aspects, such as defining data strategies, prioritizing data product backlogs, and ensuring alignment with data mesh principles. This dual ownership model allows for more effective coordination and decision-making regarding data products within domain teams, ensuring that both business requirements and data considerations are adequately addressed.

Common Misconceptions and Mistakes

Underestimating the Cultural Change

Focusing too much on the technology and overlooking the cultural change is a common pitfall when implementing a data network. While it's important to adopt modern tools and technologies, it's equally important to recognize the cultural and organizational changes required for success.

The shift to domain-specific teams and decentralized data ownership requires a significant cultural shift, including nurturing collaboration, promoting data literacy, and breaking down silos. Organizations must prioritize building a culture of data ownership and accountability where teams are empowered to take ownership of their data products. Failure to address these cultural issues can undermine the effectiveness of data mesh initiatives regardless of the sophistication of the technology employed.

Treating Data Mesh as a One-Size-Fits-All Solution

Treating data mesh as a one-size-fits-all solution is another common misconception. While data mesh provides a decentralized approach to data management, it may not be appropriate for every organization or scenario. Each organization has its own unique culture, structure, and requirements that must be considered when implementing data mesh.

It's important to tailor the approach to the specific needs and context of the organization rather than trying to force a one-size-fits-all solution. Adopting data mesh without considering these individual factors can lead to inefficiencies, stakeholder resistance, and ultimately failure to achieve the desired results.

What's more, in large organizations, both data lakes and data meshes may coexist, each serving different purposes and domains. Organizations should approach data mesh implementation with a mindset of flexibility and adaptability, recognizing that it may require iteration and customization to fit their unique circumstances.

Neglecting Data Governance and Standards

Neglecting data governance and standards is a major oversight when implementing data mesh. While data mesh emphasizes decentralization and autonomy, it still requires robust governance frameworks to ensure consistency, quality, and compliance across data products.

Without clear guidelines and standards for data management, organizations risk data silos, inconsistencies, and security vulnerabilities. Data governance includes defining roles and responsibilities, establishing data quality measures, enforcing data security protocols, and maintaining regulatory compliance. Ignoring these aspects can result in data chaos, decreased trust in data, and hindered collaboration across teams.

That's why it's critical for organizations adopting data mesh to prioritize the development and enforcement of comprehensive data governance policies and standards to support its successful implementation and operation.

Underestimating the Complexity of Implementation

Underestimating the complexity of implementation is another common pitfall in data mesh adoption. While the concept of decentralizing data ownership and encouraging domain-specific teams sounds simple, the execution can be complicated and challenging.

Implementing data mesh involves not only technical changes but also significant cultural and organizational shifts. It requires redefining roles, restructuring teams, and promoting a data-driven culture throughout the organization. In addition, integrating disparate data systems, establishing data pipelines, and ensuring interoperability between data products requires careful planning and execution.

Organizations often underestimate the time, resources, and effort required to address these complexities, leading to delays, setbacks, and suboptimal results. That's why it's essential to approach data mesh implementation with a clear understanding of its multifaceted nature and to allocate sufficient resources, expertise, and support to effectively address the challenges.

TL;DR and Further Reading

- Producers and consumers of data take ownership of it
- Data is treated as a product that delivers business value
- Data producers and consumers get additional resources and skills
- A self-service data platform supports the data producers and consumers
- Governance is decided in a federal approach by producers, consumers, and the platform

For a more in-depth look at this topic, these are some of our favorite books and websites:

- *Data Mesh: Delivering Data-Driven Value at Scale*, by Zhamak Dehghani
- *Data Mesh in Action*, by Jacek Majchrzak, Sven Balnojan, and Marian Siwiak with Mariusz Sieraczkiewicz

7

HOW TO EXECUTE YOUR STRATEGY FOR MAXIMUM IMPACT AND FLEXIBILITY

MANY ORGANIZATIONS STRUGGLE to translate their strategic vision into tangible results, often grappling with the challenge of executing strategies effectively in rapidly changing environments. This disconnect between strategy and execution can lead to wasted resources, missed opportunities, and a failure to achieve critical business objectives.

The ability to execute strategy with agility and precision is a key differentiator for great tech organizations. It directly impacts an organization's capacity to innovate, respond to market changes, and maintain a competitive edge. Effective strategy execution aligns teams, optimizes resource allocation, and ensures that daily activities contribute meaningfully to overarching business goals.

This chapter introduces a modern approach to strategy execution that leverages Kanban, Flight Levels, and hypothesis-driven development. We'll explore how to adaptively focus resources on high-stakes challenges, prioritize initiatives based on impact and success probability, and use cadences to align execution across the organization.

We begin by examining traditional, top-down approaches to strategy execution and their limitations in today's fast-paced tech landscape. We then present a comprehensive framework for turning strategy into action, including techniques for bridging knowledge and alignment gaps, transforming hypotheses into measurable results, and effectively managing stakeholders. We'll address common misconceptions about strategy execution and discuss potential pitfalls.

By the end of this chapter, you'll have a practical toolkit for executing your strategy with maximum impact and flexibility.

The Traditional Approach and Why It Falls Short

In many traditional IT organizations, strategy execution often fails to deliver the intended results, hindering growth and innovation. While these approaches aim to provide structure and clarity, they frequently lead to inflexibility, disengagement, and missed opportunities.

One major issue is the prevalence of rigid, top-down strategic planning. Senior management, such as CTOs and CEOs, typically create definitive plans with little input from other levels of the organization. This approach overlooks valuable insights from frontline employees and software development teams. Consequently, it can lead to a lack of buy-in, resistance to change, and ultimately suboptimal performance in software development projects. Moreover, this inflexibility makes it difficult for organizations to adapt to rapidly evolving market conditions and emerging technologies.

Another problematic aspect is the separation of strategy implementation from day-to-day operations. Many organizations rely on isolated projects to execute their strategies, creating a disconnect between strategic goals and routine activities. This project-based approach can result in lost momentum between initiatives, limited cross-functional collaboration, and missed opportunities for continuous improvement. In some cases, strategy execution may exist only in theory, with little to no tangible action taken to turn plans into reality.

Furthermore, traditional organizations often neglect the necessary adaptations to culture, skills, and working methods required for successful strategy implementation. There's a tendency to avoid initiatives that might disrupt existing departments or revenue streams, leading to a dilution of resources across multiple projects rather than focusing on high-impact challenges. This approach not only hinders progress toward strategic goals but also leaves the organization vulnerable to competitive threats and market shifts.

The collective impact of these traditional practices creates a significant gap between strategic intentions and actual results. Organizations struggle to make meaningful progress, adapt to change, and encourage innovation. As the tech industry continues to evolve at a rapid pace, it's clear that a new approach to strategy execution is needed—one that embraces flexibility, inclusivity, and continuous adaptation.

The General Blueprint

Adaptively Focus and Channel Resources on the High-Stakes Challenge

Successful product development organizations are characterized by their ability to adaptively focus and direct resources to high-stakes challenges. This approach is critical to achieving sustainable growth and outperforming competitors in dynamic industries.

These organizations cultivate a deep understanding of their core domains, critical value streams, evolving customer needs, and overall strategy. This knowledge provides the foundation for identifying and prioritizing high-stakes challenges—those critical issues that can make or break the organization.

The key is adaptability. While keeping a laser focus on these critical challenges, organizations must remain flexible in their approach. They continually reevaluate both the nature of the high-stakes challenges and the methods used to address them. This adaptive mindset allows for rapid reallocation of resources, including talent, funding, and technology as priorities shift or new opportunities appear.

Empowerment is central to this adaptive mindset. Teams are given the autonomy, resources, and skills they need to effectively address high-stakes challenges. This empowerment, coupled with clear strategic alignment, enables rapid decision-making about what actions to take, what tools to employ, and most importantly, what initiatives to forgo.

By adaptively focusing and channeling resources to high-stakes challenges, organizations can maximize their impact, drive targeted innovation, and remain agile in the face of market changes. This approach ensures that efforts and resources are consistently focused on the areas most critical to customer satisfaction and business success.

Address the Knowledge, Alignment, and Effect Gap in Strategy Execution

When trying to translate strategic plans into concrete actions and desired results, uncertainties, misunderstandings, and unforeseen obstacles arise that hinder the successful execution of the strategy.

According to Stephen Bungay, author of "*The Art of Action: How Leaders Close the Gaps between Plans, Actions and Results,*" the main causes are three gaps that organizations face in executing their strategy. You must be aware of these three gaps and act accordingly when setting up your strategy execution framework.

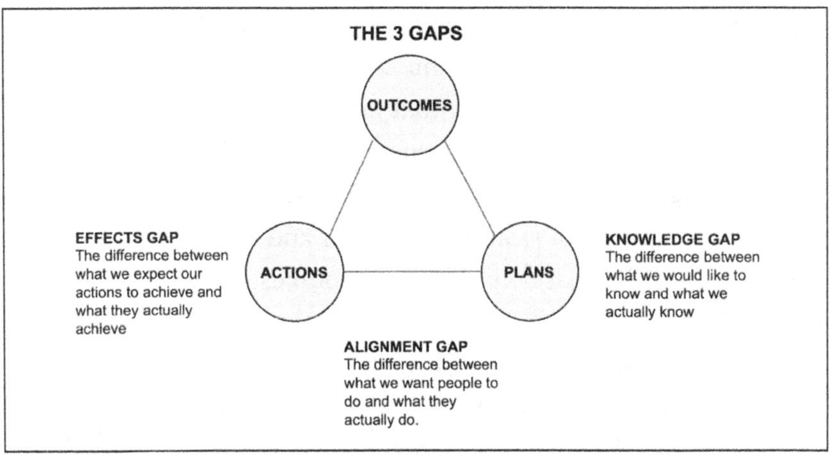

- The Knowledge Gap: The gap between what we would like to know and what we actually know. It highlights the uncertainty of fully understanding our environment, including markets, competitors, and internal capabilities.
- The Alignment Gap: This is the gap between what the strategy intends and what the organization actually does. It arises from the difficulty of communicating strategy throughout the organization and ensuring that everyone is working toward the same goals.
- The Effects Gap: This gap represents the difference between the expected results of actions and the actual results. It recognizes that even well-planned actions can have unpredictable results due to the complex nature of business environments.

The framework we propose and recommend in this chapter attempts to address these three gaps. The key points to note are:

- The Knowledge Gap is addressed through rapid feedback loops and a culture of continuous learning that supports adaptive focus by ensuring that organizations have up-to-date information to identify high-stakes challenges.
- The Alignment Gap is addressed through clear communication of strategic priorities and the use of tools such as OKRs that help channel resources effectively across domains.
- The Effects Gap is closed through hypothesis-driven development and short feedback loops that allow for rapid adaptation in response to actual results.

By adaptively focusing on high-stakes challenges and implementing these strategies, agile, domain-oriented product organizations can more effectively bridge the gaps between plans, actions, and results, leading to more successful strategy execution in dynamic environments.

Execute Your Strategy with a Hypothesis-Driven Development Backlog

When formulating a strategy, you inevitably make many assumptions about market trends, customer behavior, and the competitive landscape. Often, these assumptions are based on incomplete information. Rather than accepting these assumptions as unquestioned truths to guide your feature implementation, treat them as hypotheses that require rigorous testing and validation.

Take a scientific approach to your strategy implementation! Just as researchers subject their hypotheses to empirical testing, you should validate your strategic assumptions using data-driven methods. Think of each assumption as a bet with associated risks, potential rewards, and required resource investments. While you may already incorporate probabilities into risk assessments, apply the same rigor to evaluating your strategic initiatives.

To handle feature requests effectively, we recommend adopting hypothesis-driven development. This approach emphasizes the uncertainty inherent in product development and strategy execution. When you practice hypothesis-driven development, you make educated guesses about how certain changes or features will affect user behavior or achieve desired outcomes. Instead of continuing development based solely on assumptions or intuition, you design experiments to test these hypotheses.

By gathering empirical evidence, you can validate or invalidate your assumptions and make more informed decisions. This approach allows you to better manage uncertainty, allocate resources more efficiently, and increase the likelihood of successful strategy execution.

The goal is not to prove your initial assumptions correct but to learn and adjust your strategy based on evidence. Embrace the lessons learned from both successful and failed hypotheses. In doing so, you'll build a more resilient, adaptable organization that can thrive in uncertain environments.

Here's how it typically works:

- Formulate hypotheses: Teams identify specific assumptions or beliefs about user behavior, market dynamics, or product features in their area of responsibility that they want to test and might later develop. These hypotheses are framed as statements that can be proven true or false through experimentation. The responsible team establishes a clear, measurable signal for the success or failure of the hypothesis.

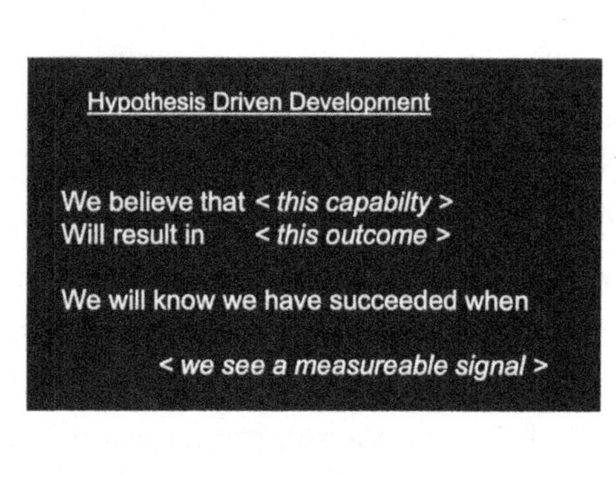

A great example is set by Thoughtworks

- Design experiments: Teams create a minimal experiment to collect data and anecdotes relevant to the hypotheses, often in the form of an MVP (Minimum Viable Product) or A/B test. These experiments can take many forms, including A/B testing, user surveys, prototype testing, or market testing.
- Execute the experiments: Teams execute the experiments and collect data on user behavior, feedback, or other relevant metrics. They ensure that experiments are conducted in a controlled environment to minimize confounding variables and bias.
- Analyze results: Once the experiments are complete, teams analyze the data and anecdotes to determine whether the hypotheses were supported or refuted. They look for patterns, trends, or statistically significant differences in the data to draw conclusions. Based on the results, they

decide whether to persevere with the idea, pivot to a new approach, or abandon the hypothesis.

- Iterate and learn: Based on the results of the experiments, teams iterate on their product or feature, making adjustments based on the insights gained from the experimentation process:
- If a hypothesis is validated, teams move to full implementation and scale the feature or product. The hypotheses remain the core backlog items throughout the entire implementation process until full-scale validation in production.
- If a hypothesis is invalidated, teams can pivot or stop based on the new information.
- The actual process is cyclical, involving strategic alignment, hypothesis generation, prioritization, experiment design, execution, analysis, learning, and strategic review.

Characteristics of good measurable signals:

- Relevance: Directly related to the hypothesis being tested and the strategic goal it supports.
- Quantifiable: Can be expressed numerically, allowing for objective measurement.
- Reliability: Consistently measures the same thing under similar conditions.
- Sensitivity: Capable of detecting meaningful changes or effects related to your hypothesis.
- Timeliness: Can be measured within a timeframe that allows for timely decision-making.
- Actionability: Provides insights that can inform clear next steps or decisions.
- Accessibility: Can be collected and analyzed using available resources and tools.

- Comparability: Enables benchmarking against baseline data or industry standards.

Customer and user anecdotes play a critical role in hypothesis-driven development, adding color and context to quantitative data. Anecdotes can inspire new hypotheses, help interpret data trends, and provide compelling examples to stakeholders.

Hypothesis-driven development should be used at every level of an organization, from strategic initiatives at the top level to individual stories at the team level. At the strategic level, it enables leaders to derive or reformulate hypotheses about market dynamics, customer needs, and the competitive landscape from the strategy that sets the direction of the organization.

These hypotheses serve as the basis for strategic decisions, ensuring that initiatives are based on empirical evidence rather than unfounded assumptions. Similarly, at the team level, hypothesis-driven development enables agile teams to create user stories based on hypotheses about user behavior, feature effectiveness, and product outcomes with teams taking primary ownership of hypothesis generation and testing within their areas of expertise.

Set in the context of strategy execution:

- Align with strategic goals: Ensure that hypotheses are tied to high-stakes challenges and strategic goals.
- Create hypothesis backlogs: Maintain a prioritized list of hypotheses to test, aligned with strategic priorities on the organizational, domain, and team levels.
- Establish an experimentation framework: Establish tools and processes for rapid experimentation and data collection.

- Define decision thresholds: Establish clear criteria for when to persevere, pivot, or stop based on experiment results.

We describe the exact process of how to prioritize and manage hypotheses across domains and teams in detail in Chapter 7 under the section, Transform Hypotheses into Results with Flight Levels and Kanban.

Done Means Someone's Need Was Met

In product- and customer-focused organizations, "done" means that a fundamental customer need or problem has been solved. It is not enough to finish building the feature and deploy it into production. The actual implementation and delivery is only an intermediate step that marks the beginning of the most important part of a team's work: Determining whether the feature

- is understood
- accepted
- used
- solves fundamental problems
- is good enough that customers are willing to pay for it

To do this, data and feedback on how customers use the feature must be collected.

In hypothesis-driven development, the concept of "done means someone's need has been met" is deeply integrated into the iterative process. Here, each development initiative begins with a hypothesis: A proposed solution to a specific problem or need identified within the target user base.

The team then formulates success criteria that define what it means for the hypothesis to be validated. Throughout the development, the team focuses on gathering data and feedback to test the hypothesis against these criteria. Success is determined by analyzing the collected data and assessing whether the implemented solution effectively addresses the identified need or problem. If the success criteria are met, the hypothesis is validated and the feature or solution can be considered "done."

However, if the criteria are not met, the team iterates on the solution, makes adjustments based on feedback, and retests until the desired outcome is achieved. This approach ensures that every development effort is guided by a clear understanding of user needs, validated by empirical evidence, and closely aligned with delivering business value.

Unfortunately, it often happens that an idea or a feature has no real effect or even a negative effect. In this case, it is recommended to remove the feature, so as not to increase the complexity of the software application without a simultaneous benefit.

Prioritize Your Backlog by Impact and Probability of Success

One of the biggest problems in most organizations, especially in product management, is having lots of ideas but not enough resources. For this reason, it is important to prioritize hypotheses and determine where to focus your people and your budget. Cost is an important prioritization criterion for many organizations. For the type of organization we are describing here, it is important as well, but for them, it is a secondary criterion in prioritization.

We recommend that you prioritize your hypotheses, which are the core work items in your strategic backlog and portfolio, based on two key factors:

- Strategic Impact Potential: It is a measure of a hypothesis' capacity to significantly advance the organization's strategy and create lasting value.

- Probability of Success: It quantifies the likelihood that a hypothesis will be successfully implemented and achieve its intended results.

Comparing hypotheses with different measurable signals is challenging because:

- Each hypothesis might focus on different aspects of the business (e.g., "Daily Active Users," "Load Time," "Customer Lifetime Value," "Net Promoter Score," "Cost per Acquisition," or "Brand Awareness").
- These measurable signals may have different scales, units, or timeframes.
- The relative importance of different measurable signals to the overall strategy may vary.
- Some signals might be leading indicators while others are lagging indicators.

We recommend against using normalization, standardization, and weighted scoring models for hypothesis prioritization because these methods often create a false sense of objectivity and precision in what is fundamentally a complex, nuanced decision-making process.

Instead, we recommend using a prioritization matrix in a highly interactive, physical workshop setting for hypothesis evaluation in our domain-driven organization. This approach uses a simple 2x2 matrix with Strategic Impact Potential and Probability of Success as dimensions, and it brings together key persons from different domains for collaborative prioritization.

The workshop is professionally facilitated by a member of the strategy team or an experienced agile coach. Participants include domain leads, key product managers, and representatives from functions such as marketing, sales, and maybe legal. Senior stakeholders are present to provide high-level strategic input, particularly in assessing the strategic impact potential.

Domain Leads place their hypotheses on the matrix, explaining their rationale for both Strategic Impact Potential and Probability of Success. This sparks cross-domain discussions, with product managers and functional representatives providing insights on feasibility, impact, and dependencies. As the discussions unfold, participants collaboratively refine the placement of the hypotheses.

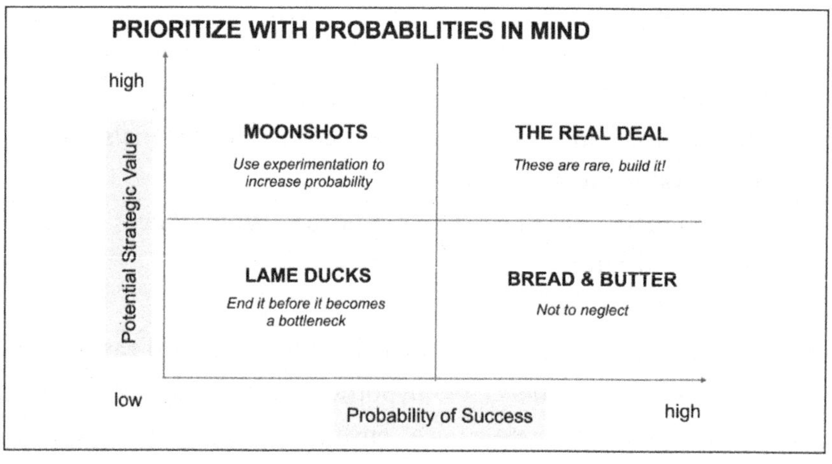

A common and crucial mistake in prioritization is that ideas and projects are isolated from each other in dedicated meetings that take the form of dog-and-pony shows and are not evaluated together in the broader portfolio context. Our approach brings together decision-makers from the specific domain, related domains, and senior management to promote a comprehensive view of the overall organizational or domain portfolio.

By visually mapping ideas against key criteria, participants gain insight into relative priorities and interdependencies that are often missed in individual assessments. This collaborative, tactile process builds consensus and shared understanding across organizational boundaries. Ultimately, this approach ensures that resource allocation and strategic decisions are made with full awareness of their impact on the entire portfolio, leading to more cohesive and effective strategy execution.

The four quadrants in the proposed 2x2 matrix are:

1. **MOONSHOTS** - Potential Breakthroughs (High Impact, Low Probability): 20-30% of capacity.

- These hypotheses could significantly advance the strategy but currently have a lower probability of success.
- The core task here is to increase the probability of success. Using lean startup thinking and design thinking, teams emphasize build-measure-learn cycles and develop minimum viable products (MVPs) to test key assumptions and find product/market fit. They focus on user-centered problem-solving and encourage rapid prototyping and iterative refinement or focus on overcoming key technical hurdles with clear go/no-go decision points. It's important to manage expectations and mitigate the risks associated with their uncertain outcomes.

2. **BREAD & BUTTER** - Quick Wins (Low Impact, High Probability): 20-25% of capacity.

- There are two types of hypotheses here: First are necessary product enhancements, maintenance activities, or legal and regulatory requirements. Second are hypotheses that are thought too small, but with a different approach, they would have the potential for higher monetization, market share, or other strategic relevance.

- On the first one, teams should take a pragmatic approach, focusing on efficiency and streamlined processes to manage the execution of these ideas. On the second one, organizations need to cultivate a "Think Big" culture and use lean startup thinking and design thinking to increase impact. External strategy, marketing, and value realization consultancies can be helpful here.

3. **THE REAL DEAL** - Strategic Priorities (High Impact, High Probability): 40-50% of capacity.

- The hypotheses in this quadrant have the greatest potential to advance the organization's strategy and are the most likely to be successful (but still can fail). In most cases, these have been quick wins or potential breakthroughs in the first place.
- They should be the primary focus for resource allocation and implementation. If these hypotheses are in the implementation phase, the word 'initiatives' or other implementation-oriented terms can be used. Agile methodologies are effective here, allowing for iterative delivery and rapid adjustment to optimize for changing requirements or market conditions.

4. **LAME DUCKS** - Low Priority Ideas (Low Impact, Low Probability): 5% of capacity.

- Hypotheses in this quadrant are least likely to drive strategic progress and have a low probability of success.
- They should generally be deprioritized or eliminated unless there are compelling reasons to pursue them like exploration or maintaining options.

REALITY TECH

The first time Matthias did this kind of assessment at one of his former employers, he and the product managers were shocked to find that a very large proportion of their initiatives were in the lower part of the 2x2 matrix: Low strategic impact, but mostly high probability of success from an implementation and customer experience perspective.

Based on this insight, the teams expanded their vey lean, execution-optimizing approach to include various creativity techniques. The company changed its approach to "failure" and encouraged product managers to think big and creatively, resulting in more innovative products, higher revenue, and increased company valuation over the medium term.

Organizational and domain leaders must ensure that they always have an appropriate and sustainable mix of ideas in each quadrant.

Another implication of this 2x2 matrix is that each team and domain in a product development organization must be able to work differently depending on the nature of the hypothesis—exploratory ideation with high uncertainty, or rapid and effective implementation combined with the ability to maintain and operate existing functionality.

Transform Hypotheses into Results with Flight Levels and Kanban

Properly managing your portfolio of strategic hypotheses and initiatives through the various stages of ideation, experimentation, implementation, and optimization is critical to your organization's success. In loosely coupled organizations, effective portfolio management depends on practices that promote transparency, collaboration, and agility:

- Visualization: Provides transparency, helps identify bottlenecks and dependencies, and facilitates alignment across domains and teams.
- Face-to-face collaboration: Creates deeper understanding, builds trust, and enables rapid problem-solving and innovation.
- Open discussion: Ensures all perspectives are heard, uncovers hidden issues, and promotes a culture of openness and continuous improvement.
- Rapid decision-making: Enables agility, allows for quick pivots based on new information, and keeps momentum.

In this section, we propose an approach that is essentially based on the Flight Level concept in combination with Kanban and that fits very well with our loosely coupled, domain-driven organizational form and our hypothesis-driven product management approach.

Flight Levels is a model developed by Klaus Leopold and provides the overall structure for linking strategy to execution across the organization. They ensure that work at all flight levels is aligned with strategic goals and that there's effective communication and coordination between flight levels. In a domain-driven organization, flight levels help maintain alignment across autonomous domains while respecting their contexts and expertise.

Kanban is an integral part of Flight Levels. It is the method used to visualize work, limit work in progress, and maximize efficiency within and across these levels. It provides the tactical tools for managing flow, identifying bottlenecks, and continuously improving processes.

The Flight Level model consists of three interrelated levels of organizational activity.

- Flight Level 3, the highest level, focuses on strategic portfolio management, where organizational goals are set and major hypotheses and initiatives are prioritized.
- Example: "We believe entering the Asian market will increase our global market share by 15% within two years."
- Flight Level 2 is the coordination level, where cross-team and cross-domain collaboration occurs to break down strategic hypotheses and initiatives into manageable pieces of work.
- Example: "We believe localizing our payment product for the Japanese market will result in a 5% market share in Japan within one year."
- Flight Level 1 is the operational level, where individual teams perform their day-to-day work and deliver value. Teams may use any process framework that is appropriate for their context.
- Example: "We believe adding Japanese language support to our UI will increase Japanese user engagement by 50%."

These levels are not hierarchical in the traditional sense but rather represent different perspectives and periods of organizational activity. Flight Levels provide a structured approach to aligning strategy and execution across the organization.

At Flight Level 3 (Strategic), leadership creates a strategic Kanban board to visualize and prioritize high-level hypotheses based on their strategic impact and likelihood of success. The team conducts biweekly reviews and quarterly planning sessions to support strategic alignment. Flight Level 3 meetings involve top leadership. Attendees typically include the CEO, C-suite executives, heads of major business units, and senior product leaders. These strategic sessions also include key domain leads to ensure alignment between high-level strategy and domain-specific knowledge.

Flight Level 2 (Self-coordination) focuses on self-coordination without relying on a single coordinator, using domain-specific Kanban boards to visualize hypotheses and initiatives while managing cross-domain dependencies. Weekly coordination meetings and monthly alignment with Flight Level 3 ensure coherence across domains. Flight Level 2 meetings bring together domain leads, product managers, and cross-functional representatives. These coordination sessions often include leaders from interdependent domains, key stakeholders from supporting functions like UX or architecture, and sometimes rotating representatives from development teams to offer ground-level insights.

At Flight Level 1 (Operational), individual teams within each domain organize their work on team-level boards, breaking down initiatives into specific tasks and experiments. Daily stand-ups help manage workflow and address impediments. This three-tiered system links strategic thinking to operational execution, facilitating a culture of hypothesis-driven development and continuous adaptation at all levels of the organization. Flight Level 1 meetings consist of the teams directly involved in day-to-day work. Attendees usually include all team members within a team. These operational gatherings focus on the tactical execution of initiatives and experiments.

Crucially, in a loosely coupled organization, attendance is flexible. Participants may vary based on the specific topics or challenges at hand. The key is to ensure that each level has the right mix of perspectives to make informed decisions while respecting the autonomy of domains and teams. Regular cross-level participation, where appropriate, helps maintain alignment and information flow throughout the organization.

The actual process looks like this:

- Leadership defines high-stakes challenges and strategic objectives on Flight Level 3.
- Domains then identify their potential contributions to these goals.
- Teams within each domain brainstorm solutions, which product managers help shape into testable hypotheses.
- These hypotheses are prioritized based on potential impact and strategic alignment, with cross-domain collaboration ensuring efficiency.
- Teams design minimal experiments for top-priority hypotheses, defining clear success metrics and timeframes.
- They execute these experiments within regular sprint cycles, collecting data throughout.
- Results are analyzed against predefined metrics, with findings presented in reviews.
- Teams collaborate with stakeholders to determine next steps.
- Learnings are documented and used to inform the next cycle of hypothesis generation and testing.
- Regular strategic reviews assess the aggregate impact of experiments on overall strategy, allowing for necessary adjustments.

This cyclical process ensures continuous alignment between strategic objectives and operational activities, fostering a culture of experimentation and data-driven decision-making across the organization.

In a domain-driven organization, each kanban board reflects the unique software development process of its specific domain. While these boards may look different, they all adhere to common kanban best practices. To create your board, start by outlining your development process as a series of columns, from initial idea to final impact. Incorporate a hypothesis-driven mindset throughout this process. On each board, both hypotheses and initiatives are ranked from top to bottom based on their importance.

This clear prioritization makes it easier to discuss blockers and dependencies across domains and teams because it's clear which initiatives take precedence over others. By following this approach, you create a visual management tool that not only represents your domain's workflow but also supports effective decision-making and cross-team collaboration.

We strongly recommend the use of physical kanban boards (supported by digital tools) coupled with face-to-face coordination meetings for effective strategic portfolio management at all three flight levels. This approach maximizes visibility and engagement, creating a tangible sense of progress and ownership among team members.

Physical boards create a focal point for discussion, making dependencies and bottlenecks immediately apparent and facilitating quick, informed decisions. Face-to-face meetings harness the power of direct human interaction, building trust and enabling rapid problem-solving through rich, nuanced communication. While digital tools provide the necessary data tracking and remote access, the physical elements ground the process in reality, encouraging spontaneous conversations and creative problem-solving.

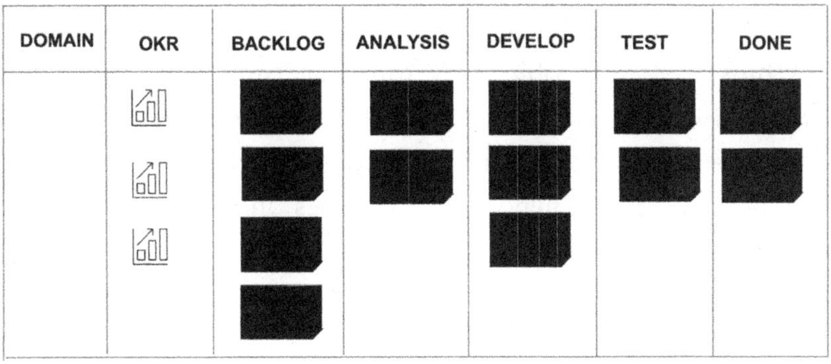

DOMAIN	OKR	BACKLOG	ANALYSIS	DEVELOP	TEST	DONE

Use Cadences to Align and Execute Strategy

Cadences are regular cycles of strategic activities that synchronize planning, execution, and review across an organization, enabling iterative and adaptive strategy implementation. In our experience, using cadences at the organizational, domain, and team levels helps maintain focus and alignment with strategic goals. These rhythmic cycles provide structure and synchronization points without imposing rigid control, striking a balance between autonomy and alignment.

The key benefits of this approach include:

- Alignment: Provides natural points for cross-domain and cross-level synchronization.
- Focus: Time-bound activities help teams focus on priorities without endless debate.
- Predictability: Establishes a rhythm that allows for better resource planning and expectation setting.
- Adaptability: Regular check-ins allow for course corrections based on new information or changing circumstances.
- Balance: Provides a middle ground between rigid annual planning and chaotic ad hoc execution.
- Accountability: Creates clear deadlines and checkpoints for commitments and goals.

To implement cadences successfully, define multi-level rhythms, set clear objectives for each time box, and conduct regular review and planning sessions. Integration with hypothesis-driven development is particularly powerful, using cadences to review hypothesis backlogs and share experimental learnings.

Recommended cadences may include:

- Organizational Level
- Strategy Review and Adjustment: Quarterly
- Cross-Domain Synchronization: Monthly
- Executive Team Sync: Weekly
- Retrospective: Quarterly
- Domain Level
- Domain Strategy Review: Monthly
- Cross-Team Synchronization: Bi-weekly
- Domain Leadership Sync: Weekly
- Retrospective: Monthly
- Team Level
- Planning and Review: Weekly or Bi-weekly
- Daily Sync: Daily (15 minutes)
- Retrospective: Monthly

Effective use of cadences in strategy execution requires ongoing evaluation and flexibility. Regularly assess how well your established cadences are serving your organization's needs and be prepared to adjust them as needed. Different types of work or different domains may benefit from different cadences; for example, innovation projects may require a different rhythm than maintenance work. Domains with custom-build software may have a different rhythm than domains with commercial-of-the-shelf software.

In addition, while consistency is important, it's wise to allow for some flexibility in adhering to cadences in exceptional circumstances. This adaptive approach ensures that cadences remain a useful tool for coordinating and driving strategy rather than becoming a rigid constraint that impedes progress.

Monitor Impact with a Range of Metrics

Product development teams have a clear understanding of the business figures and mechanisms of their domain, the adjacent domains, and the value stream in which they operate. They constantly monitor the relevant metrics so that they know how their business is doing at all times.

This practice involves the systematic collection and analysis of data related to various aspects of the product, such as user engagement, performance, and business outcomes. By using a variety of metrics, teams can gain insight into how their product is performing and whether it is meeting its goals. These metrics can include user retention rates, conversion rates, customer satisfaction scores, response times, and revenue generated, among others.

By tracking these metrics over time, teams can identify trends, identify areas for improvement, and make data-driven decisions to optimize the product's performance and increase its value to users. In addition, by monitoring metrics, teams can assess the impact of new features or changes, validate hypotheses, and prioritize future development efforts based on observed results.

To effectively monitor their progress, teams use a mix of leading and lagging indicators to ensure they have both predictive insights and retrospective assessments. In addition, teams often monitor KPIs that they cannot directly influence, providing valuable context and understanding of external factors impacting their product. Proper visualization of data is essential, allowing teams to compare data in both absolute and relative terms, facilitating deeper insights and informed decision-making.

Manage Stakeholders Continuously and Carefully

Managing external stakeholders is critical to successful agile portfolio management in loosely coupled, domain-driven organizations. These stakeholders include executive leadership, finance teams, legal departments, external partners, customers, investors, and various internal departments not directly involved in agile processes.

Effective stakeholder management ensures organizational alignment, secures resources, mitigates risk, and facilitates decision-making. To achieve this:

- Demonstrate value: Regularly share success stories and key learnings and link portfolio outcomes to broader organizational goals.
- Encourage a collaborative environment: Encourage open dialogue and stakeholder questions, and proactively and transparently address concerns.
- Identify and categorize stakeholders: Map all potential stakeholders and assess their level of influence, their interest in the portfolio, how active they are in portfolio management, their relationships with each other, and the domain leaders.
- Develop a communication strategy: Tailor communication methods and frequency to each stakeholder group. Use visual tools such as simplified kanban boards for high-level updates.
- Engage stakeholders regularly: Host regular briefings or showcases and invite stakeholders to observe key Flight Level meetings.

- Educate stakeholders on the process: Provide training on agile and hypothesis-driven development concepts. Explain the benefits of Flight Levels and the kanban approach.
- Solicit and incorporate feedback: Regularly solicit input from stakeholders and demonstrate how their feedback influences decisions and outcomes.
- Manage expectations: Clearly communicate the iterative nature of the process and explain how priorities and hypotheses may evolve over time.

We do not recommend having a dedicated stakeholder manager to coordinate efforts. Instead, responsibility for stakeholder management is shared among different roles. Flight Level 3 participants manage high-level stakeholders, while domain leads and product owners manage stakeholders relevant to their specific areas.

The key is to establish stakeholder management as a core responsibility and ensure that it's an ongoing, proactive process integrated into the overall strategic portfolio management approach.

REALITY TECH

From Sophie's extensive experience in a corporate environment, keeping stakeholders at bay was as simple as introducing regular show-and-tells. This interactive session allowed the team to get immediate feedback and address any concerns, avoiding months of invisible work that could have ended up going down the wrong path. In other circumstances, direct user feedback may be more important. Everyone has to decide what works best for the people involved. The most experienced and successful teams prioritized transparency, openly discussing work in progress and potential roadblocks. The focus of their dialogue was on problem-solving rather than listing the issues that could turn a project into a "mission impossible."

In addition, a key element in creating trust between teams and stakeholders was a shared conversation about the duration and scope of the tasks at hand. While setting often unrealistic deadlines is an unavoidable practice, these high-performing teams engaged in discussions with senior management. The role of management on these teams was to provide clarity on deliverables and support continuous value delivery. In essence, meeting the team at eye level and encouraging autonomy proved to be the cornerstone of high-performing teams.

How to Interact with Non-Digital Parts of an Organization

In a hybrid organization where agile product development teams coexist with traditional departments, effective collaboration is critical for successful product launches and scaling. Agile teams must bridge the gap with non-agile units such as sales, marketing, and legal through strategic communication and alignment.

We recommend creating liaison roles or cross-functional teams to facilitate interaction between the domains and traditional IT departments. These facilitators should be well-versed in both agile methodologies and traditional business processes.

To effectively coordinate with traditional parts of your organization:

- Establish regular touchpoints such as daily, weekly, bi-weekly, or monthly syncs to align goals and timelines. More frequent and brief is better than less frequent and lengthy.
- Implement a common visualization tool, such as a high-level kanban board to provide a common reference point. This allows for better understanding and alignment across diverse teams. Start collaboration early in the product development process by involving non-agile departments in hypothesis formulation and testing.

- Use incremental delivery methods even when working with traditional IT departments. Break large initiatives into manageable chunks for regular review and adjustment. Establish clear handoff processes and documentation standards that balance agile flexibility with traditional structure.
- Educate non-agile departments about agile principles to avoid misunderstandings and manage expectations. Conversely, ensure that agile teams respect and accommodate the formal processes required by legal or finance.
- Allow for longer lead times in traditional IT departments when planning. Allocate sufficient resources for communication and alignment activities, recognizing the time required for effective cross-functional collaboration.

By focusing on these strategies, organizations can create a harmonious environment where agile product development teams can effectively collaborate with non-agile departments, ensuring smooth product launches and scaling efforts while maintaining agile integrity.

Valid Variants for Different Situations

Teams with Low-priority Initiatives Help Other Teams

Each team within the software development organization has a distinct product responsibility, and every product undergoes various phases in its life lead, each requiring different levels of effort.

While some products may require intensive development efforts at the outset but stabilize over time, others undergo continuous development and demand ongoing attention from their respective teams. Unfortunately, organizations often overlook this product life lead, leading to the continuous development of products that may not warrant significant effort from a strategic standpoint.

This misalignment results in resource wastage and dissatisfaction among both management and team members. To address this issue, teams must collaborate and support each other. Teams can assist one another by participating in the development of functionalities for a specified period without taking over operational responsibilities.

However, it's essential to maintain consistency in coding standards, technology stacks, and architectural principles across teams to facilitate effective collaboration. This approach optimizes for strategic alignment while also considering resource efficiency within the organization.

Objectives and Key Results (OKRs) Can Support Strategic Execution

Objectives and Key Results (OKRs) are a goal-setting framework that defines measurable objectives and the key results needed to achieve them.

From Sophie's experience, OKRs can complement Flight Levels and kanban in strategic portfolio management and strategy execution by providing a structured approach to goal alignment across organizational levels.

At Flight Level 3, organizational OKRs set the strategic direction. These cascade down to domain-specific OKRs at Flight Level 2, and further down to team goals at Flight Level 1. By visualizing OKRs on kanban boards at each level, organizations create a clear link between strategic goals and day-to-day work.

This integration allows teams to see how their tasks contribute to broader organizational goals. Regular reviews of OKR progress facilitate adaptation and ensure alignment with evolving business needs. Combining OKRs with Flight Levels and kanban creates a powerful system for translating strategy into actionable, measurable results at all levels of the organization.

Common Misconceptions and Mistakes

Rigid Implementation of OKRs

From Matthias' practical experience, OKRs seem promising in theory for strategic portfolio management and strategy execution, but in practice, they often create more problems than they solve. Organizations often turn OKRs into a bureaucratic nightmare and lose sight of their original purpose. Rigid implementation of OKRs can stifle the flexibility and responsiveness that flight levels and kanban are designed to cultivate.

Teams can become too focused on meeting arbitrary metrics rather than delivering real value. The process of cascading OKRs across organizational levels can become time-consuming and complex, distracting from real work. In addition, the quarterly rhythm of traditional OKRs may not align well with the more dynamic flow of work visualized in kanban systems.

Instead of improving strategic alignment, poorly implemented OKRs can create artificial barriers and increase administrative overhead. Organizations may benefit more from focusing on clear, adaptable goals and using flight levels and kanban to maintain strategic alignment and operational effectiveness without the added complexity of formal OKRs.

Assuming Complete Autonomy Means No Coordination

Some organizations misinterpret loose coupling as a license for teams to work in silos. They believe that each domain can run independently without any cross-team coordination. This leads to misaligned priorities and duplication of effort. Instead, recognize that autonomy requires deliberate alignment.

Establish regular cross-domain synchronization events and use visual management tools to share progress and dependencies. Encourage teams to collaborate on common goals while keeping decision-making authority. Build a culture of proactive communication where teams voluntarily share information and seek input from others as needed. This balanced approach preserves the benefits of loose coupling while ensuring that the organization moves cohesively toward its strategic goals.

Equating More Hypotheses with Better Outcomes

Organizations sometimes fall into the trap of generating numerous hypotheses without proper validation or follow-through. They mistake quantity for quality in hypothesis-driven development. This approach leads to scattered efforts and inconclusive results. Instead, focus on generating fewer, more impactful hypotheses that are aligned with strategic goals. Implement a rigorous process for prioritizing and testing hypotheses.

Ensure that each hypothesis has clear success criteria and a defined timeline for evaluation. Encourage teams to deeply explore and learn from each hypothesis, rather than quickly moving on to the next. Stimulate a culture where invalidating a hypothesis is seen as valuable learning, not failure. This approach leads to more meaningful insights and better-informed strategic decisions.

Failure to Evolve the System

Some organizations set up flight levels and kanban systems but then treat them as static structures. They fail to recognize that these systems should evolve with the organization. This rigidity leads to outdated processes and misaligned workflows. Instead, view your flight levels and kanban systems as living entities that require regular refinement.

Conduct periodic reviews to assess whether the current structure still meets your organizational needs. Encourage teams to suggest and implement improvements to their boards and workflows. Create feedback loops that allow insights from the operational level to influence strategic decisions.

Embrace continuous improvement and apply it not only to products but also to your management systems. This adaptive approach ensures that your strategy execution and portfolio management remain effective as your organization grows and changes.

Overemphasis on Cost and Effort

Overemphasis on cost and effort is a common pitfall in strategy execution and portfolio management. Organizations often prioritize initiatives based primarily on resource requirements and difficulty of implementation, neglecting potential value and strategic impact. This approach results in a portfolio filled with "easy wins" that may not contribute significantly to long-term goals.

It stems from a desire for quick, visible progress and a misguided attempt to maximize resource utilization. Instead, shift the focus to value-based prioritization. Evaluate initiatives based on their alignment with strategic goals and potential business impact. Use techniques such as cost of delay to quantify the value of timely delivery. Implement a balanced scorecard approach that considers multiple factors beyond cost and effort.

Encourage teams to propose high-impact initiatives, even if they're challenging. Create a culture that values strategic outcomes over simply doing the work. This value-driven approach ensures that your portfolio drives meaningful progress toward organizational goals, rather than just keeping teams busy.

TL;DR and Further Reading

- Adaptively focus and channel resources on the high-stakes challenge
- Address the knowledge, alignment, and effect gap in strategy execution
- Execute your strategy with a hypothesis-driven development backlog
- Done means someone's need was met
- Prioritize your backlog by impact and probability of success
- Transform hypotheses into results with Flight Levels and kanban
- Use cadences to align and execute strategy
- Monitor impact with a range of metrics
- Manage stakeholders continuously and carefully
- Learn how to interact with non-digital parts of an organization

For a more in-depth look at this topic, these are some of our favorite books and websites:

- *Rethinking Agile: Why Agile Teams Have Nothing To Do With Business Agility,* by Klaus Leopold
- *The Art of Action: How Leaders Close the Gaps Between Plans, Actions, and Results,* by Stephen Bungay

- *Good Strategy Bad Strategy: The Difference and Why It Matters,* by Richard P. Rumelt
- *Measure What Matters: How Google, Bono, and the Gates Foundation Rock the World with OKRs,* by John Doerr

8

HOW TO INNOVATE AND DELIVER BUSINESS VALUE, NOT JUST FEATURES

THOSE WHO HAVE WORKED in tech for a considerable time know that the traditional approach to IT has revolved around managing projects based on scope, time, and budget. This methodology has its roots in an era when business problems were primarily addressed with software, either custom-built and now considered 'legacy' or through 'one size fits all' solutions, such as large-scale SAP projects.

These complex undertakings were often accompanied by extensive documentation, governance, and administration, primarily managed by the 'IT organization'—the bridge between business and integration partners.

Historically, managing according to scope, time, and budget was seen as essential, leaving little room for innovation. Initiatives were driven by process digitization, cost efficiency, or workload management—essentially, tasks aimed at managing one's organization.

However, the emergence of tech giants like Amazon, Google, and Spotify challenged the traditional role of IT. These companies demonstrated seamless expansion and continuous innovation, offering new services and products that fit together digitally, raising the question: What makes them so successful?

The Traditional Approach and Why It Falls Short

In many traditional IT organizations, the approach to innovation and value delivery is rooted in outdated practices that often hinder rather than help. While these methods were once considered best practices, they now struggle to meet the demands of rapidly evolving markets and customer expectations.

One major issue is the disconnect between IT teams and end-users. Layers of intermediaries attempt to capture and translate customer needs, inadvertently severing the direct link between developers and users. This shift in focus prioritizes internal success metrics and stakeholder satisfaction over genuine user needs. Project managers become consumed with mastering the "iron triangle" of scope, time, and budget, often at the expense of delivering real business value. Success is measured by ticking boxes on a requirements document rather than achieving tangible outcomes that matter to customers.

Another problematic aspect is the misalignment of incentives and measurements. Teams are rarely challenged to improve on business metrics like increased user engagement or revenue growth. Instead, progress is tracked through tactical measures such as the number of days spent or features completed. This approach fails to accurately reflect the true value of the project and can lead to a false sense of accomplishment. Moreover, the focus on incremental innovation within existing business models neglects opportunities for pivoting or developing new models, leaving organizations vulnerable to disruption.

The risk-averse culture prevalent in traditional IT setups further compounds these issues. With failure often viewed as a career killer, leaders and team members alike tend to play it safe. This mindset suppresses fundamental changes and potential cannibalization of existing products or services, even when such changes are necessary for long-term success. The result is an environment that prioritizes justifying mistakes over addressing underlying issues, stifling true innovation and adaptability.

Collectively, these traditional practices create the perfect storm of inefficiency and missed opportunities. While intended to ensure predictability and control, they instead create an environment that is slow to respond to market changes, resistant to necessary transformation, and ultimately ill-equipped to deliver real value to customers.

To thrive in today's dynamic business landscape, IT organizations need a radically different approach—one that prioritizes customer satisfaction, embraces calculated risks, and measures success through tangible business outcomes.

The General Blueprint

Get Out of the Building and Understand Real Customer Needs

Too many IT initiatives are developed far from the end-user without understanding the customer's problem, need, or task. Solutions built without this understanding often fail to solve customer problems satisfactorily. Engaging directly with end-users through methods like in-person visits or remote sessions can provide invaluable insights.

Popularized by Steve Blank in the context of customer development and lean startup methodology, "getting out of the building" emphasizes the importance of directly engaging with customers and users in their environments. This practice is particularly vital in tech organizations where rapid innovation and market responsiveness are key to success.

By physically (or virtually) leaving your office and interacting with customers, you can:

- Validate assumptions about user needs and preferences.
- Gather real-world insights that data alone might miss.
- Identify new opportunities for innovation.
- Build stronger relationships with your user base.

REALITY TECH

In a project Sophie was leading, the team had been building software for months under high pressure which was delivered in scope, time, and budget. Regardless of this achievement, no one in the market was actually using the software. The reason wasn't that the software was buggy, slow, or features were poorly designed: The solution didn't solve the problem of the specific user group but the problem that was assumed the user group had. This was a simple misunderstanding that could have been avoided by taking the time to understand the real user's needs.

In contrast, Sophie experienced a highly motivated team that built a community around an internal app that delivers simple employee services such as vacation approval, etc.—after every release, the feedback from the internal forum, emails, and helpdesk tickets were evaluated and improvements were implemented right into the next release. These small gestures created a lot of positive feedback both from end users as well as management, and in turn, created a highly motivated team.

Observing customers using your product is a powerful way to gain insights into their real-world experiences and identify opportunities for improvement. Yet, it gives many people an awkward feeling to directly interact with their potential user group. Guiding your team and encouraging them to do so is crucial.

User interaction can be done through in-person visits to their workplace or remote screen-sharing sessions. During these observations, users should be encouraged to walk through their typical workflow while narrating their actions and thoughts out loud. The observing team members should take note of any pain points, workarounds, or inefficiencies in the process and ask clarifying questions to better understand the customer's reasoning and motivations.

These insights can then be shared with the broader team to inform product improvements and streamline the user experience. Offering an incentive and expressing gratitude for the customer's time and participation can help build goodwill and encourage future engagement.

This simple approach ensures that solutions are relevant, valuable, and effectively address customer needs. Teams can get creative on setting up this interaction by using design thinking methods or building a small prototype—anything that helps to understand users and the market you are trying to approach.

Focus on Business Value and Outcomes

As for many large corporations, people are focussing on managing the process and people rather than focussing on the actual value delivered. If you find yourself challenged by this statement—maybe it is indeed a good starting point to re-discuss your success metrics and shift your team's focus on business value creation. A challenging but effective way to shift the focus toward value creation is the idea of changing your success metrics.

As IT usually understands its quality deliverables in terms of uptime, meantime-to-restore, etc., the focus of the business and tech teams must shift toward business-driven metrics. Metrics such as user growth, revenue, or conversion rates (for marketing sales) can be effective metrics to measure value, not just output. In other words: the most stable IT application does not help if no one uses it.

Some key learning from our practice includes:

- All team members must use the same metrics
- Key metrics are always on display and everyone works on improving them
- Iterative and short development cycles help to improve the numbers
- Data and User Feedback is used to improve metrics

A simple question you can ask your teams is: What have we improved for users last week? Even though this question might be provocative for many, it should be possible to answer if you are following the idea of a product-driven approach.

Everyone Understands the Business to Be In

The practice of moving toward business metrics for value-driven development automatically triggers the question of whether everyone on the team and the domain understands the business you are in.

A tool that has been extensively used in practice is the Business Model Canvas. It can help the team (again, we talk about cross-functional teams) to gain broader insights into their product and its interaction with others. Understanding the broader business context ensures that development efforts are aligned with strategic goals and customer needs.

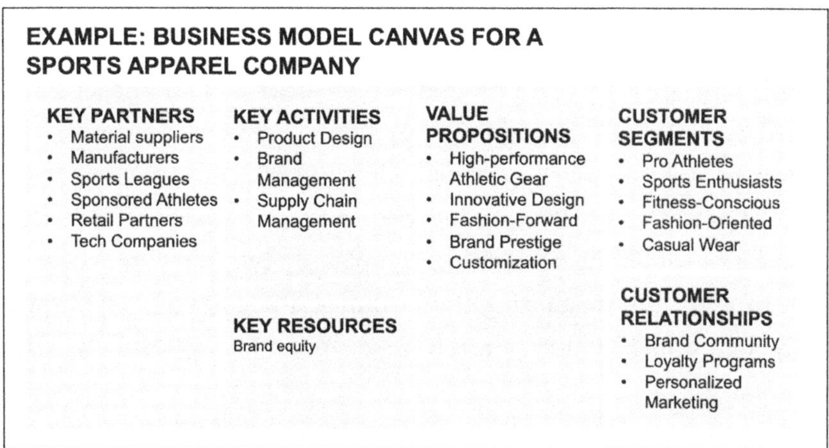

Once filled with the first draft, the Business Model Canvas invites the team to challenge and understand their assumptions and undermine them with numbers. For example: If thinking about which channels should be used to make your product available, it makes sense to dive into the world of 'Sports Enthusiasts'—how they shop, how they consume, whom they follow on Social Media, etc. Before investing efforts into either of them, a short test can give insights into which channel can be worked on with priority.

A/B Testing Is Your Weapon of Choice for Value Delivery

In the fast-paced world of software development, A/B testing has emerged as an essential practice to maximize value delivery and rapidly gather feedback on whether you're heading in the right direction.

This method, now considered an industry best practice, allows you to compare two or more variations of a product feature by exposing different user groups to each version simultaneously. Through A/B testing, you gain clear, quantitative insights into how each variation performs in terms of key metrics like user engagement, conversion rates, or other relevant outcomes.

Despite its proven effectiveness, A/B testing often faces skepticism, particularly in organizations under tight deadlines or those dominated by "HIPPO" (Highest Paid Person's Opinion) decisions. The power of A/B testing lies in its ability to turn subjective opinions into objective data. By running controlled experiments—whether it's testing different advertising campaigns, tweaking the color or text of a button, or altering the layout of a page—you can empirically determine which version resonates most effectively with users.

Think of A/B testing as a scientific experiment, just carried out digitally. You isolate a single variable, make a change, and observe the outcome to see which version achieves the desired results. This approach not only provides data-driven insights but also encourages a culture of continuous improvement where decisions are informed by evidence rather than gut feeling.

However, the story doesn't end with quantitative data. Numbers can tell you what is happening, but they often fall short of explaining why it's happening. To gain a complete understanding of user behavior, you need to complement A/B testing with qualitative feedback mechanisms. Methods such as user interviews, surveys, and usability testing delve into the underlying reasons behind user actions, uncovering sentiments, motivations, and preferences that aren't visible in the raw data.

The approach 'Get out of the building and understand customer behavior' also stands strong in the context of A/B testing. The magic lies in the combination of quantitative data from A/B tests with qualitative insights. Out of this, you can create a holistic view of your desired user experience. A/B testing helps you to make informed decisions based on actual user behavior, while qualitative feedback provides the necessary context and depth, revealing the 'why' behind those actions. Together, these approaches empower you to develop more nuanced and effective product features, ultimately leading to better decision-making and more successful products.

Introducing A/B testing into your organization requires a few critical components. First, you need robust analytical tools such as Google Analytics or Adobe Analytics to track and measure user interactions. Next, platforms like Optimizely or Mixpanel can facilitate multi-variant testing, allowing you to experiment with different versions of a feature, manage feature flagging, and segment users based on various criteria. Finally, a solid continuous integration/continuous delivery (CI/CD) pipeline is essential to ensure that new features and variations can be quickly and efficiently deployed for testing.

Build Small, Think Big, Sell the Story

In many organizations, there's a tendency to overthink and overengineer experiments, often resulting in delays and missed opportunities, and again leading to timeline glitches, but to kick-start a new idea, you don't always need formal stakeholder approval. In fact, experimenting with minimal resources—whether through a prototype, a Minimum Viable Product (MVP), or a simple test—can be more effective in the long run.

By launching quickly and focusing on the insights gained, you generate valuable data that can be used to build a compelling narrative and persuade stakeholders to support the larger vision. This approach not only accelerates innovation but also bridges the gap that often exists between management expectations—like timelines and milestones—and the realities faced by those executing the work.

To overcome this common contradiction, management must play a dual role. On one hand, they need to manage stakeholders by communicating progress and potential. On the other hand, they must create a safe space for teams to experiment, test, and validate ideas without fear of failure. The key to success lies in alignment and mutual trust, ensuring that both sides are working toward the same goals and supporting each other throughout the process.

By thinking big but starting small, you can create a more agile and innovative culture where small wins build momentum and help sell the story to those who can champion your vision on a larger scale.

Three Horizons, Three Ways of Working, Three Budgets, and Three Reward Systems

In any organizational context, prioritizing scaling and nurturing its core business is paramount to initiating the first wave of growth. As previously emphasized, clear comprehension of one's core business, made transparent across the organization, is imperative for early success.

While scaling, defining subsequent steps for growth becomes essential. The McKinsey 3 Horizon model eases this process, enabling companies to concurrently focus on three key areas to ensure sustained business development. Especially in turbulent times, it allows a structured approach for innovation considerations within and outside the current business model.

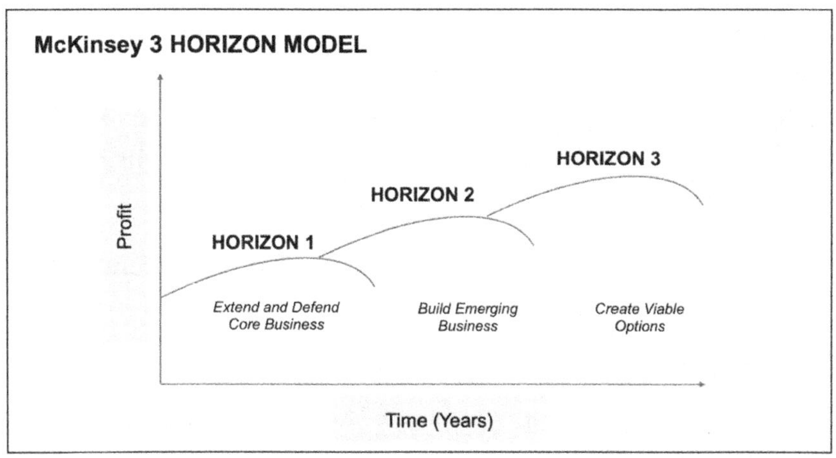

- Horizon 1 concentrates on refining the company's most profitable income stream—the core business.
- Horizon 2 is dedicated to cultivating future income streams that may become integral to the future core business, often needing investments.
- Horizon 3 involves research and experimentation in different contexts, representing initiatives furthest along the time horizon.

Effective management and discussion of these horizons ensure the progression of initiatives from, for example, Horizon 3 to Horizon 2.

An illustrative scenario involves a small team collaborating with an early-stage tech startup on a specific use case. After 24 months, a decision is made to acquire the technology and integrate it into the core business. The model advocates a 70-20-10 approach: allocating 70% of the budget to innovation within the existing business model (H1), 20% to innovation in near-term income streams (H2), and the remaining 10% to experimentation (H3).

In order to ensure the quality of ideas, you want as much experimentation and therefore 'failure' in H3. Consider different reward systems for every horizon to make sure no one is playing it too safe; otherwise, your ideas will be sugar-coated and will not help you to progress.

Spot Weak Signals and Think Five Years Ahead of Trends

The sheer number of trends, particularly in the tech space, is overwhelming. The critical question arises: Which tech trends are worth an investment, and which ones are possibly fading or subject to eventual cannibalization?

Drawing from Pascal Finette's concept, organizations must excel at identifying and analyzing weak signals. For instance, the ascent of AI paved the way for GenAI, while the prominence of Cloud Computing likely laid the foundation for the emergence of Quantum Computing.

Today, the trajectory of AI development is not linear but exponential. Yet, many companies still struggle with fundamental AI prerequisites, notably data. Like any successful enterprise, having a roadmap that acknowledges potential disruptors is imperative. Proactively engaging with innovation trends and gauging their impact over the next three to five years enables effective future preparation. Moreover, it facilitates the structural adaptation of your current business model to forthcoming changes (e.g., Horizon 3 ideas).

Common Misconceptions and Mistakes

Focus on Speed but Not on Business Value

The temptation to create pressure on the team to deliver at least 'something' is a practice we have been experiencing throughout our careers. The teams usually deliver something of mediocre quality to immediately scale it afterward.

While experimentation allows for a wide range of approaches to validate ideas, careful consideration is crucial before basing your future business on an improvised prototype. Although many stakeholders may not differentiate between results produced by a prototype versus fully functional software, it's essential to allow teams the time to develop something of genuine value that can be utilized and expanded upon for future requirements.

We Are Autonomous...We Do Whatever We Want

In agile organizations that promote autonomy and flexibility, there's a growing tendency for teams to drift away from the core product vision. With the freedom to explore and experiment, some teams may inadvertently start pursuing ideas that stray too far from the original task or product strategy.

This can lead to a lack of focus, where efforts are spent on projects or features that don't align with the company's objectives or the user's needs. This misconception arises from the belief that autonomy means complete freedom without boundaries. While agile practices encourage innovation and iteration, they also require a strong anchor in the form of a clear product vision and strategy. Without this, teams can end up working in silos, developing ideas that may not contribute meaningfully to the overall product goals.

To prevent this, it's essential to establish guardrails that guide creative efforts while ensuring alignment with the broader strategy.

Here are some strategies to address this:

- **Reinforce the Product Vision**: Regularly communicate the core product vision to all teams. Ensure that everyone understands the fundamental goals and user problems the product is designed to solve. This keeps innovation focused and relevant. Remember circling back to the Business Canvas!

- **Set Strategic Boundaries**: While autonomy is important, it should come with strategic boundaries. Define clear parameters within which teams can explore and experiment, ensuring that their efforts remain aligned with the product's objectives.
- **Encourage Contextual Innovation**: Encourage teams to innovate within the context of the product's mission. This means focusing on enhancements or new ideas that directly contribute to the product's value proposition rather than veering off into unrelated territories.
- **Regular Check-Ins**: Establish regular check-ins where teams present their ideas and progress in the context of the overall strategy. This not only keeps everyone aligned but also cultivates a culture of accountability.

By balancing autonomy with strategic focus, organizations can harness the creative potential of their teams while ensuring that all efforts contribute to the product's success. This approach ensures that agility enhances rather than detracts from the achievement of the company's goals.

TL;DR and Further Reading

There can be no simpler recommendation than encouraging your teams to get out of the building and understand the user. As simple as it sounds, it is a make or break for many. This helps to better understand the business and create a common idea about what needs to happen next.

In the next step:

- Change your success metrics into common metrics between business and tech
- Use extensive A/B testing and invest in data literacy
- Innovate strategically and with structure
- Accept failure to be part of your journey

For a more in-depth look at this topic, these are some of our favorite books and websites:

- *The Lean Startup: How Today's Entrepreneurs Use Continuous Innovation to Create Radically Successful Businesses,* by Eric Ries
- *The Art of Business Value,* by Mark Schwartz
- *Value Proposition Design: How to Create Products and Services Customers Want,* by Alexander Osterwalder
- *Accelerate: The Science of Lean Software and DevOps: Building and Scaling High Performing Technology Organizations,* by Nicole Forsgren PhD, Jez Humble, Gene Kim

9

HOW TO DELIVER TWICE AS FAST

MANY TRADITIONAL IT organizations and even some great tech organizations struggle to deliver software quickly enough to meet market demands and stay competitive. This chapter addresses the critical challenge of significantly reducing lead times and increasing throughput in software development.

The ability to deliver software fast directly impacts a company's capacity to innovate, respond to customer needs, and outpace competitors. Faster delivery not only improves time-to-market but also enhances product quality, team morale, and overall business agility.

We'll explore an approach to software delivery that leverages Lean and kanban principles, focusing on continuous optimization of lead times, throughput, and quality. Key strategies include limiting work in progress, reducing batch sizes and dependencies, automating processes, and creating optimal work environments for developers.

By the end of this chapter, you'll have a practical toolkit for dramatically improving your software delivery speed, enabling your organization to thrive in an increasingly competitive and fast-moving tech landscape.

The Traditional Approach and Why It Falls Short

In software delivery, traditional IT organizations often cling to practices that ultimately hinder their ability to keep pace with modern demands. These approaches, rooted in outdated beliefs about productivity and risk management, create the perfect storm of inefficiency and missed opportunities.

At the heart of the traditional approach lies a misguided focus on developer utilization over lead time optimization. Organizations operate under the assumption that keeping developers constantly busy equates to productivity and cost-effectiveness. However, this strategy backfires spectacularly. It leads to excessive multitasking and increased work-in-progress, paradoxically extending lead times and reducing overall output quality. This utilization-centric mindset often results in too many projects being tackled simultaneously, further exacerbating the problem. As tasks compete for resources, each item takes longer to complete, creating a vicious cycle of delays and bottlenecks.

The traditional approach also falters in its handling of project risks and quality management. Risks are frequently postponed until later stages of development based on the misguided belief that they'll resolve themselves or show early progress. This delay inevitably leads to exponentially higher costs and difficulties when issues finally surface, often resulting in major project overruns or even failures. Similarly, quality and maintainability are often sacrificed in the name of short-term gains, creating a technical debt that haunts future development efforts.

Perhaps most tellingly, traditional organizations often lack automation in critical areas such as infrastructure, quality assurance, and release processes. This deficiency, born from resistance to change or shortsighted cost-saving measures, results in error-prone manual processes that slow down every aspect of software delivery. It's a stark example of how traditional approaches, in their attempt to maintain control, actually relinquish it to inefficiency and human error.

Collectively, these traditional practices create an environment where IT organizations struggle to deliver software efficiently, adapt to market changes, or cultivate innovation. The disconnect between the intended outcomes and the actual results is stark, highlighting the urgent need for a fundamental shift in approach.

As we'll explore in the next section, great tech organizations have found ways to overcome these limitations, paving the way for faster, more responsive software delivery.

The General Blueprint

Continuously Measure and Optimize Lead Times, Throughput, and Quality

Continuously measuring and optimizing lead times, throughput, and quality is crucial for enhancing software development efficiency. As H. James Harrington said, "Measurement is the first step that leads to control and eventually to improvement." Delivered business value is the ultimate performance indicator, but it's a lagging metric that only reveals success at the end. To gain real-time insights into your organization's performance, these key metrics should be monitored continuously:

- **Lead Time**: Measures how long it takes to complete a work item, from commitment to deployment. Shorter lead times mean higher efficiency, faster experimentation, and quicker value delivery. Reducing lead time is achievable through strategies like automation, breaking work into smaller packages, and focusing on completing tasks sequentially.
- **Throughput**: Answers the question "How many..." by tracking the amount of work completed in a given period. It's a productivity measure, showing how many tasks—like features or bug fixes—a team completes over time, helping in resource allocation and planning.
- **Quality**: Encompasses multiple metrics that reflect the product's overall health, particularly from the user's perspective, including availability, speed, usability, and functionality. High quality should not be compromised, as poor quality negatively impacts customer satisfaction, lead time, and throughput.

Regularly tracking these metrics creates a culture of continuous improvement, enabling teams to identify bottlenecks, set realistic goals, and prioritize efforts. This data-driven approach enhances decision-making, leading to faster delivery of high-quality software, increased visibility, improved predictability, and higher customer satisfaction.

Limit Work in Progress and Context Switching

"Context switching is one of the most challenging issues in getting things done. A person who is interrupted takes 50% longer to accomplish a task. Not only that, he or she makes up to 50% more errors."—Gerald Weinberg[1]

Limiting work in progress (WIP) and reducing context switching

1. Gerald Weinberg, "Quality Software Management: Systems Thinking"

are powerful strategies for reducing software development lead times. This approach involves limiting the number of concurrent tasks for individuals, teams, domains, and the overall organization and minimizing switching between different tasks or initiatives.

This strategy reduces lead time by:

- focusing efforts on completing tasks rather than starting new ones
- reducing cognitive load and context-switching overhead
- quickly identifying bottlenecks for faster resolution
- improving flow efficiency[2] while reducing task queue time[3]

To put this into practice, organizations can implement WIP limits on kanban boards or in project management tools. Teams should be encouraged to complete current tasks before starting new ones and to adhere to a strict priority order. Creating dedicated focus time for developers, free of meetings or interruptions, is critical. Time-boxing techniques can be used to allocate specific periods of time for different types of work.

The results of this approach are largely positive. It leads to faster completion of individual tasks and overall projects, improved quality due to increased focus, and improved predictability of delivery schedules. Team members experience less stress and burnout, and project status becomes clearer as blockers are more easily identified.

However, there are potential challenges to consider. Initial resis-

2. The proportion of time a work item spends actively being worked on compared to its total lead time. It measures how smoothly work progresses through a system without delays or waiting periods.
3. The duration a task spends waiting to be started or resumed after being put on hold. It represents the inactive periods in a task's lifecycle before it's actively worked on.

may come from team members accustomed to multitasking. There may be a temporary perception of reduced productivity because fewer tasks are being performed simultaneously. This approach also requires better prioritization and communication to effectively manage stakeholder expectations.

By limiting WIP and reducing context switching, organizations can:

- significantly reduce cycle times
- improve work quality
- create a more focused, efficient development process

While this requires a change in mindset and practices, the benefits are substantial. Teams can achieve higher productivity and faster delivery, resulting in improved customer satisfaction and competitive advantage.

This approach aligns well with agile and lean principles, which emphasize the importance of flow and continuous improvement. It encourages teams to focus on delivering value quickly and consistently rather than trying to juggle multiple priorities at once. Over time, this can lead to a more predictable and efficient software development process, benefiting both the organization and its customers.

Two illustrations that demonstrate Limiting WIP and Focusing on Getting Things Done:

DOMAIN	OKR	BACKLOG	ANALYSIS	DEVELOP	TEST	DONE
			Limit Work In Progress			

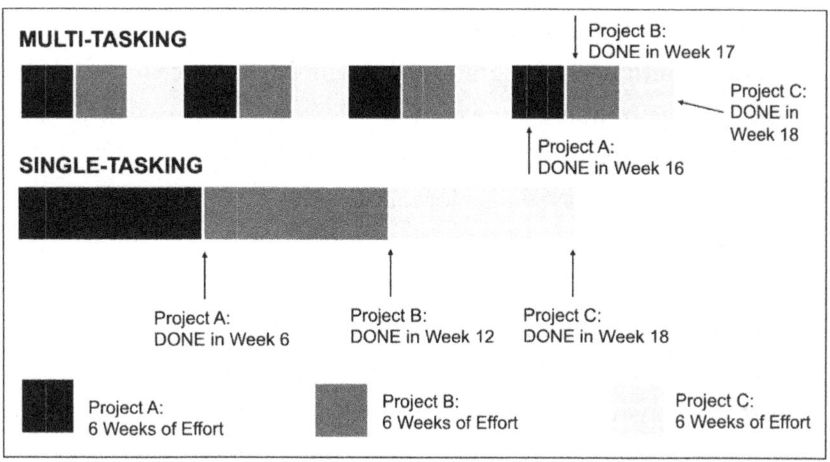

Reduce Batch Sizes

"Smaller batches mean faster throughput, which means shorter cycle times, which means faster feedback, which means less waste and higher quality." — Gene Kim[4]

Reducing batch size in software development means breaking work

4. Gene Kim, "The Phoenix Project: A Novel About IT, DevOps, and Helping Your Business Win"

into smaller, more manageable chunks. Teams, domains, and the overall organization focus on delivering smaller chunks of work quickly rather than large features infrequently. This approach reduces cycle time by enabling faster feedback loops, easier integration, and faster problem identification.

Smaller batches move more smoothly through the development pipeline, reducing bottlenecks and wait times while minimizing release risk and enabling more frequent delivery of value to customers.

To achieve this, organizations can:

- break large features into smaller user stories
- adopt continuous integration and delivery practices
- encourage frequent code commits
- use feature flags
- practice trunk-based development
- set shorter sprint cycles

The results include faster time to market, reduced risk, more frequent customer feedback, improved team morale, and improved market responsiveness. However, challenges can arise, such as increased planning effort, potential feature fragmentation, the need for sophisticated testing infrastructure, and possible stakeholder resistance.

Reduce Dependencies and Communication

"The secret to efficient IT operations is to reduce coordination between teams to an absolute minimum." — Gene Kim[5]

Reducing dependencies and communication between teams, domains, and their applications or microservices is a strategy for streamlining software development processes and reducing overall lead time. This approach involves designing systems and workflows that minimize the need for constant coordination between teams and reduce the coupling between different parts of the system.

This strategy reduces lead time by reducing the need for synchronization and waiting between teams. When dependencies are reduced, teams can work more autonomously, make decisions faster, and deliver their components without being blocked by other teams or systems.

In practice, organizations can implement clear domain boundaries and APIs, use modular architecture and microservices, adopt asynchronous communication patterns, empower teams with decision-making authority, implement service-level objectives (SLOs) instead of tight coupling, and use feature flags and toggles for independent deployments.

The benefits include increased team autonomy and productivity, faster decision-making and implementation, reduced bottlenecks and latency, and improved system resilience and scalability. However, challenges can arise, such as the potential for duplication of effort or inconsistencies, the need for strong documentation and clear interfaces, a potential increase in overall system complexity, and the need for more sophisticated monitoring and observability.

5. Gene Kim, "The Phoenix Project: A Novel About IT, DevOps, and Helping Your Business Win"

Reduce Bureaucracy and Streamline the Product Development Process

"If you're spending more time managing the process than doing the work, you've lost the battle." —Jason Fried[6]

Reducing bureaucracy and streamlining the product development process, particularly in the pre-development stages such as specification, prioritization, and budgeting, is critical to reducing cycle times in software development organizations. This approach involves simplifying decision-making processes, reducing unnecessary documentation, and empowering teams to make quick, informed decisions.

By minimizing bureaucratic overhead, organizations can:

- significantly reduce the time spent on non-value-added activities
- allow teams to focus more on the actual development work

This streamlining accelerates the flow of ideas from conception to implementation, enabling faster responses to market needs and customer feedback.

To put this into practice, organizations can implement lean product development principles, adopt agile methodologies beyond the development teams, use lightweight documentation processes, and create cross-functional teams with decision-making authority. Cultivating a culture of trust and experimentation where teams are allowed to make decisions without excessive oversight is also critical.

The results of this approach include faster time-to-market for new

6. Jason Fried, "It Doesn't Have to Be Crazy at Work"

features and products, increased innovation as barriers to trying new ideas are reduced, and improved employee satisfaction as they spend less time on bureaucratic tasks. However, it can also lead to challenges in maintaining consistency across projects, the potential loss of detailed historical records, and the need for more sophisticated coordination mechanisms in larger organizations.

Automate Infrastructure, Quality Assurance, and Release Processes

"Continuous delivery is the ability to get changes of all types—including new features, configuration changes, bug fixes and experiments—into production or into the hands of users safely and quickly in a sustainable way." —Jez Humble and David Farley[7]

Automating infrastructure, quality assurance, and release processes is a key strategy for reducing lead times in software development. This approach encompasses various practices and technologies, including Continuous Integration/Continuous Deployment (CI/CD), cloud technology, Infrastructure as Code (IaC), and security-as-code.

CI/CD involves automatically integrating code changes, running tests, and deploying to production environments. Cloud technology provides scalable, on-demand computing resources, enabling rapid provisioning and deployment. IaC allows infrastructure to be managed and versioned like software code, ensuring consistency and repeatability. Security-as-code integrates security practices directly into the development pipeline.

7. Jez Humble and David Farley, "Continuous Delivery: Reliable Software Releases through Build, Test, and Deployment Automation"

These practices:

- reduce lead time by dropping manual, error-prone processes and enabling rapid, consistent deployments
- allow for faster feedback loops
- quickly identify and resolve issues
- allow more frequent releases
- reduce the cognitive load on developers, allowing them to focus on creating value rather than managing infrastructure or deployment processes

To implement this approach, organizations can start by adopting CI/CD tools and practices, gradually moving toward a fully automated pipeline. Implementing cloud-based infrastructure and containerization technologies can ease deployment and scaling. Using IaC tools allows for version-controlled, repeatable infrastructure setups. Integrating automated security scanning and compliance checks into the pipeline ensures that security is built-in from the start.

The consequences of this approach are generally positive. It leads to faster, more reliable releases, improved software quality due to consistent testing, and enhanced security through standardized processes. It also increases developer productivity and satisfaction by reducing tedious manual work.

State-of-the-art lead times for releasing and testing code into production are remarkably short in high-performing software development organizations. Elite performers can achieve lead times of less than one hour from code commit to production deployment. Automated testing cycles typically complete within 10 to 15 minutes, covering unit, integration, and end-to-end tests. Deployment frequency can reach multiple times per day, with some organizations deploying hundreds or even thousands of times daily. The time to recover from failures is often less than one hour for top performers. These metrics, based on industry benchmarks like the annual "State of DevOps" reports, represent aspirational targets.

However, there are challenges to consider. Initial implementation can be time-consuming and may require significant upfront investment in tools and training. There's a learning curve for teams to adapt to new practices and technologies. Over-reliance on automation can sometimes lead to a lack of understanding of underlying systems, making troubleshooting more difficult when issues arise.

Increase the Cadence of Process Steps

"If it hurts, do it more frequently, and bring the pain forward." — Jez Humble

Increasing the cadence of process steps in software development organizations means shortening the time intervals between various stages of the software lifecycle, from ideation to deployment to production. This approach extends beyond the development process itself to include earlier stages such as planning, requirements gathering, and decision making, as well as later stages such as testing and release.

By increasing cadence, organizations can reduce cycle time by minimizing delays between stages and promoting a more continuous flow of work. This approach helps identify and resolve bottlenecks faster, reduces the accumulation of work in progress, and enables faster feedback loops. It also promotes a more agile response to changing market conditions or customer needs.

In practice, organizations can implement shorter planning cycles, more frequent stakeholder meetings, and rapid prototyping. They can apply agile methods to all departments, not just development teams. Regular, short check-ins can replace long, infrequent meetings. Decision processes can be streamlined by empowering teams to make more decisions autonomously and release cycles can be shortened, moving toward continuous delivery where possible.

The results of increased process cadence include faster time to market for new features, improved responsiveness to customer feedback, and better alignment between different parts of the organization. It can lead to increased innovation as ideas are implemented and tested more quickly, but it can also put more pressure on team members and require a cultural shift to embrace rapid change and continuous improvement.

Provide the Best Tools and Workspace Environments to Improve Developer Productivity

"Give developers the best tools money can buy. Compared to the cost of a developer, the cost of a top-of-the-line workstation and a big monitor is nothing." —Joel Spolsky[8]

Providing the best tools and workspace environments to improve developer productivity is a strategic approach to reducing cycle time in software development organizations. This includes equipping developers with powerful hardware, efficient software tools, ergonomic workspaces, and state-of-the-art AI-based coding assistants.

This strategy reduces cycle time by minimizing technical barriers, automating repetitive tasks, and extending developer skills. High-end tools, including AI-powered coding agents, can streamline workflows, reduce errors, and even generate code, tests, and infrastructure configurations. These AI assistants can quickly generate boilerplate code, suggest optimizations, and assist with

8. Joel Spolsky, "Joel on Software

debugging, freeing developers to focus on higher-level problem-solving and innovation.

To put this into practice, organizations can invest in powerful computers, multiple monitors, and ergonomic furniture. They can provide licenses for advanced development environments, code analysis tools, and AI-powered coding assistants. These AI tools can be integrated into the development workflow to generate application code, build test cases, generate test data, and even help write infrastructure-as-code scripts.

The results of this approach include significantly increased developer productivity, faster code generation, and potentially higher code quality as AI assistants can help enforce best practices. It can also lead to more innovative solutions because developers have more time to focus on complex problems. However, it requires a significant investment in both hardware and software licenses.

There's also a learning curve associated with using AI tools effectively, and organizations need to address potential concerns about over-reliance on AI-generated code.

The Right Share between Individual Focus Time, Creative Group Work, and Socializing

"The ability to perform deep work is becoming increasingly rare at exactly the same time it is becoming increasingly valuable in our economy. As a consequence, the few who cultivate this skill and then make it the core of their working life will thrive." —Cal Newport[9]

Achieving the right balance between individual focus time, creative group work, and social time is critical to reducing cycle time in software development organizations:

9. Cal Newport, "Deep Work: Rules for Focused Success in a Distracted World"

- Individual focus time allows developers to dive deep into complex problems, write code without interruption, and maintain high productivity on specific tasks.
- Creative group work facilitates problem-solving, brainstorming, and knowledge sharing, leading to innovative solutions and better overall product design.
- Social time builds team rapport, improves communication, and can lead to spontaneous idea generation.

To put this into practice, organizations can implement policies such as "no meeting days" for uninterrupted focus, schedule regular brainstorming sessions for creative group work, and create casual spaces for social interaction. They can use time-blocking techniques to ensure a balanced distribution of these activities throughout the week. Training managers and team leaders to recognize and respect these different work modes is also critical.

This approach reduces cycle time by optimizing productivity during focus time, accelerating problem-solving through effective collaboration, and encouraging a positive team dynamic that increases overall efficiency. It also helps prevent burnout by providing necessary breaks and social interactions.

The results include improved code quality through better focus, more innovative solutions through effective group work, and stronger team cohesion. However, it requires careful scheduling and may initially feel disruptive to those accustomed to constant availability. Some team members may struggle with the structure, requiring flexibility in implementation.

Valid Variants for Different Situations

Sometimes, Delivery Comes First

When strict deadlines are necessary—like aligning a feature launch with a product release—it's vital to be transparent with your team. Rushing multiple initiatives without proper context frustrates everyone. For example, everyone understood the importance of Apple's website being ready for its September product launch, even with limited testing or testing workarounds due to confidentiality.

However, it's crucial to explain the context and prioritize tasks. If every task is treated as equally urgent, it can lead to burnout and demotivation. Clear communication and prioritization keep teams focused and motivated.

Common Misconceptions and Mistakes

Agile Teams Do Not Make Agile Organizations

A large number of agile teams that are working alongside each other do not make up an entire organization—even if it looks like it from the top or from the outside. As long as those teams do not work on the bigger picture together, they simply are teams in themselves.

The big question that needs to be answered is: What is the product you are building? What are the sub-products and what are the features? For a company with an online sales channel: Is the website the product or a module thereof? Based on our experience, this question needs to be answered and it also needs to be agreed on and communicated. As simple as it sounds but as long as there is no common understanding about this, it might just be a large number of teams working on similar content. Name it as you would like, but bringing in everyone on that same baseline is a project in itself.

Agile Software Development Teams Are Not Necessarily High-Performance Teams

Critics may question what baseline was used to measure something as twice as fast. Agility is frequently equated with speed, leading to the misconception that tasks suddenly get completed in no time. However, the reality is that progress may sometimes seem slower than desired.

First and foremost, effective leadership of in-house teams is crucial. Continuous delivery hinges on ensuring that teams are not bogged down by excessive meetings or internal events, which can hinder their ability to innovate.

Secondly, agile organizations often cultivate a participative leadership style, encouraging open discussions. While creating space for dialogue is important, it's vital to discern when discussions contribute tangible outcomes versus when they devolve into abstract philosophical debates that don't directly impact ongoing work. It is a thin line that we are walking on.

TL;DR and Further Reading

To get started, try to start small. Use one task/increment and follow it through your organization. Try to understand where bottlenecks are. With this rather simple approach, you will most likely be able to identify quick fixes and understand that you can't push through topics unlimited.

Start by trying to understand how your organization operates and how it flows. Based on our experience, Senior Management seems to be very far away from understanding how their organization flows.

- Continuously measure and optimize lead times, throughput, and quality
- Limit work in progress and context-switching
- Reduce batch sizes
- Reduce dependencies and communication
- Reduce bureaucracy and streamline the product development process
- Automate infrastructure, quality assurance, and release processes
- Increase the cadence of process steps
- Provide the best tools and workspace environments to improve developer productivity
- Rightly share between individual focus time, creative group work, and socializing

For a more in-depth look at this topic, these are some of our favorite books and websites:

- *This Is Lean: Resolving the Efficiency Paradox*, by Niklas Modig and Par Ahlstrom
- *Kanban from the Inside*, by Mike Burrows
- *The Principles of Product Development Flow: Lean Product Development*, by Donald G. Reinertsen

10

HOW TO DELIVER ON TIME: STOP ESTIMATING AND START FORECASTING

ACCURATE TIMELINES and resource forecasts are critical challenges in tech organizations, yet traditional estimation methods often lead to missed deadlines and budget overruns. This persistent problem causes frustration, erodes trust between teams, and can significantly impact an organization's ability to deliver value consistently.

The ability to reliably predict timelines and resource needs is crucial for strategic planning, resource allocation, and maintaining stakeholder confidence. Inaccurate estimates can lead to missed market opportunities, decreased competitiveness, and wasted resources.

This chapter introduces a paradigm shift from estimation to forecasting, leveraging mathematical methods such as Monte Carlo simulations. This approach provides more reliable predictions with quantified probabilities, aligning with the agile and data-driven nature of great tech organizations. We'll also consider the #noestimates movement and why a middle ground of data-driven forecasting is often more practical.

By the end of this chapter, you'll have a robust framework for replacing guesswork with probabilistic forecasting, enabling more reliable planning and decision-making in your tech organization.

The Traditional Approach and Why It Falls Short

The pursuit of predictability and control often leads to practices that paradoxically undermine project success. These traditional approaches frequently result in delayed deliveries, budget overruns, and stakeholder dissatisfaction.

At the heart of this issue lies the reliance on detailed specifications and precise estimates. Organizations invest significant time and resources in creating comprehensive project plans, believing this will provide clarity and enable accurate resource allocation. However, this approach often backfires. The rigidity of detailed specifications fails to account for the inherent uncertainty in software development, leading to scope creep as requirements inevitably evolve. Moreover, the pressure to provide low estimates, coupled with optimism bias, results in unrealistic timelines that set projects up for failure from the start.

The consequences of these practices ripple throughout the development process. Teams find themselves struggling to meet impossible deadlines, often sacrificing quality or essential features in the process. The lack of historical data and experience in estimation further accelerates these issues, as teams resort to guesswork rather than informed forecasting. This cycle of inaccurate estimates and missed deadlines erodes trust between development teams and stakeholders, creating a culture of skepticism and micromanagement.

Collectively, these traditional practices create the perfect storm of inefficiency and frustration. While intended to provide control and predictability, they instead introduce rigidity and unrealistic expectations into a process that demands flexibility and continuous adaptation. The result is a disconnect between the intended outcomes and the realities of modern software development, leaving organizations ill-equipped to deliver value in a timely and efficient manner. It's clear that a new approach is needed—one that embraces uncertainty and leverages data-driven insights to guide project planning and execution.

The General Blueprint

Monte Carlo Simulations Replace Estimates

Humans are often inaccurate in estimations due to inherent biases, limited information, and the unpredictable nature of complex tasks. Automated forecasting methods can be used instead of manual estimation. We recommend Monte Carlo simulation as a faster, less complex data-driven method for predicting delivery dates and quantities.

A Monte Carlo simulation takes two things as input:

- The backlog of an initiative.
- Historical data on the effort and duration of such backlog items in the past.

The values of the historical backlog items can be thought of as a cube, with all the historical data as the sides of the cube. For example, if you have 53 different historical values, the cube would have 53 sides with possible outcomes.

The Monte Carlo simulation now simulates a project run by:

- determining a random value for each backlog item from the historical data. It rolls the expected value
- It does this until a value is determined or rolled for each backlog item
- At the end of a run, the sum of all estimated values is totaled
- This result is only one of many possible outcomes
- The Monte Carlo simulation is repeated many times by a tool, up to 10,000 times, and you get a correspondingly large number of results

Some results are either very low or very high because the estimates were often obtained by chance. Because the simulation has been run very often, a statistically significant distribution of results is obtained, which can be assigned by probabilities of occurrence.

The effort and duration results can now be converted to dates, which can be assigned probabilities. This can be used to answer the question "When can you implement the required items?" For example: "There is a 43% probability that we can deliver the backlog items by June 1. By October 12, however, we would have a 95% probability, and by December 3, a 100% probability."

Another way to look at this is to answer the question, "How many items can we complete by the target date of June 1?" The answer could be "By June 1, we can complete 43 items with a probability of 100%, 58 items with a probability of 80%, and 102 items with a probability of 50%."

Don't worry! You don't have to simulate this yourself in Excel or with a cube. Monte Carlo simulations are not widely used as an estimation method, but there are a few tools, mostly from the kanban community. We can recommend 55 Degrees "ActionableAgile™" Analytics (separate app or embedded in Jira or Azure) and Portfolio Forecaster (for Jira Cloud, Server, & Data Center).

However, when selecting historical data, care must be taken to select the correct period. In this period, the organizational setup of the team or domain should be as close as possible to the setup with which the planned backlog items are to be implemented. Otherwise, incorrect input parameters would distort the simulation. It is better to choose a shorter but comparable period than a longer period with more but less comparable data.

Mature kanban implementations that have a constant flow of work items provide a good basis for implementing Monte Carlo simulations in software development estimation. The constant flow of work allows for the collection of reliable historical data on task completion times, resource utilization, and workflow patterns, which are essential inputs for Monte Carlo simulations. With an established workflow and historical data, teams can more accurately model and predict project outcomes using probabilistic methods such as Monte Carlo simulations.

Valid Variants for Different Situations

How to Predict Without Historical Data

When historical data is not available, performing Monte Carlo simulations for software development estimation becomes challenging, but not impossible. In such cases, teams can explore alternative approaches to gather relevant input for the simulation:

- Estimated inputs: In this approach, team members use their expertise to estimate the various backlog items. Instead of treating these estimates as single-point values, they are used as input parameters for Monte Carlo simulations. Each backlog item estimate becomes a data point within the simulation that is run multiple times (e.g., 10,000 runs) with random values drawn from probability distributions based on the provided estimates. This approach leverages the collective expertise of the team while capturing the inherent variability and uncertainty associated with each backlog item, enabling the generation of probabilistic forecasts for project schedules, resource requirements, and delivery outcomes.

- Analog inputs: Look for similarities between the current initiative and past initiatives to make informed comparisons and estimates. While not as precise as historical data, analogous estimating provides a basis for extrapolating potential outcomes.
- Prototyping-based inputs: Conduct prototyping or proof of concepts to gather empirical data on the time and effort required for specific tasks or features. This approach allows teams to iteratively refine their estimates based on real-world experimentation.
- Iterative refinement: Start with initial estimates based on available information and refine them iteratively as the project progresses and more data becomes available. This adaptive approach allows teams to adjust their estimates based on actual project performance and feedback.

How to Predict Cost and Budget

Knowing the time required to complete the scope of work allows you to derive the necessary budget and associated costs. Typically, organizations have established cost rates for both internal and external teams that provide a basis for calculating the financial requirements of the project.

By multiplying the estimated time to complete the scope by the corresponding cost rates, teams can estimate the total cost of the software development part of the initiative. This approach enables accurate budgeting and cost estimating, which facilitates financial planning and resource allocation throughout the project lifelead. In addition, a clear understanding of cost implications allows stakeholders to make informed decisions regarding project investments, resource utilization, and overall project feasibility.

Perception Is Reality—Deliver the Most Important Things First

Focusing on delivering the most critical features with the highest business value first is a strategic approach to mitigating conflicts and discussions near the release date in software development projects. By prioritizing these critical elements, teams ensure that the core functionality essential to meeting stakeholder needs and achieving project goals is delivered early in the development process.

This prioritization allows for flexibility in the project schedule, as less critical features can be delayed or adjusted as needed without jeopardizing the overall project's success. With this approach, teams can more effectively adapt to unforeseen challenges or changes in requirements, minimizing the risk of delays or conflicts as the release date approaches.

TL;DR and Further Reading

To get started on measuring your performance, a look into the classic DORA metrics for a single team can be a good starting point (remember we pointed out Release Frequency and Change Lead Time as the two most critical ones).

Instead of creating a KPI and drilling it down to every individual, allow yourself the time to understand what it takes to set up the numbers, and most importantly, to have an understanding of what you are measuring. Later on, once you've collected enough data, Monte Carlo simulations replace estimates.

For a more in-depth look at this topic, these are some of our favorite books and websites:

- *When Will It Be Done?: Lean-Agile Forecasting to Answer Your Customers' Most Important Question*, by Daniel S. Vacanti
- Troy Magennis work on https://www.focusedobjective.com/

11

HOW TO SHIP SOFTWARE CONTINUOUSLY IN HIGH QUALITY

MANY TRADITIONAL IT organizations struggle to deliver high-quality software quickly and consistently, often caught between the pressures of rapid innovation and maintaining system stability. This challenge can significantly impact an organization's ability to compete effectively, respond to market changes, and maintain customer satisfaction. Great tech organizations have found success by embracing continuous delivery practices, which enable them to ship software frequently, reliably, and with confidence.

This chapter explores a blueprint for implementing continuous delivery centered around key concepts such as CI/CD, trunk-based development, and shift-left testing. We'll examine how these practices, combined with automation, observability, and a culture of continuous improvement, can transform your software delivery process.

By the end of this chapter, you'll have a clear roadmap for implementing continuous delivery in your organization, enabling you to ship high-quality software faster and more reliably than ever before.

The Traditional Approach and Why It Falls Short

Software development and release processes in traditional IT organizations have long been governed by established practices that often fall short in today's fast-paced tech landscape. These traditional approaches, characterized by infrequent releases and rigid structures, create a cascade of challenges that hinder efficiency and innovation.

At the heart of this issue lies the practice of rare, large-scale releases, typically occurring quarterly or even less frequently. This approach, born from a desire to manage complexity and coordinate efforts, paradoxically leads to unplannable and unmanageable processes. As changes accumulate over months, deployments become increasingly complex and error-prone. Quality assurance teams find themselves navigating a labyrinth of interconnected changes, increasing the risk of overlooking critical issues. Moreover, this extended release cycle creates a significant lag in delivering value to customers, potentially resulting in missed market opportunities and user dissatisfaction.

The problem is compounded by the intricate web of dependencies that exist in traditional IT setups. Releases often require coordination across multiple applications, teams, infrastructure components, and specialists. Each dependency introduces potential bottlenecks and failure points, extending timelines and increasing the risk of errors. The need for input from various experts—such as database administrators, network engineers, and security specialists—further complicates the process, often leading to delays and miscommunications.

Another critical weakness in the traditional approach is the low level of automation. Many organizations still rely heavily on manual interventions, often performed by external vendors who may lack intimate knowledge of internal systems.

This reliance on manual processes not only slows down the release cycle but also introduces a high risk of human error and inconsistency.

The result is extended downtimes, increased costs, and reduced overall efficiency in the software delivery pipeline.

Collectively, these traditional practices create a vicious cycle of poor quality, unmet expectations, and strained collaborations.

The rigid adherence to predetermined release schedules and elaborate planning processes often leads to a disconnect between the delivered product and evolving business requirements.

This misalignment frequently surfaces during user acceptance testing, where stakeholders see the functionality for the first time only to find it doesn't meet their current needs.

The ensuing blame game further erodes trust between IT and business units, poisoning collaborative efforts.

As the limitations of these traditional approaches become increasingly apparent, it's clear that a new approach is needed—one that can keep pace with the demands of great tech organizations and deliver value continuously and reliably.

The General Blueprint

Increase the Frequency of Releases, and Thus, Reduce Their Size

"Releasing software frequently reduces its costs and risks while yielding better results for users." —Mary Poppendieck and Tom Poppendieck[1]

Increasing the frequency of releases while reducing their size is a fundamental mental shift in modern software development practices compared to the traditional approach of few, but large releases. Often associated with continuous integration and continuous delivery (CI/CD), this approach involves releasing smaller batches of changes more frequently—first monthly, then weekly, daily, hourly, up to several hundred releases per day, with each code commit being pushed into production as a single release.

The benefits of this strategy are many and powerful:

- Smaller releases contain fewer changes, making it easier to identify and fix problems quickly, thereby reducing risk.
- More frequent releases allow teams to gather user feedback sooner, enabling rapid iterations and improvements.
- With smaller changes, testing becomes more focused and thorough, resulting in improved quality.
- Teams can respond more quickly to market demands and competitive pressures, increasing overall agility.
- Regular, successful releases build team confidence and reduce deployment anxiety.

To put this approach into practice, organizations need to make

1. Mary Poppendieck and Tom Poppendieck, "Lean Software Development: An Agile Toolkit" (2003), p. 71

several changes, most of which are discussed in the following chapters.

- Work should be broken down into smaller, independently deployable units.
- Extensive automated testing must be implemented to ensure quality with each release.
- Establishing CI/CD pipelines that automatically build, test, and deploy code changes is critical.
- Feature flags can be used to separate deployment from release, allowing for incremental rollouts.
- Security practices must be integrated earlier in the development process.
- Robust monitoring and observability tools should be implemented to quickly detect and respond to problems.

Organizations can start by gradually increasing release frequency, perhaps moving from quarterly to monthly, then bi-weekly, and so on. It's critical to adapt processes, tools, and culture to support this change. This may involve restructuring teams, investing in automation tools, and fostering a culture that values small, incremental improvements.

This can be done in many small evolutionary steps, each of which has an effect. It is important to proceed in a disciplined manner and not to be satisfied with compromises. Continuous does not mean occasional. The best organizations release each code or infrastructure change as an isolated change to the production environment.

Automate Deployments to Be Faster and More Reliable

"Automating deployment is the key to rapid, repeatable, and reliable delivery of software." —Nicole Forsgren, Jez Humble, and Gene Kim[2]

Automating deployments is a crucial practice for releasing more often and having much shorter releases. This involves creating a streamlined, repeatable process for moving code from development to production environments without any manual intervention. This approach leverages tools and scripts to handle tasks such as building code, running tests, configuring environments, and deploying applications.

To achieve automated deployments, organizations typically implement Continuous Integration/Continuous Deployment (CI/CD) pipelines. These pipelines use tools like Jenkins, GitLab CI, or GitHub Actions to orchestrate the deployment process. The pipeline starts with code commits triggering automated builds and tests. If successful, the code is automatically deployed to staging environments for further testing, and eventually to production.

Key steps in implementing automated deployments include:

- Standardizing development environments.
- Implementing version control for all code and configurations.
- Creating comprehensive automated test suites.
- Designing infrastructure-as-code for consistent environment setups.
- Implementing monitoring and rollback mechanisms.

---

2. Nicole Forsgren, Jez Humble, and Gene Kim, "Accelerate: The Science of Lean Software and DevOps: Building and Scaling High Performing Technology Organizations" (2018), p. 41

The benefits of automated deployments are substantial and far-reaching. They significantly increase the speed of deployments, allowing changes to be pushed to production in minutes rather than hours or days. Automated processes improve reliability by reducing human error and ensuring consistency across deployments.

Developer productivity is enhanced as they can focus more on writing code instead of managing complex deployment procedures. Faster deployments enable quicker feedback loops, allowing for rapid detection and resolution of issues. The practice of frequent, smaller deployments reduces risk by limiting the scope of potential problems. Additionally, automated processes provide better audit trails and reproducibility, improving compliance with regulatory requirements.

By automating deployments, organizations can significantly improve their software delivery performance, leading to faster time-to-market, higher quality products, and increased customer satisfaction.

Cloud technology greatly enhances the automation of deployments, making them faster and more reliable. It provides powerful tools and services for continuous integration and continuous deployment (CI/CD) pipelines, enabling teams to automate the entire process from code commit to production release. Cloud platforms provide scalable infrastructure that can be instantly provisioned and configured through Infrastructure as Code (IaC), ensuring consistent and repeatable deployment environments.

Features such as containerization and orchestration services (e.g., Kubernetes) facilitate rapid and consistent application deployment across environments. In addition, cloud-native services for monitoring, logging, and rollback mechanisms improve deployment reliability by enabling rapid detection and resolution of issues. This combination of automation, scalability, and built-in tools in cloud environments dramatically reduces deployment times, minimizes human error, and increases the overall reliability of the software delivery process.

When initiating automation efforts, organizations often struggle with the decision of whether to address their biggest pain points or pursue quick wins. While both approaches have merit, a balanced strategy that focuses on quick wins is often more effective, especially in the early stages. Starting with smaller, easily achievable automation tasks has several advantages:

- It allows teams to build momentum, quickly demonstrate value, and gain critical experience with automation tools and processes.
- These early wins help build trust and stakeholder buy-in, making it easier to secure resources for larger, more complex automation projects down the road.
- Quick wins often address common, repetitive tasks that, while not necessarily the biggest pain points, can significantly improve daily workflows and developer satisfaction.
- As the team gains proficiency and the organization sees tangible benefits, they can gradually tackle more significant challenges.

This approach creates a positive feedback loop where each success fuels enthusiasm for more automation, ultimately leading to a more comprehensive and impactful automation strategy across the organization.

Use Trunk-Based Development to Reduce Time-consuming Merge Conflicts

Trunk-based development offers a streamlined alternative to traditional branch-and-merge strategies. In this approach, developers work primarily on a single branch, often called the "trunk" or "main" branch, rather than creating long-lived feature branches. Developers integrate their changes directly into the main branch continuously at least once a day.

This method emphasizes small, incremental changes, and relies on feature switches to hide unfinished work in production. Unlike complex branching strategies, where multiple branches exist simultaneously and require extensive merging, trunk-based development minimizes merge conflicts by keeping all developers working on the latest version of the codebase. It supports continuous integration and delivery practices, allowing teams to maintain a consistently deployable master branch. While it requires discipline and robust testing practices, trunk-based development leads to faster development cycles, fewer integration problems, and improved collaboration among team members.

To ensure code quality and seamless integration, radical pair programming and four eyes on the code reviews are crucial. These practices ensure that code fits seamlessly into the main trunk and mitigates the risk of compromising the build.

While other methodologies like GitFlow exist, we focus on trunk-based development in this book: By prioritizing early and high-quality commits, organizations can create reverse pressure to follow the main development flow, ultimately becoming more efficient in their software development processes and increasing quality.

Regardless of your level of expertise, the key lies in owning the code as an organization. Defining clear processes, especially when managing multiple development teams, ensures efficiency and adherence to the main development flow.

Shift Left – Teams Test Early and Continuously

"Shift left" in software development emphasizes moving testing earlier in the development lifecycle. This approach encourages teams to test early and continuously throughout the development process rather than waiting until the end. By integrating testing from the start, developers can catch and fix issues sooner when they're less costly and time-consuming to address.

This continuous testing approach includes unit tests, integration tests, and even some system tests being performed as code is written. It often involves automated testing tools and practices like Test-Driven Development (TDD), which encourages developers to define test cases and expected outcomes before writing any code. This approach requires intense collaboration and discussion with stakeholders to align on requirements and expectations.

While it's not necessary to rigidly apply TDD in every situation, the core idea of early testing is invaluable. By testing features early in the development process, teams can identify and eliminate unwanted functionality or bugs much sooner than traditional methods, which often catch issues only during User Acceptance Testing.

As developers become more proficient with this approach, they should be able to clearly articulate how a feature should behave and what outcomes it should produce. This skill not only improves the testing process but also enhances overall software design and quality. Ultimately, while TDD may not be a universal solution, its principles of early testing and clear requirement definition can significantly improve software development processes.

Automate Testing to Be Faster and to Improve Quality

Not only does the deployment need to be automated, but also the many manual, complex, and often difficult-to-repeat functional and non-functional tests. This is done by the software developers of the software development teams themselves. There are no dedicated testers, test teams, or QA departments.

- At the team level, automated testing in YBIYRI environments involves creating a suite of tests that cover all aspects of the service. This includes functional, performance, and reliability testing. Cross-functional engineers must be proficient in writing and maintaining these tests, as they're responsible for both building and running the service. This approach ranges from unit and integration testing to end-to-end testing and even includes production monitoring and alerting, which can be considered a form of continuous testing in production.
- Domain-level automated testing focuses on ensuring that services interact correctly within their domain and with adjacent domains. This includes extensive integration testing and contract testing between services. Teams often use consumer-driven contract testing tools to ensure that changes in one service don't break dependencies in another.
- At the organizational level, automated testing in a loosely coupled YBIYRI culture means cultivating shared responsibility for quality across teams. It involves creating common tools, practices, and platforms that enable teams to efficiently implement and execute their tests. This may include shared test environments, centralized test data management, and common CI/CD pipelines that

incorporate various types of automated tests that are the responsibility of platform teams.

To achieve effective test automation in software development teams, organizations should invest in training to ensure that all team members can write and maintain automated tests.

Integrating testing into the development process and promoting practices such as Test-Driven Development (TDD) is critical. Implementing robust CI/CD pipelines that automatically run all relevant tests and using feature flags to safely test new features in production are also key strategies.

The benefits of this approach are many:

- It enables faster and more reliable releases because teams can deploy their changes with confidence. They can be fast and secure
- It improves service quality and reliability, resulting in a better user experience
- It reduces the time spent on manual testing and production issues
- It improves the ability to quickly identify and resolve issues
- It enables a better understanding of service behavior across the team

When starting or focusing on automated testing efforts, teams should start with basic unit and integration testing for critical paths in their service. They can then gradually expand to more comprehensive end-to-end testing and implement automated performance testing for key scenarios.

Cloud technology significantly enhances automated testing in software development by offering scalable, flexible, and cost-effective resources. It enables rapid scaling of testing environments, allowing teams to run parallel tests and reduce execution time. The pay-as-you-go model ensures cost-effectiveness, while global accessibility facilitates remote collaboration.

Cloud environments provide consistency, eliminating "it works on my machine" issues, and integrating seamlessly with CI/CD pipelines. They offer diverse testing scenarios across multiple platforms, support performance testing with simulated high loads, and provide efficient test data management. Many cloud platforms also integrate AI services for intelligent test generation and predictive analytics. The ability to quickly provision and dispose of testing environments speeds up the overall process.

Monitoring and Observability Is the New Testing

"Monitoring is the new testing" represents a paradigm shift in how we approach software quality assurance and reliability. Traditionally, software testing has focused primarily on pre-deployment activities such as unit testing, integration testing, and end-to-end testing. These testing practices were designed to catch bugs and ensure that the software met functional and non-functional requirements before it was released into production.

However, in great tech organizations, software is constantly pushed into production. In this dynamic and complex environment, it is impossible to rely solely on pre-deployment testing: Pre-deployment testing cannot fully simulate real-world conditions, especially from a non-functional perspective. Pre-production environments rarely fully replicate production environments, and all of the dependencies and data-related issues may only manifest when the software is exposed to real-world data at scale. This is where the concept of "monitoring is the new testing" comes into play.

Instead of relying solely on pre-deployment testing, organizations, domains, and teams are now placing a strong emphasis on monitoring the behavior and performance of their software in production environments. Teams are instrumenting their applications and infrastructure with comprehensive monitoring tools that collect metrics, logs, traces, and other telemetry from production environments.

This data provides real-time insight into software performance, security, user experience, and potential problems or anomalies. By analyzing the monitoring data, software development teams can observe the behavior of their software in production.

This visibility enables teams to quickly identify and diagnose problems, understand root causes, and take immediate action to mitigate or resolve issues.

Monitoring systems are configured with intelligent alerting mechanisms that can automatically detect anomalies, performance degradation, or deviations from expected behavior. These alerts trigger rapid incident response processes, enabling teams to resolve issues quickly and minimize the impact on users.

By analyzing monitoring data and incident reports, teams can identify patterns, bottlenecks, or areas for improvement in their software or infrastructure. This feedback loop allows teams to continuously refine and optimize their systems, resulting in improved quality and reliability over time.

Shift Your Thinking from Mean Time Between Failures to Mean Time To Resolution

"Failures are a given and everything will eventually fail over time" — Werner Vogels[3]

Organizations that have largely automated their deployments and testing, and whose software development teams can effectively monitor the behavior of their code in production, can make the next fundamental mental shift in their approach to system reliability and incident management.

In doing so, the organization changes its focus from what it optimizes during the release process—from mean time between failures (MTBF) to mean time to resolution (MTTR).

Traditionally, organizations have focused on MTBF, which measures the average time between system failures. This metric emphasizes failure prevention and strives for perfect uptime, often reflected in service level agreements (SLAs) based on availability percentages (e.g., 99.9% uptime). While this seems logical, it can lead to overly cautious practices, slower release cycles, and a fear of change.

This traditional approach often results in extensive testing phases, including development, integration, user acceptance, smoke testing, regression testing, and performance testing. While thorough, these lengthy testing periods can significantly delay the release of new features and updates. Paradoxically, despite the effort invested in testing, it's still impossible to test for every possible scenario, leaving room for unforeseen problems in production.

The shift to prioritizing MTTR recognizes that failures are inevitable in complex, distributed systems. Instead of trying to

---

3. https://www.allthingsdistributed.com/2016/03/10-lessons-from-10-years-of-aws.html

prevent all failures, this approach focuses on how quickly and effectively an organization can detect, respond to, and resolve problems when they occur. This mindset aligns well with modern practices such as continuous delivery, microservices architectures, and cloud-native applications.

Key aspects of this shift include:

- Improved monitoring and observability to quickly identify problems
- Automated alerting systems to immediately notify the right people
- Well-defined incident response processes
- Emphasis on post-incident learning and system improvement
- Building resilience into systems through practices such as chaos engineering

By focusing on MTTR, organizations can become more agile and resilient. They can release changes more frequently with the confidence that they can quickly address any issues that arise. This approach enables a culture of learning from failure rather than fearing it.

This shift is particularly appropriate for advanced teams that are confident in their ability to fix and release quickly. It allows for a reduction in extensive pre-release testing efforts, relying instead on practices such as trunk-based development and pair programming to maintain code quality. The focus shifts from preventing every possible problem to effectively monitoring and quickly fixing problems as they occur.

It's important to note, however, that this shift does not mean abandoning efforts to prevent failures altogether. Instead, it balances prevention with a pragmatic acceptance that some failures will occur and prepares the organization to handle them effectively when they do.

Implementing this approach can be challenging, especially when it comes to stakeholder and business user buy-in. It requires building trust through a demonstrated ability to fix problems quickly and pragmatically. Organizations must carefully manage this transition to ensure that all stakeholders understand the benefits of this new approach and are comfortable with the shift in focus from prevention to rapid resolution.

This mindset is particularly valuable in "you-build-it-you-run-it" environments, where teams are responsible for both the development and operation of their services. It empowers these teams to take calculated risks, innovate faster, and ultimately deliver more value to users while maintaining high standards of reliability and user experience.

Use Feature Flags to Reduce the Risks of Deployments

Feature flags, also known as feature toggles, are a powerful technique that allows software development teams to move from mean time between failures (MTBF) to mean time to resolution (MTTR).

With feature flags, teams can control the execution, visibility, and activation of specific functionality in production without deploying new code. At its core, a feature flag is a conditional statement like an if-then-else statement in the codebase that determines whether a particular feature should be enabled or disabled.

The mechanism behind feature flags is simple. Developers implement conditional statements around new features in the code at the very beginning of the development of this new feature. These flags are controlled by a configuration file or database that stores their on/off state. When the application runs, it checks the state of each flag to decide whether to execute the new code.

This setup allows dynamic changes to the behavior of the application, often managed through a user interface without the need for redeployment. Feature flags are not limited to "on" and "off" states. In more sophisticated feature flag systems, there can be multiple states or conditions.

Here are some common states and uses of feature flags:

- On/Off (Boolean): The simplest form, where a feature is either enabled or disabled.
- Percentage rollout: The feature is enabled for a percentage of users or requests. This allows for gradual rollouts.
- User Targeting: The feature is enabled for specific users or groups of users, often based on criteria such as role, location, and account type (e.g., free vs. premium).
- Time-based: The feature is enabled or disabled based on time conditions.
- A/B or Multivariant Testing: Multiple variants of a feature are available, and users are assigned to different groups to compare results.
- Environment-based: The feature behaves differently depending on the environment (development, staging, production).
- Device or Platform: The feature is enabled or configured differently based on the user's device or platform (iOS, Android, Web, etc.).
- Custom Rules: Complex logic that combines multiple conditions (e.g., "enable for premium users in the U.S. using a Chrome browser").
- Killswitch: A special type of flag used to quickly disable a feature in case of critical issues.

In the context of this chapter on increasing release frequency, automating deployments, and improving testing in great tech organizations, feature flags offer several key benefits and are a powerful, highly recommended practice:

- Decouple deployment from release: Feature flags allow teams to deploy code to production without immediately enabling new features. This separation enables more frequent deployments and reduces the risk associated with each release.
- A/B testing: Feature flags make it easy to perform A/B testing, allowing teams to compare different versions of a feature and make data-driven decisions.
- Quick rollbacks: If problems arise with a new feature, it can be quickly disabled without requiring a full code rollback or re-deployment.
- Accelerate time to market: New features can be deployed as soon as they're ready, even if they're not complete, allowing for faster iteration and feedback cycles.
- Support trunk-based development: For features that take a long time to develop, feature flags enable incremental deployment of partially completed work.
- Customization: Feature flags can be used to offer different feature sets to different user groups or to manage premium features in a software-as-a-service model.
- Operational control: In a you-build-it-you-run-it environment, feature flags give teams more control over how their service behaves in production, allowing them to respond quickly to operational issues.
- Support chaos engineering: Feature flags can be used to selectively enable or disable certain system behaviors during chaos experiments, providing fine-grained control over test scenarios.

- Gradual rollouts: Teams can use feature flags to slowly introduce new features to a subset of users, allowing for controlled testing of functional and especially non-functional requirements in production and gathering real-world feedback before a full release. Teams can evaluate capacity, performance, reliability, third-party integration, and network impact, and perform cost analysis.
- Shadow traffic: Teams test new versions of services or applications under real-world conditions on production without impacting users. In this approach, live production requests are duplicated and sent to both the current production version and a new version running in parallel. While the production version processes the request and responds to the user as normal, the new version processes its copy of the request, but its response is discarded or logged for analysis rather than returned to the user. Teams can evaluate the performance, compatibility, and reliability of new releases using actual production traffic patterns, data, and volumes.

Implementing feature flags in an organization requires a thoughtful approach. It's best to start small, perhaps with a simple flag for a non-critical feature. Educating the team about the concept and its benefits is critical to successful adoption.

Choosing the right tool, whether a third-party feature flag management solution or a simple in-house system, is an important decision. Integrating feature flags into existing CI/CD processes ensures seamless integration into the development workflow. Establishing governance around flag creation, naming conventions, and lifecycle management is essential to maintain order as usage grows.

Monitoring and measuring the impact of feature flags on system performance and user experience provides valuable insights. As the team becomes more comfortable with the concept, gradually expanding its use to more complex scenarios can yield greater benefits.

REALITY TECH

Feature flags were used very successfully in one of the organizations where Matthias worked. Initially, feature flags were only introduced for some simple code changes in the frontend where it was thought to be feasible. However, it quickly became apparent that contrary to initial expectations, feature flags could also be used very effectively in the backend and even for changes to data and data structures with comparatively little effort. As a result, branch environments were abolished, trunk-based development was introduced, and feature flags became mandatory for isolating changes in production. These were not just on/off, but with very sophisticated conditions including gradual rollouts and shadow traffic. There were very few bugs that could be traced back to feature flags, and if there were any, it was because they were not used for a "simple" change.

However, feature flags come with potential pitfalls that organizations must navigate carefully:

- Technical debt can accumulate if too many flags are left in the codebase, making it difficult to maintain. This can be mitigated by regularly reviewing and removing obsolete flags, and setting expiration dates for flags when they're created.
- Increased complexity is another concern, as overuse of flags can lead to convoluted code paths. Using flags judiciously

and considering architectural changes for major variations can help avoid this problem.
- Testing overhead can increase exponentially with many flags, requiring robust automated testing that covers different combinations of flags.
- Performance can be affected by too many runtime checks, which can be addressed by optimizing flag evaluation and caching results where possible.
- Inconsistent user experiences can occur when different users see different versions of the application, requiring clear communication about features in testing and ensuring graceful degradation when features are turned off.
- Security risks can arise when feature flags expose sensitive information about upcoming features, underscoring the need for proper access controls over flag management.
- Lack of cleanup can be an issue if code associated with obsolete flags is not removed, highlighting the importance of including flag removal in the definition of done for features and scheduling regular code cleanup activities.

By understanding and carefully managing these aspects of feature flags, organizations can effectively use this technique to improve their development process, enhance the user experience, and maintain greater control over feature releases. When used judiciously, feature flags become a powerful tool in the modern software development toolkit, enabling teams to move faster with greater confidence and flexibility.

Eliminate Your Staging Environments

By adhering to continuous integration and feature flags, along with maintaining a single main trunk, the need for staging environments becomes more and more obsolete, and we recommend reducing as many staging environments as possible, leading to significant savings in cost, time, and effort.

Many companies employ multiple staging environments, such as development, integration, and user acceptance/pre-production to prevent bugs and issues from reaching the live environment. However, the setup of a pre-production environment typically involves replicating the live environment, resulting in delays for development teams and exacerbating deployment queues, contrary to the best practices advocated in earlier sections. Eliminating this pre-production stage represents a pivotal step toward accelerated development.

REALITY TECH

In one of the organizations where Matthias used to work, all but one staging environment was successfully phased out over time, and all functional and non-functional testing took place in the production environment. The sole purpose of this environment was to test whether the release package (which consisted of a single change) would be executable in the production environment.

While the concepts we've discussed (such as feature flags, gradual rollouts, automated testing, and shadow traffic) significantly enhance an organization's ability to test and deploy safely in production, the complete elimination of staging environments is a nuanced and often controversial topic.

With robust implementation of these practices, organizations can significantly reduce their reliance on traditional staging environments. The production environment itself becomes a controlled testing ground through feature flags, gradual rollouts, and shadow traffic. This approach, sometimes called "testing in production," allows for more realistic testing under actual user conditions and loads. However, eliminating staging environments may not be suitable or possible for all organizations due to several factors:

- Regulatory requirements: Some industries have strict regulations that mandate separate testing environments.
- High-risk changes: Certain critical changes may still benefit from isolated testing before any production exposure.
- Data sensitivity: Testing with production data may not always be feasible due to privacy concerns or data protection regulations.
- Complex integrations: Some integrations with external systems may be difficult or costly to test directly in production.
- Team comfort and culture: The shift to testing primarily in production requires a significant cultural change that not all teams may be ready for.

Instead of complete elimination, many organizations opt for a hybrid approach. They maintain a minimal staging environment for specific use cases while leveraging production for most testing through the techniques we've discussed.

The goal is to shift as much testing as possible to production in a controlled manner, reducing the reliance on staging environments and the associated maintenance overhead. This approach allows for more realistic testing while maintaining a safety net for scenarios where isolated testing is necessary or preferred.

Ultimately, the decision to eliminate staging environments should be based on an organization's specific needs, risk tolerance, regulatory environment, and technical capabilities. While some organizations can operate effectively without traditional staging environments, for many, a strategic reduction rather than complete elimination may be more appropriate.

Develop All Code in Pairs to Improve Quality at Source

Pair programming, a widely adopted industry standard in tech-driven companies, is often underutilized and not sufficiently emphasized in development teams. In pair programming, individuals work together, often in pairs or even triplets to review and discuss solutions before merging or integrating code. This collaborative approach cultivates constructive critique and innovation regardless of the participants' seniority levels.

We highly recommend this practice for several reasons:

- Real-time code review: Errors are caught immediately, reducing the need for later bug fixes.
- Knowledge sharing: Programmers learn from each other, spreading best practices and domain knowledge.
- Improved design: Two minds collaborating often leads to better solutions and cleaner code.
- Reduced distractions: Pairs tend to stay more focused on the task at hand.
- Built-in mentoring: Junior developers can learn directly from more experienced colleagues.
- Increased code quality: The continuous peer review typically results in higher quality code from the start.

While some may view programming as a solitary endeavor, many tech professionals enjoy the challenge and camaraderie of collaborating with peers. Pair programming sessions not only facilitate knowledge sharing but also spark tech innovation by exploring diverse perspectives.

It's essential to recognize that pair programming should complement, not replace, individual expertise. Additionally, it proves invaluable in candidate selection, providing insights into both technical skills and cultural fit. This practice significantly enhances hiring processes by offering a firsthand glimpse into candidates' capabilities and collaborative dynamics.

To motivate and encourage pair programming, leaders should focus on creating a supportive environment that values collaboration. Start by explaining the benefits to the team and addressing any concerns they might have. Implement pair programming gradually, perhaps beginning with specific tasks or time slots. Recognize and reward successful collaborations, and share positive outcomes with the broader team. Encourage rotation of pairs to maximize knowledge sharing and prevent siloes. Provide comfortable workspaces conducive to side-by-side work, whether in-person or virtual.

Most importantly, lead by example—participate in pair programming sessions yourself to demonstrate its value and normalize the practice within your organization. Remember, the goal is to create a culture where pair programming is seen not as an obligation, but as a valuable tool for personal growth and project success.

Establish a Federated Incident Management Process

In distributed software organizations structured around domains and value streams, a federated incident management process provides an effective approach to handling technical issues and outages. It leverages domain-specific knowledge for faster and more effective incident resolution and scales incident management capabilities across a complex, distributed system.

This decentralized method distributes responsibility for incident response across different domains or teams while maintaining a coordinated, organization-wide framework for communication, escalation, and learning. This structure aligns well with the "You Build It, You Run It" (YBIYRI) principle, ensuring that teams are responsible for their services from development through operations.

There are several key components to implementing a federated incident management process:

- Domain-Specific Ownership: Each domain team takes primary responsibility for incidents within their bounded context.
- Unified Classification System: Implement a standardized incident classification framework across all domains.
- Local Incident Response: Domain teams develop their incident response procedures tailored to their specific needs.
- Cross-Domain Coordination: Establish mechanisms for managing incidents that span multiple domains.
- Platform Support: Provide shared tools and services for incident management across all domains.
- Knowledge Sharing: Implement processes for sharing incident postmortems and lessons learned.
- Clear Escalation Paths: Define procedures for escalating complex or high-impact incidents.
- Continuous Improvement: Regularly review and refine the incident management process.
- Training and Simulation: Conduct cross-domain training and simulated incidents.
- Consistent Metrics: Implement uniform metrics to measure incident response effectiveness.

Cross-domain coordination is a crucial component of managing incidents that span multiple domains in a DDD-oriented organization. At its core, cross-domain coordination relies on a triage system to swiftly identify incidents requiring multi-domain attention. When such an incident occurs, a virtual "war room" is activated, facilitating real-time communication among affected domains. An Incident Commander oversees the response efforts, coordinating with designated representatives from each impacted domain.

Clear communication protocols and shared tooling ensure smooth information flow and collaborative problem-solving. For particularly complex situations, well-defined escalation paths guide the involvement of additional resources or senior leadership.

By implementing a federated incident management process, distributed organizations can maintain their domain-driven structure while ensuring effective, coordinated responses to technical issues across the system. This approach not only aligns with the principles of DDD but also enhances the organization's ability to resolve incidents quickly and effectively, resulting in improved system reliability and customer satisfaction.

Harden Your Systems & Organization with Chaos Engineering

As large and distributed applications add complexity to production, many large technology companies have embraced the concept of "chaos engineering." It introduces the idea that by injecting interference and disturbances on purpose, the entire organization will learn how to deal with it. This involves the deliberate, automated, and random introduction of failures or adverse conditions into the system to test its resilience. This can include simulating network outages, high latency, or resource exhaustion.

These incidents help not only the incident process to be streamlined but also to create resilience in your software code, including potential fall-backs or a short-lived 'workaround' like buffers, etc.

Chaos engineering, as an advanced practice, is particularly valuable in YBIYRI environments. Their chaos engineering helps ensure that engineers truly understand how their service behaves under stress and can respond effectively to incidents.

REALITY TECH

At one of the organizations Matthias used to work for, chaos engineering was applied to the production environment with great success. Due to the cloud-native architecture with redundant microservices in multiple availability zones, this usually had no noticeable impact on the users of the system, but provided a lot of learning for the teams, except for one time. At noon on a Wednesday, the service that delivered the home page was offline for about 30 minutes. The chaos engineering tool had struck, and the company realized that this service was running on a single instance in a single availability zone, contrary to specifications. Root cause analysis revealed that this was not a technical problem, but an organizational one: Matthias had made too many compromises in the team setup, and the team was too small and young for this important service, taking his advice to be frugal too literally.

Implementing chaos engineering should start with controlled experiments in non-production environments. Teams can then gradually introduce experiments into production, starting with low-impact scenarios. Using tools to automate chaos experiments and carefully monitoring and learning from each experiment are critical steps to improving system resilience.

Netflix has been one of the first to use this idea vigorously throughout its entire tech setup, achieving great results on uptime and resilience.

Cloud technology serves as an ideal platform for chaos engineering, offering numerous advantages that enhance system resilience testing. Its flexibility allows for the rapid creation and destruction of test environments that mirror production systems. Cloud platforms provide a rich array of services and tools, including managed Kubernetes and built-in features for load balancing and auto-scaling, which are perfect for implementing and testing microservices architectures under various failure conditions.

Sophisticated monitoring and observability tools enable real-time insights during experiments. The programmable nature of cloud infrastructure supports codified, versioned, and automated chaos experiments.

Many tech companies have dedicated chaos engineering teams, similar to security teams, that not only work on potential chaos scenarios but also assist and train development teams to increase their resilience. Such a chaos engineering team and its tooling are usually part of the platform organization.

Introduce a Zero-bug Policy to Optimize Quality and Reduce Bug Management Efforts

To ship code continuously and in high quality, we recommend adopting a zero-bug policy. In a zero-bug policy:

- When a bug is identified, it's evaluated immediately by the responsible owner of the product.
- The bug is then placed in one of two categories:
- Fix-worthy: In this case, the bug is considered important enough to be fixed immediately.
- Not fix-worthy: If the bug is considered minor or not impactful enough, it's discarded.
- There's no bug backlog. Bugs are not kept in a tracking system for later prioritization or fixing.
- If a bug is fixable, it becomes a top priority and is fixed

immediately by the team, often with the same urgency as a production incident.

This doesn't mean that software is always 'bug-free' (which is anyway never possible) but it eludes the discussion if a bug is relevant or not. This allows 'real' bugs to be addressed early in the process and therefore have a lower cost when fixed rather than dragging them along for a long time. At the same time, overall software quality increases since bugs (that are significant) will be fixed right away rather than late in the process, or even worse, when already live.

REALITY TECH

In one organization where Matthias worked, there were over 3,200 defects, some of them very old, stored in a defect management system. There were constant discussions about these bugs, especially when priorities changed and some old bugs had to be retested. Often, these were no longer reproducible sometimes because the bugs no longer existed, sometimes because the bug description was too poor. All this effort disappeared when Matthias declared bug bankruptcy, explaining that he would never be able to fix all bugs, but that from now on, a "zero bug policy" would be followed.

A key benefit is the substantial reduction in administrative overhead. By eliminating the bug backlog, teams save significant time and effort that would otherwise be spent on bug prioritization, discussions, and alignment meetings. There's no need for regular bug triage sessions or debates about which issues to address next. This streamlined process also eliminates the need for retesting old bugs, which can be time-consuming and often frustrating when the original context has been lost.

Implement a Continuous Improvement Process for Your Release Process

In this book, we advocate for an adaptive, learning, self-organized, and self-critical organization and strongly recommend monthly reviews and retrospectives on your release, testing, and operations processes driven by the senior engineers of the domain teams with attendance from platform engineers. During these self-critical reviews, quick wins as well as the biggest pains are identified, prioritized, and assigned to work on.

While the concept of continuous delivery is compelling, achieving it necessitates full organizational alignment and commitment to these new principles. Therefore, we recommend actively reflecting on and refining the release process as a continuous learning endeavor for all involved parties.

Just as with continuous improvement in manufacturing processes, the team should regularly reflect on how to become better and more efficient in their release practices. This iterative approach ensures that the organization evolves toward smoother and more effective release processes over time.

Valid Variants for Different Situations

Dedicated QA Resources and Teams

As with many 'dedicated' teams—we have seen the best team performances when QA was an integral task for any developer. A dedicated QA team creates the temptation to hand over code to another party without being properly tested. If we are manifesting our principles along continuous software delivery, code should always be produced in pairs and only checked into the main trunk when it is bug-free.

We do know that reality often looks different in large organizations. Whereas we don't recommend outsourcing QA to another party as an acceptable practice, it can be a compromise to have dedicated testers in every team. This is more a philosophical idea and matter of maturity in an organization rather than an either/or but we do want to point out that the traditional way of having testers is a concept that can be challenged when adopting DevOps principles. Again, regardless of your organizational setup, automated tests over manual testing are preferred and should be pushed through.

Bug Prioritization Instead of a Zero-Bug Policy

For some organizations, it is difficult to implement a zero-bug policy. A valid variant for us might look like this: Bug reporting begins with a centralized issue tracking system, where bugs are tagged to the person who discovers and reports them with relevant domain and service information.

This ensures that they're routed to the appropriate team. Each domain team performs a frequent, rapid triage of new bugs in their area, typically daily or every few days, to ensure timely response. In some cases, especially for more complex issues that might span multiple domains, the initial reviewer might involve other team members or even representatives from other domain teams to ensure accurate tagging.

Bugs are then classified based on severity and priority. This classification is a collaborative effort between the product owner and technical team members. Once classified, bugs are integrated into the team's backlog alongside feature work. High-priority bugs may be added to the current sprint, while others are scheduled for future sprints.

During regular backlog refinement meetings, teams review both new features and existing bugs, adjusting priorities as needed based on current project goals and customer feedback. During sprint planning, teams decide which bugs to address in the upcoming sprint, balancing them against feature development work. Critical bugs may take precedence over planned feature work.

Throughout the development process, the status and priority of bugs are continually reassessed. As the system evolves, some bugs may become relevant. For bugs that span multiple domains or services, the affected teams work together to determine the best approach and which team should take the lead in resolving the issue.

To maintain oversight and drive improvements, teams track metrics such as bug resolution time, recurrence rates, and bug density per domain. This data informs process improvements and helps identify areas that need more attention. For customer-reported issues, there's a process for keeping customers informed of progress, often through integration between the bug tracking system and customer support tools.

Lower-priority bugs that don't warrant immediate fixes are regularly reviewed as part of the team's technical debt management process. For significant bugs, teams conduct root cause analysis sessions to prevent similar problems in the future and improve overall system quality.

This process seamlessly integrates bug fixes into the development workflow, maintaining the agility and responsiveness required in a great tech organization. By structuring the bug management process in this way, teams can effectively balance addressing current issues with ongoing feature development and system improvement.

Common Misconceptions and Mistakes

DevOps Is a Set of Tools

Many organizations adopt DevOps with a long list of tools to be implemented. Be it a static security code scanner or GitHub, all of these tools are useless if you do not adopt the philosophy of DevOps in the first place. DevOps is a work ethos and a journey for your entire team. It is about people, processes, and technology.

Having DevOps 'implemented' doesn't mean that this is a complete task. On the contrary, it requires you to continuously improve your organization to become better: Be it the flow for software development, reduction of bugs, release cadence, or any other metric we have pointed out: The fact is that DevOps is more a philosophy than a set of tools: Using JIRA won't make you Agile. Using GitHub won't make you an expert in source code control, etc.

Lack of Discipline and Ambition Leads to Insufficient Continuous Delivery

As with any of our practices to improve software quality and development flows, a lack of discipline creates the 'worst' of both worlds, meaning that the concepts discussed in this book, if only half-heartedly implemented, might lead to even worse results than doing nothing at all.

While a complete adoption leads to a continuous improvement of what you have, doing something halfway should be avoided. As we have pointed out earlier, it doesn't make any sense to adopt continuous deployment if your deployments in the data center allow you to deploy only once every three months. Your static three-month release lead might just do the job for you.

TL;DR and Further Reading

A simple first step can be advocating pair programming and creating a common culture and idea of how your developers should be working together. As you might have noticed, engineering culture can be very diverse, and opinions may differ—bringing everyone on board what long-term principles you want to look out for can be a good beginning.

- Increase the frequency of releases and thus reduce their size
- Automate deployments to be faster and more reliable
- Use trunk-based development to reduce time-consuming merge conflicts
- Shift left. Teams test early and continuously
- Automate testing to be faster and to improve quality
- Monitoring and observability is the new testing
- Shift your thinking from mean time between failures to mean time to resolution
- Use feature flags to reduce the risks of deployments
- Eliminate your staging environments
- Develop all code in pairs to improve quality at source
- Harden your systems and organization with chaos engineering
- Introduce a zero-bug-policy to optimize quality and reduce bug management efforts
- Implement a continuous improvement process for your release process

For a more in-depth look at this topic, these are some of our favorite books and websites:

- https://trunkbaseddevelopment.com/
- *Continuous Delivery: Reliable Software Releases through Build, Test, and Deployment Automation*, by Jez Humble and David Farley
- *Accelerate: The Science of Lean Software and DevOps*, by Nicole Forsgren, Jez Humble, and Gene Kim
- *The Phoenix Project: A Novel About IT, DevOps, and Helping Your Business Win*, by Gene Kim, Kevin Behr, and George Spafford
- *The Unicorn Project*, by Gene Kim

12

HOW TO ALIGN CROSS-CUTTING CONCERNS LIKE ARCHITECTURE, SECURITY, AND GOVERNANCE

IN LOOSELY COUPLED, domain-oriented tech organizations, aligning cross-cutting concerns such as architecture, security, and governance poses a significant challenge. These organizations must strike a delicate balance between domain autonomy and overarching organizational requirements to ensure cohesion and effectiveness at scale.

Failure to address this challenge can lead to inconsistent practices, security vulnerabilities, and architectural fragmentation, ultimately hampering innovation, scalability, and the organization's ability to deliver value efficiently. Conversely, over-centralization can stifle domain-specific innovation and agility, undermining the benefits of a loosely coupled structure.

This chapter introduces a federated approach to managing cross-cutting concerns, emphasizing the establishment of a collaborative architecture and governance community. We explore strategies for creating guidelines that enable product teams to deliver sustainable, secure business value while maintaining a clear separation between macro and micro-level concerns. We outline how to balance short-term and long-term needs, define guiding principles for accelerated decision-making, and leverage tools like technology radars to assess and evolve your tech landscape.

By implementing the strategies outlined in this chapter, you'll be equipped to cultivate a cohesive yet flexible tech organization that can innovate rapidly while maintaining architectural integrity, robust security, and effective governance.

The Traditional Approach and Why It Falls Short

In some traditional IT organizations, the approach to aligning cross-cutting concerns like architecture, security, and governance often stems from a desire for control and standardization. However, these well-intentioned efforts frequently result in practices that hinder rather than help the organization.

Central governance bodies, typically far removed from day-to-day operations, create policies and standards to reduce costs and ensure compliance. While this centralization seems logical for managing complexity, it often leads to overly rigid, impractical guidelines. These standards, born from a 'control and reduce' mindset, focus more on what teams shouldn't do rather than enabling innovation. The result is a set of imprecise, over-detailed policies that prove challenging to implement in real-world scenarios.

To enforce these standards, organizations implement bureaucratic coordination and approval processes, such as Change Approval Boards. These mechanisms, designed to maintain stability and compliance, often become bottlenecks that slow down development and deployment. Moreover, the emphasis on comprehensive documentation over working software and automated controls further widens the gap between business needs and IT delivery. This approach, rooted in outdated project management methodologies, consumes valuable time that could be spent building and testing actual solutions.

REALITY TECH

In one of her first jobs, Sophie had to create a document as an IT deliverable that clearly outlined which document needed to be signed by which level of the hierarchy and by whom before anyone started writing a single line of code.

The collective impact of these traditional practices creates an environment of mutual distrust and inefficiency. Policies, crafted under the assumption that people can't be trusted, erect barriers to delivery rather than facilitating success. This "law and order" approach to IT governance stifles innovation and creates resistance among development teams, leading to workarounds or outright non-compliance. The disconnect between well-intentioned governance and practical implementation ultimately undermines the security and efficiency these measures aim to achieve.

As organizations grapple with the limitations of this traditional approach, it's clear that a new paradigm is needed—one that balances necessary oversight with the agility and innovation required in great tech environments.

The General Blueprint

Establish a Federated Architecture and Governance Community

So far, we introduced two important structural elements:

- Autonomous product teams that focus on maximizing effectiveness and minimizing lead times.

- Platform teams that optimize efficiency across the organization by providing shared tools and services that reduce redundancy and streamline common processes.

What we need in addition is a third very essential element to ensure alignment between these autonomous teams, particularly concerning overarching issues such as architecture, technology stack, and security and compliance.

We call this element a "Federated Architecture and Governance Community" (FAGC). We use the word 'community' to emphasize its decentralized, federated, and inclusive nature. However, it is important to us that this community does not simply meet on Friday afternoons to share knowledge or opinions.

Community members make important decisions as representatives and delegates of their respective domains or functions, and therefore, have important rights and responsibilities.

Important rights and responsibilities are:

- Decision-making authority: Members have the authority to make binding decisions on architectural and governance issues that affect the entire organization.
- Representation: They are responsible for accurately representing the needs, challenges, and perspectives of their respective domains or functions.
- Communication: Members must effectively communicate decisions, rationales, and policies to their domains and teams and ensure implementation.
- Alignment: Members must align domain-specific practices with organization-wide standards and principles.
- Accountability: Members are accountable for the results of

their decisions and their impact on both their domain and the broader organization.
- Conflict Resolution: They are responsible for addressing and resolving conflicts between domain-specific needs and organization-wide goals.

By exercising these rights and responsibilities, FAGC members play a critical role in shaping the technical direction of the organization, ensuring coherence across domains, and driving sustainable business value through effective architecture and governance practices.

The composition of a Federated Architecture and Governance Community should reflect the diverse needs and expertise across the organization while remaining flexible and inclusive.

Here's a typical structure composition:

- Chief Technology Officer (CTO): Provides overall technical vision and alignment with business strategy.
- Domain Representatives: These are senior technical leads or architects from each major domain or product area.
- Enterprise Architecture Representatives: Maintain a holistic view of the organization's technical landscape.
- Platform Team Representatives: These are subject matter experts from shared-platform or infrastructure teams.
- Data Governance Specialists: These are experts in data management, privacy, and compliance.
- A Security Architect: Ensures security considerations are integrated into all decisions.

The composition of the FAGC prioritizes deep technical expertise and hands-on experience over hierarchical positions, ensuring that members are primarily Subject Matter Experts (SMEs) who are actively involved in the day-to-day technical challenges and innovations within their respective domains.

This focus on technical proficiency and practical knowledge, rather than managerial titles, ensures that decisions are grounded in real-world experience and current technological realities, enabling a community that values expertise, practical insights, and collaborative problem-solving over hierarchical authority.

At its center is a Core Group that meets regularly, typically bi-weekly to discuss and make high-level decisions that shape the organization's architectural and governance landscape. Complementing this, Working Groups are formed as smaller, focused teams to tackle specific issues or projects, allowing for deep dives into areas of concern. To ensure broader engagement and knowledge dissemination, the FAGC also hosts periodic Open Forums, inviting a wider audience from across the organization.

These sessions facilitate broader input and knowledge sharing and help maintain transparency in the community's activities and decisions. Consider implementing a rotation system where some positions (especially domain representatives) change periodically to ensure fresh perspectives and broad representation over time. Regarding decision-making, we recommend a consensus-based approach for major decisions, with clear escalation paths for unresolved issues.

Different domains can have their own specific FAGC. This approach recognizes that different domains may have unique technological needs and contexts. These domain-specific FAGCs need to align with the overall guidelines.

Wardley Maps and Domain-Driven Design (DDD) are valuable tools for a Federated Architecture and Governance Community, offering complementary frameworks that enhance strategic decision-making and complex system management.

Wardley Maps provide a visual representation of the organization's technology and business landscape, showing how components evolve and interconnect. This helps the FAGC in strategic planning, resource allocation, and anticipating future changes. As a communication tool, Wardley Maps excel at conveying complex ideas across different domains and stakeholders, ensuring alignment between technology strategies and business goals.

Domain-Driven Design, on the other hand, focuses on the intricate details of each business domain. It helps the FAGC identify and define bounded contexts, which is crucial for effective federated governance. DDD promotes the use of a ubiquitous language within each domain, improving communication between technical and business teams. Its strategic design patterns, like Context Mapping, are invaluable for managing relationships between different domains in a federated structure. DDD also provides tools for managing complexity in large systems, ensuring that software models closely reflect the business domain.

The Primary Goal of Common Guidelines Is to Enable the Product Teams to Deliver Sustainable Business Value Securely

In managing cross-functional concerns such as macro architecture, security, and governance, the primary goal is to enable product teams to deliver sustainable business value securely. This is achieved through a Federated Architecture and Governance Community that provides common guidelines that optimize the entire organization while supporting loosely coupled teams.

The FAGC serves as a cross-domain and cross-functional body with several key responsibilities:

- Establishing high-level architectural principles and governance frameworks.
- Facilitating collaboration across domains or teams.
- Ensuring interoperability and compliance across the enterprise.
- Adapting governance and architecture approaches based on feedback and evolving needs.

These guidelines are not restrictive rules, but an evolving framework that balances team autonomy with organizational coherence. They empower product teams to innovate efficiently within a secure and sustainable structure that recognizes these teams as the primary value creators.

Crucially, all units and persons involved in creating and enforcing these policies must see themselves as enablers. Their role is to create a global balance that allows for local autonomy and enables an environment where teams can work effectively toward long-term business goals.

By making this goal explicit and adhering to these principles, the FAGC ensures that the policies remain relevant, adapt to new technologies and business needs, and support the organization's collective learning and evolving needs. This approach enables the organization to maintain consistency in critical areas such as security and interoperability, while driving innovation and long-term value creation.

Clear Separation and Balance between the Macro and Micro Levels

When establishing a Federated Architecture and Governance Community in a loosely coupled organization, one of the most critical aspects to consider is the clear separation and balance between the macro and micro levels of decision-making and governance.

It is important that the FAGC focus on the macro level and avoid acting on the micro level to provide essential organizational alignment and consistency while preserving the autonomy, agility, and domain-specific expertise of individual teams and domains.

- At the macro level, the FAGC focuses on overarching principles, standards, and guidelines that ensure organizational coherence and alignment. This includes defining high-level architectural patterns, security policies, and governance frameworks that apply across all domains. The goal is to provide a consistent foundation that enables interoperability, maintains compliance, and supports the organization's long-term vision.
- At the micro level, individual domains and teams retain autonomy to make decisions specific to their areas of expertise. This includes selecting technologies, implementing specific solutions, and optimizing processes within their bounded context. At the micro level, innovation thrives, and teams can tailor their approaches to best serve their particular use cases and customer needs.

The key to success is to strike the right balance between these two levels. The FAGC should establish clear boundaries that define what falls under macro governance and what remains within the purview of individual domains. This separation prevents the FAGC from becoming overly prescriptive or creating bottlenecks in the decision-making process.

Wardley Maps and Domain-Driven Design (DDD) play crucial roles in separating and aligning micro and macro architecture within an organization. Wardley Maps provide a macro-level view, helping visualize the overall technological landscape and strategic positioning of various components. This macro perspective guides high-level architectural decisions and long-term planning. DDD, conversely, excels at the micro level, focusing on individual domains and their specific contexts.

It helps define clear boundaries between different parts of the system, ensuring that each domain's architecture is tailored to its unique needs. When used together, these tools create a powerful synergy: Wardley Maps inform the overarching architectural strategy and evolution, while DDD ensures that this strategy is effectively implemented at the domain level, respecting the nuances and complexities of each business area.

This combination allows organizations to maintain a coherent macro architecture while enabling the flexibility and specialization needed at the micro level, striking a balance between organizational consistency and domain-specific optimization.

To achieve this balance:

- Define the FAGC scope clearly and develop a decision-making framework that clearly outlines when issues should be escalated to the FAGC level.
- Focus on creating interfaces and standards at the macro level rather than dictating specific implementations.
- Implement a lightweight review process for significant domain-level decisions that could impact the broader organization.
- Encourage knowledge sharing between domains to spread best practices organically.
- Periodically review and adjust the balance to ensure it continues to meet the needs of the organization as it evolves.

By maintaining this clear separation and balance, the FAGC can provide the necessary guidance and alignment at the organizational level while empowering the domains to innovate and optimize in their specific contexts. This approach enables a culture of responsible autonomy, where teams are aligned with organizational goals but have the freedom to make decisions that best suit their unique challenges and opportunities.

Balance Short-Term and Long-Term Goals and Needs

The Federated Architecture and Governance Community aims to maintain a 50/50 focus between addressing immediate challenges and planning for future architectural and organizational needs. This balance is critical to ensuring both short-term efficiency and long-term innovation.

A key practice in this framework is to alternate the focus of the core bi-weekly FAGC meetings between short-term issues and long-term strategic decisions. Short-term meetings address immediate challenges and ongoing projects, while long-term meetings focus on strategic planning and future architecture. For long-term meetings, a guiding question is: "What will our architecture and organization look like in three years if we continue to act/work as we do now?"

To effectively balance short-term and long-term considerations, the FAGC engages in several key activities

- Strategic Impact Analysis: For every major decision, assess both the immediate benefits and the long-term implications.
- Technology horizon scanning: Regularly review and update a technology radar to identify emerging trends and their potential long-term impact.

- Document architectural decisions: Record all major decisions, explicitly stating their short-term rationale and long-term strategic direction.
- Balanced performance metrics: Develop and track KPIs that measure both immediate performance and progress toward long-term goals.
- Future scenario planning: Conduct quarterly workshops to envision future states of the organization's technology landscape and plan backward.
- Innovation incubation: Dedicate resources to researching and developing potentially disruptive long-term innovations.
- Continuous architecture review: Host monthly forums where teams present their current work and its alignment with the long-term architectural vision.
- Integrate external perspectives: Engage with industry experts, academic partners, and thought leaders to gain insight into long-term trends.

These activities ensure that while immediate needs are addressed, the organization is also preparing for future challenges and opportunities. The framework emphasizes the importance of regular review and adjustment. Quarterly assessments assess the balance between short-term and long-term focus, while an annual review allows for adjustments to the framework itself.

Define Guiding Principles to Accelerate Day-to-Day Decisions

Defining guiding principles to accelerate day-to-day decisions across teams and domains is a core mission of the Federated Architecture and Governance Community. These principles serve as a compass for teams, enabling faster and more consistent decision-making across the organization.

In this context, guiding principles are high-level, enduring guidelines that reflect the organization's values, technical vision, and strategic goals. They are not prescriptive rules, but rather a framework for decision-making.

Examples of such principles include favoring loosely coupled systems over tightly integrated ones, designing for observability from the start, treating security as everyone's responsibility, optimizing for maintainability over premature optimization, and embracing cloud-native technologies where appropriate.

REALITY TECH

During his time at Scout24 as CTO of AutoScout24, Matthias used these principles to clarify strategy and accelerate local decision-making. They were developed primarily by his Chief Architect in an interactive, inclusive, and incremental process.

To establish these guiding principles:

- Gather input from various stakeholders, including technical leaders, product managers, and domain experts.
- Align the principles with the organization's overall strategy and values.
- Discuss and refine policies in FAGC meetings.
- Limit the number of principles (typically eight to 12) to ensure they're memorable and impactful.
- Document the rationale for each principle.

Acting on these principles involves communicating broadly and frequently, using them as reference points in architectural reviews and decision-making processes, including them in onboarding and training materials, encouraging teams to discuss their application in specific contexts, and periodically reviewing their real-world impact.

Different areas may have their own specific principles that complement the organization-wide principles. These should align with the global principles while addressing domain-specific needs, be developed collaboratively by domain teams and the FAGC, be clearly communicated as domain-specific enhancements, and be reviewed periodically to ensure continued alignment with the global principles.

When teams violate these principles:

- Engage in a dialog to understand the reasons for the deviation.
- Assess whether the principle needs clarification or refinement.
- Evaluate whether the specific situation warrants an exception.
- If an exception is not warranted, provide guidance on how to conform to the principle.
- Use the incident as a learning opportunity, possibly updating documentation or training.
- In persistent cases, escalate to higher levels of management while maintaining a collaborative approach.

The goal is not rigid enforcement, but enabling a culture where principles guide thoughtful decision-making. Principles should evolve as the organization learns and grows, with the FAGC playing a key role in managing this evolution.

REALITY TECH

Scout24, Matthias' former employer, released version 3, which, for good reasons, represents a significant development and adaptation to new circumstances and requirements.

Track and Assess Your Technology Landscape with a Technology Radar

A technology radar is a strategic tool used to visualize and track emerging technologies, trends, and their potential impact on an organization. Popularized by Thoughtworks, it has been adapted by many organizations to meet their specific needs.

The purpose and benefits of a technology radar include:

- Providing a structured view of emerging technologies and trends.
- Facilitating strategic discussions about technology adoption.
- Helping to prioritize technology investments.
- Driving innovation and keeping the organization technologically competitive.
- Aligning technology decisions with business strategy.

Implementing and maintaining a technology radar involves defining categories such as Tools, Techniques, Platforms, Languages, and Frameworks, and establishing rings such as Adopt, Trial, Assess, and Hold. The process requires regular input from teams across the organization, periodic review sessions, and frequent updates, typically quarterly or semi-annually. Once updated, the radar should be widely communicated throughout the organization.

For individual domains and teams, the technology radar serves as a guide for technology selection and experimentation, informs training and skills development priorities, helps align technology stacks with organizational direction, and cultivates cross-domain knowledge sharing and collaboration.

Different domains may have their own specific technology radars, recognizing that each domain may have unique technology needs and contexts. This approach requires a structured way of managing both global and domain-specific tech radars. The global radar, maintained by the FAGC, focuses on enterprise-wide technologies and trends and provides overall strategic direction. Domain-specific radars, maintained by individual domain teams, focus on technologies specific to their needs and may go beyond the global radar.

The integration of global and domain-specific radars involves regular synchronization meetings between the FAGC and domain representatives. Domain radars feed into the global radar for broadly relevant technologies, while the global radar informs the domain radars for strategic direction. Clear documentation is required where domain radars diverge from the global radar.

Both global and domain radars should be published transparently throughout the organization, with clear communication about their relationship. These radars serve as valuable discussion tools in cross-domain meetings.

In cases of conflict between global and domain radar recommendations, a resolution process should be established, with the FAGC acting as a mediator when necessary, balancing organizational needs with domain-specific requirements.

Continually Evolve Your Architecture and Technology Stacks

In today's rapidly changing technology landscape, static architectures and systems quickly become obsolete, unable to meet new challenges or take advantage of new opportunities.

This constant evolution is driven by several factors:

- Business needs: As business strategies and goals change, the technology that supports them must adapt.

- User Expectations: Evolving user needs and expectations drive changes in system capabilities.
- Technological Advancements: New tools, frameworks, and platforms emerge that offer improved efficiency, scalability, or functionality.
- Market pressures: Competitive forces may require technology upgrades to maintain market position.
- Regulatory changes: New regulations or compliance requirements may drive architectural changes.

While evolution is necessary, it's critical to balance change with stability. Organizations must maintain core systems while introducing incremental improvements, ensure backward compatibility where possible, and proactively manage technical debt.

This balance is often achieved through approaches such as:

- Incremental improvements: Making small, continuous updates to existing systems.
- Modular architecture: Designing systems with loosely coupled components that can be updated independently.
- Microservices: Adopting a microservices architecture to make it easier to update and scale individual services.
- Cloud-native technologies: Leveraging cloud platforms for greater flexibility and scalability.
- Continuous Integration/Continuous Deployment (CI/CD): Implementing practices that enable frequent, reliable updates.

The Federated Architecture and Governance Community plays a key role in managing this evolution. They monitor technology trends, facilitate discussions about potential changes, ensure alignment with organizational strategy, balance short-term needs with long-term vision, and guide the adoption of new technologies.

This approach presents challenges, including maintaining system stability during change, managing increasing complexity, ensuring that team skills keep pace with technological advances, and balancing the costs of change against the potential benefits. However, the benefits are significant: improved ability to meet changing business needs, enhanced competitiveness, improved user experience, and increased system resilience and scalability.

Embracing continuous architecture and technology stack evolution enables organizations to remain agile and responsive to change. This approach requires constant vigilance, strategic planning, and a culture that values continuous learning and adaptation.

Key to this process is the recognition that evolution is not just about adopting the latest trends, but about making strategic choices that align with organizational goals and user needs. It involves carefully evaluating new technologies and architectural patterns, understanding their potential impact, and integrating them in ways that enhance rather than disrupt existing systems.

This constant evolution also requires a shift in mindset across the organization. Teams must be prepared to learn and adapt continuously. Knowledge sharing becomes critical, as does creating a culture of experimentation and calculated risk-taking.

Ultimately, the goal is to create a flexible, resilient technology foundation that can adapt to changing needs while delivering consistent value.

Integrate Security Across Domains

Security is a key consideration in the context of a Federated Architecture and Governance Community and plays a critical role in ensuring the overall integrity, compliance, and risk management of an organization's technology landscape. As a pervasive concern that affects all aspects of architecture and governance, security cannot be overlooked or treated as an afterthought.

Key aspects of security in the context of the FAGC include:

- Security as a Shared Responsibility: The FAGC should promote a culture where security is everyone's responsibility, not just a specialized team's concern.
- Security by Design: Encourage the integration of security considerations from the earliest stages of architecture and design processes.
- Federated Security Governance: Like other aspects of governance, security should balance organization-wide standards with domain-specific implementations.
- Security Guidelines and Principles: Develop and maintain a set of security guidelines and principles that apply across all domains.
- Threat Modeling: Incorporate threat modeling into the architectural review process, considering potential security risks in new designs and changes.
- Compliance Framework: Establish a framework for ensuring compliance with relevant security standards and regulations across all domains.
- Security Reviews: Include security experts in architectural reviews and decision-making processes.
- Incident Response Planning: Develop and maintain an organization-wide incident response plan, with clear roles and responsibilities across domains.
- Continuous Security Education: Promote ongoing security training and awareness programs for all teams.

- Security Metrics and Reporting: Establish key security metrics and ensure regular reporting to track the organization's security posture.
- Third-party Security Management: Develop guidelines for assessing and managing the security of third-party components and services used across domains.
- Data Protection and Privacy: Ensure that data protection and privacy considerations are integral to all architectural decisions, especially considering regulations like GDPR.

Regular communication and collaboration between domain security teams and the FAGC is essential to ensure that domain-specific security measures are robust and aligned with the organization's overall security strategy. The FAGC can facilitate cross-domain security knowledge sharing and help spread best practices and lessons learned throughout the organization.

Your Architecture, Tech Stack, and Delivery Principles Are Key to Attracting Talent

The most successful tech organizations in this world are very vocal about the technologies that they use. At the same time, they are active contributors in Free and Open Source Communities and are making their code available for other parties to consume.

Basically, they 'show off' to the world the great software they have built over the years. A much-underestimated way to attract talent is by displaying and talking about technology for tech talents.

A very good example is the Tech Radar[1] invented by Thoughtworks. They created an industry benchmark for introducing a simple chart where new technologies are being assessed or old ones crossed out.

---

1. https://www.thoughtworks.com/radar

Another benchmark was created by Spotify—not only has their organizational model been discussed and copied all over the world —their developer portal, backstage.io[2], has been the number one go-to portal for creating great developer platforms, basically giving anybody the code baseline to build it by themselves.

Thoughtworks and Spotify, only to name two of many, have been able to hire some of the most sought-after tech talents in the world ('just') by publicly talking about tech and promoting their tech stack to the external world.

Common Misconceptions and Mistakes

No Overall Guidance on Architecture, Governance, and Security Is Necessary

As with many misconceptions around agile teams, the people involved will 'sort it out by themselves' is simply wrong.

We have experienced this on both extremes:

- Over-regulation
- No regulation at all

Unfortunately, both ways were wrong. The one team was not able to deliver anything since almost any idea was blocked due to compliance while the other team was able to deliver something, but it was almost unacceptable.

For sure, as an owner of a customer-facing application containing end-user data such as credit card information, you do not want to have a data leak and user data appearing somewhere in the dark net. Nonetheless, the security requirements often implemented are

2. www.backstage.io

far from working consistently and practically—in one direction or the other.

Looking into big tech discussions around governance, tech stacks, etc. seems to be non-existent. Our experience is quite the contrary: Governance, Security, Data Protection, etc. are taken very seriously. In comparison to many other organizations, teams are being assisted in delivering their products rather than giving them a list of things that they are not supposed to do.

Security and Governance Is Better Done Manually, Just to Be on the Safe Side

The temptation to stay in a classic structure when it comes to security and governance measures is high. Established working models with IT consulting companies (for your Pen-Testing) and manual checks by 'designated roles' were established many years ago. Too often, these issues have been neglected by product teams, putting organizations at risk, e.g., with security flaws, license violations, etc. These routines and checks are applied to all parts of the organization regardless if they are taking these topics seriously or not.

Our strong recommendation goes into incentivization if sticking to the rules. Units that are overachieving on security checks might as well be allowed to be self-sufficient in their security measures. The better they are at putting self-induced measures upon them, the easier is the one-size-fits-all approach. Teams will automatically move into ideas on how to optimize and automate their work if they would just be allowed to. Being able to steer efforts for governance-related work and getting incentivized might be well worth considering.

Long-Term Health of the Architecture Is Neglected

The migration away from legacy mainframe or monolithic applications has often been the consequence of neglecting operational architectural work over extended periods. This negligence has resulted in multi-million dollar projects taking years to transition from, for instance, mainframe to cloud-native infrastructure.

The significant resources used and the prolonged duration of such transitions should let us rethink whether the next multi-million dollar migration is just around the corner.

Regularly scrutinizing your technology stack is imperative, particularly in assessing vendor reliability, scalability, and cost efficiency.

Two key factors underscore this necessity:

- The wealth of available technologies offers diverse solutions to our challenges, yet the selection process demands critical thinking due to the vast array of options.
- The rapid evolution of technology challenges the idea of building for the long term.

Experience teaches us that year-long mainframe upgrade endeavors often falter as the technology becomes outdated even before implementation. Maintaining flexibility in migration initiatives, including the willingness to explore alternative technological pathways, emerges as a prudent strategy worthy of consideration.

TL;DR and Further Reading

Creating a first step when it comes to compliance and governance can be difficult. We recommend reviewing and checking what ideas might need to be reworked and where things can be improved. A small recommendation: it is easy to establish policies while it is much harder to get rid of some. Trying to become leaner and focus on the big topics is a core recommendation of ours.

- Establish a federated architecture and governance community
- The primary goal of common guidelines is to enable the product teams to deliver sustainable business value securely
- Clear separation and balance between the macro and micro level
- Balance short-term and long-term goals and needs
- Define guiding principles to accelerate day-to-day decisions
- Track and assess your technology landscape with a technology radar
- Continually evolve your architecture and technology stacks
- Integrate Security Across Domains
- Your architecture, tech stack, and delivery principles are key to attracting talent

For a more in-depth look at this topic, these are some of our favorite books and websites:

- *Building Evolutionary Architectures,* by Neal Ford, Rebecca Parsons, and Patrick Kua
- *Data Mesh: Delivering Data-Driven Value at Scale,* by Zhamak Dehghani
- *The Architect Elevator (https://architectelevator.com/)*

13

HOW TO DRIVE CHANGE AND CONSTANTLY IMPROVE THE ORGANIZATION

ORGANIZATIONS FACE the constant challenge of driving meaningful change and creating continuous improvement to stay competitive and relevant. Many struggle to balance the need for stability with the imperative for innovation, often resulting in stagnation or disruptive, poorly executed transformations.

Effective change management and continuous improvement are critical for tech organizations aiming to scale successfully. They directly impact an organization's ability to adapt to market shifts, leverage new technologies, and maintain a culture of innovation. Failure to master these skills can lead to decreased productivity, missed opportunities, and ultimately, a loss of market position.

This chapter introduces a holistic approach to driving change and improving tech organizations, centered around the concept of becoming a learning organization. We'll explore strategies for establishing feedback loops, visualizing change in an agile manner, and cultivating a mindset that embraces failure as a growth opportunity. The chapter will guide you through implementing iterative and incremental change, balancing grassroots and top-down initiatives, and effectively communicating across all levels of the organization.

By applying the principles and practices outlined in this chapter, you'll be equipped to transform your tech organization into an adaptive, resilient entity capable of thriving in an increasingly complex and competitive business environment.

The Traditional Approach and Why It Falls Short

When it comes to organizational change, traditional IT organizations are often stuck in outdated paradigms that hinder true transformation. These approaches frequently fall short of addressing the dynamic needs of great tech companies.

One major issue lies in the linear view of change management. Rooted in Kurt Lewin's "unfreeze—change—refreeze" model, this approach assumes organizations move from one stable state to another. However, in today's rapidly evolving tech landscape, this static mindset fails to enable the continuous adaptability required for success. Organizations find themselves constantly playing catch-up, unable to cultivate a culture of ongoing improvement.

Another significant problem is the superficial nature of change initiatives. While structural reorganizations are common, they often neglect the deeper aspects of work culture and ethics. Simply reshuffling the same people with unchanged attitudes rarely yields transformative results. This surface-level approach is further exacerbated by resistance from those in power who fear losing budget, headcount, or status. The standardization of leadership positions creates a rigid hierarchy that stifles innovation and true organizational evolution.

Perhaps most tellingly, change management is frequently treated as an afterthought, relegated to external consultants and symbolic gestures like project T-shirts or kick-off events. This lack of genuine engagement from top management in understanding employees' needs leads to a disconnect between change initiatives and the people they affect. As a result, organizations often find themselves grappling with "mindset problems" too late in the process when resistance has already taken root.

These traditional practices collectively create a culture of cosmetic change, where new labels are applied to old structures without addressing fundamental issues. The disconnect between the intention of change and its actual implementation leaves IT organizations ill-equipped to handle the demands of the great tech landscape.

To truly drive change and constantly improve, a radically different approach is needed—one that embraces continuous adaptation and places people at the heart of transformation.

The General Blueprint

Establish Feedback Loops That Show the Current State of the Organization

To improve an organization, it is essential to have indicators and signals that show how the organization and its components are doing and how key characteristics and capabilities are developing. For this purpose, feedback loops are installed.

A feedback loop is a continuous process of collecting, analyzing, and responding to input from all parts of the organization about its current state and the effectiveness of changes being implemented. These loops are like a continuous conversation that helps the organization understand how it is doing. They inform everyone about the core metrics and capabilities that the organization is optimizing for. We recommend focusing on the benefits that are generated, how fast the organization is delivering, how productive it is, and if it maintains quality. Most importantly, they provide insight into what motivates the employees.

To make these feedback loops effective, we must use both data and anecdotes. We need hard numbers to understand our performance, but we also need real-life examples to see the bigger picture. It's not just about collecting feedback now and then. It is essential to make this a regular occurrence, with frequent feedback sessions to ensure we remain on track.

Formalizing these feedback loops is crucial. This involves establishing a structured approach to gathering feedback to ensure it is not overlooked. However, it is also important to allow for informal feedback. In some cases, the most valuable insights can emerge from casual conversations or anecdotes shared between colleagues. Furthermore, it is vital to consider inclusivity. It is essential that everyone in the organization feels comfortable providing feedback regardless of their position. There should be no fear of negative consequences for speaking up. By embracing feedback loops in this way, we can create a culture of continuous improvement and empowerment.

There are different types of feedback loops, such as metrics in dashboards, moderated retrospectives, and surveys. Some provide feedback in real-time, some are queried daily, others are in longer leads. The results can overlap and be contradictory. This feedback must be understood as signals that need to be analyzed.

Individual feedback should be anonymized, but aggregated feedback should be available to all. This allows results to be both validated and critically examined.

Visualize and Manage Change in an Agile Way

Feedback without follow-up and action is worthless and discourages employees from continuing to provide feedback. Feedback should lead to change initiatives, sometimes just to better understand certain aspects of the feedback or the organization.

However, managing change initiatives can be challenging and often suffers from the same shortcomings as other initiatives. To overcome these challenges, we recommend applying agile principles to change management processes. Just as agile methods are used to manage product development, they can also be applied to change initiatives. This includes visualizing change initiatives, setting clear priorities, and limiting work in progress to ensure focus and effectiveness.

One effective approach to visualizing and managing change initiatives is using kanban. Kanban principles such as visualizing workflow, limiting work in progress, and managing flow should be applied to change management processes. By using a physical kanban board and holding regular stand-up meetings, teams can track the progress of change initiatives, identify bottlenecks, and adjust as needed. This approach promotes transparency, collaboration, and alignment, enabling organizations to drive change more effectively.

In addition to visualizing change initiatives, it's important to prioritize them. By prioritizing and ranking change initiatives based on their impact and feasibility, organizations can focus their efforts on the most important initiatives and maximize their chances of success.

Establish a Flexible, Open-Minded, and Self-Critical Mindset That Appreciates Failure, Growth, and Change

Establishing a flexible, open-minded, and self-critical mindset is essential for effectively implementing feedback loops and driving change within an organization. Flexibility means being willing to adapt to new information, ideas, and approaches, even if they challenge existing beliefs or practices. It involves embracing change as a natural part of growth and evolution rather than resisting it out of fear or complacency. Self-criticism is about being honest and reflective about one's performance, decisions, and behaviors. It means being willing to acknowledge mistakes, shortcomings, and areas for improvement without defensiveness or blame.

Embracing failure, growth, and change requires a mindset shift from viewing them as threats to embracing them as catalysts for innovation and progress. Failure becomes an opportunity to learn and iterate rather than a source of shame or discouragement. Growth becomes a journey of continuous improvement, where individuals and organizations strive to reach their full potential through ongoing development. Change becomes a constant driving force for adaptation and evolution in response to shifting internal and external dynamics.

Leaders play a critical role in shaping the culture of their organizations:

- By leading by example and embodying the values they wish to instill, they set the tone for others to follow.
- Clear communication is essential to convey expectations and reinforce the importance of key values such as openness, adaptability, and continuous learning.
- Encouraging collaboration and diversity creates an environment where different perspectives are valued,

leading to more innovative solutions and more resilient teams.
- Leaders who actively lead change initiatives rather than outsourcing them demonstrate their commitment to organizational transformation.

Feedback can sometimes make leaders feel uncomfortable. However, leaders need to face this feedback. Ignoring uncomfortable feedback can lead to missed chances for learning and trust. Instead, leaders should listen, reflect, and address concerns. This shows humility and a commitment to getting better.

Drive Change Continuously, Iterative and Incremental

Rather than implementing large-scale changes all at once, we recommend breaking initiatives down into smaller, more manageable steps that can be tested, evaluated, and refined over time. By adopting a continuous change mindset, organizations enable a culture where change is seen as normal and expected rather than disruptive or unsettling. This helps employees adapt more easily to new ways of working, which cultivates a sense of agility and resilience in the face of evolving challenges and opportunities. If nothing changed, employees would find it strange.

The iterative nature of this approach allows organizations to break change initiatives into manageable increments, allowing for focused efforts and efficient use of resources. By setting clear timelines and goals for each iteration, teams can maintain momentum and avoid getting bogged down in lengthy, resource-intensive projects. In addition, iterations provide opportunities for feedback and reflection, allowing teams to course-correct and adjust their approach based on real-world results and stakeholder insights. This iterative process helps ensure that change initiatives remain aligned with organizational goals and priorities while allowing for flexibility and adaptability in response to changing circumstances.

In addition, an incremental approach to change allows organizations to prioritize the most important aspects of the initiative and build on them over time. By starting with small, targeted changes and incorporating stakeholder feedback, organizations can refine and expand their efforts in ways that maximize impact and minimize risk. This incremental approach allows organizations to focus on delivering tangible value early and often while maintaining a sense of momentum and progress throughout the change process.

Don't Boil the Ocean and Become Ready by Starting

"How do you eat an elephant? One bite at a time." —Creighton Abrams

Rather than getting bogged down in extensive analysis and planning, organizations should take action and gain experience through hands-on implementation.

The principle of "not boiling the ocean" underscores the importance of learning through action. Rather than trying to anticipate every possible outcome or scenario, organizations can gain valuable insights by actually implementing change initiatives and observing their impact firsthand. This experiential learning approach allows teams to test hypotheses, identify challenges, and iterate their approach in real-time, ultimately leading to more effective and informed decisions.

To mitigate the risks associated with change, it's important to limit the "blast radius" of any initiative. This means starting with small experiments or pilots that are limited in scope and impact. By framing change initiatives as experiments, organizations can create a mindset of curiosity and learning, where it's okay to try new things and adjust your course based on feedback and results. This approach enables a culture of innovation and agility, where failure is seen as an opportunity for growth and adaptation.

In addition, applying change incrementally and selectively helps further mitigate risk while allowing organizations to compare the effectiveness of different approaches. By focusing on a single process, application, team, or domain, organizations can isolate variables and more effectively measure the impact of change. This allows for more targeted interventions and ensures that resources are efficiently allocated to areas where they are most needed.

Leverage Grassroots and Top-Down Initiatives

In change management, it is essential to use both bottom-up and top-down initiatives. A common question is whether to go top-down or bottom-up. We recommend using both approaches. Change and improvement must start at the top of the organization. Leaders set the vision and goals. Strategies often come from them.

Bottom-up initiatives are equally important. These come from people who are close to customers, products, and processes. They have valuable insights and ideas. Grassroots initiatives shouldn't wait for approval from the top. They can begin as small, informal projects. These "guerrilla" initiatives can show early successes. These successes can then support larger, top-down initiatives. Encourage those bottom-up initiatives and label them as organizational experiments based on clearly defined hypotheses.

Both approaches have a significant impact on the "frozen middle." This is the middle management layer that is often resistant to change. This resistance is due to mixed signals from higher up. Combining top-down vision with grassroots innovation can help unfreeze this middle layer. It aligns the entire organization around common goals and continuous improvement.

Grassroots initiatives improve innovation and problem-solving by harnessing the creativity and insights of employees directly involved in operations, leading to faster responses to problems and a better understanding of customer needs. These initiatives increase employee engagement and motivation by making employees feel valued and invested in the organization, cultivating a sense of ownership and accountability.

In addition, grassroots efforts promote adaptability and agility, helping the organization respond effectively to change and new opportunities. They also reduce resistance to change because employees are more likely to support initiatives they have helped to create, and they develop future leaders by allowing employees to gain experience in project management, decision-making, and collaboration.

Set Objectives That Inspire and Force the Organization to Move Faster Than It Would Have Organically

"The greatest danger for most of us is not that our aim is too high and we miss it, but that it is too low and we reach it." — Michelangelo

Setting goals that inspire and push the organization to move faster is critical to getting things done. Ambitious goals motivate teams to exceed their usual performance. They create a sense of urgency and purpose, which helps the organization innovate and grow faster.

To make this happen, start by setting clear and challenging goals. Make sure these goals are aligned with the organization's vision. Communicate these goals effectively to all employees. Use inspiring language to highlight the potential impact and benefits.

Break these goals down into smaller, more manageable tasks. Set deadlines to keep the momentum going. Encourage teams to take ownership of their tasks. Provide regular feedback and support.

Recognize and celebrate successes along the way. This keeps morale high and reinforces the importance of the goals. Continually review and adjust goals based on progress and feedback.

By setting and pursuing ambitious goals, the organization can achieve more than it could through gradual, organic growth.

Communicate All the Time on All Channels to All Types of Employees

"Thought is not said, said is not heard, heard is not understood, understood is not agreed, agreed is not applied, applied is far from retained." — Konrad Lorenz

Effective communication is critical to change management. Leaders must communicate constantly across all channels to all types of employees. Without clear and frequent communication, change efforts can fail because people may not understand, agree with, or apply the changes.

Leaders or anyone driving change need to talk about change more often than they think is necessary. They should communicate in a variety of ways. Sometimes, their messages should be visionary while sometimes very specific.

They should communicate through all available channels. Use email, town hall meetings, intranet posts, videos, lunches, and coffee breaks. This will ensure that the message reaches everyone. It's important to tailor communications to different groups of employees. Innovators and early adopters are eager for change. Early adopters are curious but cautious. Late adopters are skeptical, and laggards are often resistant.

Leaders should use a mix of regular, prepared communications and spontaneous ad-hoc messages. Regular updates keep everyone informed and aligned. Spontaneous communications address immediate concerns and demonstrate responsiveness.

By communicating effectively and frequently, leaders can ensure that all employees understand, accept, and support the changes. This helps the organization move forward together, making the change process smoother and more successful.

Be Clear on What to Learn, What to Unlearn, and What to Keep

Change projects often unsettle employees. They tend to focus only on why and what should change. This can make people feel that everything that has contributed to the organization's success is bad and subject to change. Employees may also apply new methods and tools to areas where they are not appropriate.

It is often ignored that some things in the organization are good and should not change. Some practices must continue to ensure the current success of the organization. It is critical to clearly define and communicate what will change and when.

Leaders should identify what needs to be learned, unlearned, and retained. Learning means acquiring new skills and knowledge needed for the future. Unlearning involves letting go of outdated habits and practices. Keeping involves maintaining valuable practices that contribute to the organization's success.

Leaders should explain why certain practices need to change and provide support for unlearning old habits. They should also recognize and preserve the organization's strengths.

Trust and Invest in the People You Have and Bring In Experienced Outsiders

"Train people well enough so they can leave, treat them well enough so they don't want to." —Sir Richard Branson

We often hear, "My people don't have the right mindset and skills for this change." This may be true, but in most cases, we recommend trusting and investing in your current people while bringing in external talent that has made a similar change before.

When it comes to managing organizational change, trusting and investing in existing employees while also bringing in experienced outsiders is critical. Your current employees know the organization well and are invested in its success. Trust them to contribute ideas and insights to drive change. Invest in their development through training and support to build their skills and confidence.

At the same time, experienced outsiders bring fresh perspectives and specialized knowledge. They can offer valuable insights and best practices from their past experiences. By combining the strengths of your internal team with the expertise of external professionals, you create a powerful synergy that accelerates the pace of change and increases the likelihood of success.

Take Care of Your Team and Peers

"I've learned that people will forget what you said, people will forget what you did, but people will never forget how you made them feel." —Maya Angelou

Caring for your team and peers is essential to creating a positive and supportive work environment. When team members feel valued, supported, and respected, they are more motivated, engaged, and productive. It builds trust and strengthens relationships, creating collaboration and teamwork. By prioritizing the well-being and professional development of your team members and colleagues, you create a culture of care and mutual respect that benefits everyone.

To care for your team and peers, start by actively listening to their needs, concerns, and feedback. Show empathy and understanding, and offer support and encouragement when needed. Provide opportunities for professional growth and development, such as training, mentoring, and coaching. Recognize and celebrate their accomplishments and milestones, both individually and collectively. This boosts morale and motivation, reinforces positive behaviors, and manifests a sense of accomplishment.

In addition, create a supportive and inclusive work environment where everyone feels valued and appreciated. Encourage open communication, collaboration, and teamwork, and address any conflicts or issues promptly and constructively. Recognize their efforts and contributions and develop a culture of continuous learning and improvement. Importantly, be transparent and honest in your interactions and lead by example by demonstrating integrity, fairness, and accountability in your actions.

Celebrate! Progress, Success, and Failure

"Celebrate what you want to see more of." —Tom Peters

Celebrating progress, success, and even failure is critical to organizational change management. It builds morale, motivation, and engagement among team members. Recognizing and celebrating progress highlights employees' hard work and dedication, reinforces positive behaviors, and creates a culture of appreciation and recognition.

Similarly, celebrating success reinforces the organization's values and goals by highlighting achievements and milestones along the change journey. It also provides an opportunity to reflect on what went well and why, facilitating learning and continuous improvement.

In addition, celebrating failure may seem counterintuitive, but it's just as important. Failure is an inevitable part of the change process and provides valuable learning opportunities. By celebrating failure, organizations create a safe environment where people feel comfortable taking risks, experimenting, and learning from mistakes. It nourishes innovation, resilience, and a growth mindset, encouraging individuals to embrace challenges and turn setbacks into opportunities for growth and improvement.

To effectively celebrate progress, success, and failure, leaders can organize regular team meetings or events to recognize achievements and milestones. They can publicly acknowledge individual and team contributions and provide praise and rewards for outstanding performance. In addition, leaders can create rituals or traditions that mark important moments in the change journey, such as ringing a bell or sharing success stories. Importantly, celebrations should be inclusive, involving all team members and stakeholders in the recognition process.

Valid Variants for Different Situations

Revolutionary Changes May Be Necessary If You Have Missed an Important External Change

Sometimes organizational change management requires revolutionary changes when an important external change has been overlooked. This could be due to market shifts, technological advances, or changes in customer preferences that were not anticipated.

It's critical to recognize the need for revolutionary change when incremental and iterative approaches are no longer sufficient to address the new reality. While incremental change focuses on making small, incremental improvements, and iterative change involves repeating leads of testing and refining, revolutionary change requires bold, transformative action to adapt to significant changes in the external environment.

When faced with the need for revolutionary change, it's important to act quickly and decisively. This may involve rethinking fundamental aspects of the organization, such as its business model, products or services, processes, or organizational structure. Leaders must clearly and transparently communicate the urgency and rationale for these changes and align stakeholders around a shared vision for the future. While revolutionary change can be disruptive and challenging, it also presents opportunities for innovation, growth, and competitive advantage.

Common Misconceptions and Mistakes

Change Is Only Possible When Everyone Is Comfortable and In Agreement

The misconception that "change is only possible when everyone is comfortable and in agreement" is false and can hinder progress. Change often involves discomfort and resistance because it challenges the status quo and requires individuals to step outside their comfort zones. Waiting for universal agreement before implementing change can lead to missed opportunities for growth and innovation.

Instead of waiting for everyone to be comfortable and in agreement, leaders should focus on the group of innovators and early adopters in their organization and gain their buy-in and support. The rest should manage resistance effectively. This includes communicating the rationale for change, addressing concerns and objections openly and transparently, and involving stakeholders in the decision-making process whenever possible. It's important to create a safe space for people to express their opinions and feelings about the change while providing support and resources to help them overcome any challenges or uncertainties.

Leaders should also recognize that not everyone will embrace change at the same pace or to the same degree. While some individuals may be early adopters and champions of change, others may need more time and support to come on board. By recognizing and respecting different perspectives and reactions to change, leaders can cultivate a culture of inclusiveness and collaboration that encourages participation and engagement from all stakeholders.

After all, change is often messy and complex, and it's unrealistic to expect everyone to be comfortable and in agreement from the start.

Manager-Initiated Changes Are a Prohibited Intrusion into Team Autonomy

The misconception that "manager-initiated change is a forbidden intrusion into team autonomy" is flawed, especially in agile organizations. While autonomy is important for empowering teams and encouraging innovation, it does not mean that managers should refrain from providing feedback and initiating change altogether. In fact, managers play a critical role in providing direction, guidance, and support to teams, and their input can be valuable in driving organizational change and achieving strategic goals.

Rather than viewing manager-initiated change as an intrusion into team autonomy, it's important to see it as feedback and an opportunity for collaboration and alignment. Managers bring a broader perspective and strategic insight that can help teams understand the rationale behind proposed changes and how they align with organizational goals. By involving teams in the decision-making process and soliciting their input and feedback, managers can ensure that changes are implemented in a way that respects and supports team autonomy while driving overall organizational success.

In addition, agile organizations often embrace change as a natural and necessary part of the iterative development process. Managers and teams work together to continuously improve and adapt to changing circumstances, using feedback and data to inform decisions and drive progress. Rather than viewing manager-initiated change as a threat to autonomy, teams should view it as an opportunity for learning, growth, and collaboration.

Teams, Managers, and Individuals Isolate Themselves from Feedback

Especially in agile organizations where continuous feedback is essential for growth and improvement, teams, managers, and individuals who insulate themselves from feedback are dangerous. Feedback serves as a valuable source of insight that helps teams and individuals identify strengths, areas for improvement, and growth opportunities.

By isolating themselves from feedback, teams, managers, and individuals miss valuable learning opportunities and hinder their ability to adapt and evolve in a dynamic environment.

Rather than isolating themselves from feedback, they should actively seek it and embrace it as a tool for development and success. This means creating a culture of openness, trust, and accountability where feedback is welcomed and encouraged at all levels of the organization. Leaders should set an example by soliciting feedback from their teams and peers and demonstrating a willingness to listen, learn, and adapt based on the input received.

In addition, feedback should be timely, specific, and constructive to be effective. Teams and individuals should regularly seek feedback, both formally and informally, and use it as a basis for reflection, learning, and improvement. Creating channels and processes for giving and receiving feedback, such as regular check-ins, retrospectives, and peer reviews can help create a culture of continuous feedback and improvement.

Feedback Loops Contain No Incorrect or Unaccepted Metrics

Rather than ignoring or using the wrong metrics in feedback loops, organizations should prioritize the selection of relevant, accurate, and accepted metrics. This includes identifying key performance indicators (KPIs) that align with organizational goals and objectives, as well as stakeholder needs and expectations. Metrics should be specific, measurable, achievable, relevant, and time-bound (SMART) to allow clear tracking of progress and identification of areas for improvement.

Organizations should regularly review and refine feedback loops to ensure they remain relevant and aligned with evolving goals and priorities. This includes monitoring performance against established metrics, identifying trends and patterns, and adjusting as needed to optimize effectiveness and drive continuous improvement.

TL;DR and Further Reading

Without any due, the easiest way to establish trust is by being a role model. Asking actively for feedback and being present in the process of change is not only well-meant advice, it is the baseline for your success in building a great tech organization.

- Establish feedback loops that show the current state of the organization
- Visualize and manage change in an agile way
- Establish a flexible, open-minded, and self-critical mindset that appreciates failure, growth, and change
- Drive change continuously, iteratively, and incrementally
- Don't boil the ocean and become ready by starting
- Leverage grassroots and top-down initiatives
- Set objectives that inspire and force the organization to move faster than it would have organically
- Communicate all the time on all channels to all types of employees
- Be clear about what to learn, what to unlearn, and what to keep
- Trust and invest in the people you have and bring in experienced outsiders
- Take care of your team members and colleagues
- Celebrate! Progress, Success, and Failure

For a more in-depth look at this topic, these are some of our favorite books:

- *Leading Change*, by John P. Kotter
- *Switch: How to Change Things When Change Is Hard*, by Chip and Dan Heath

14

HOW TO ESTABLISH A HIGH-PERFORMANCE CULTURE THAT ATTRACTS TALENT

> "The culture itself will help attract the right people, repel the wrong ones, enable brand distinction and determine corporate performance."
>
> TONY HSIEH, FORMER CEO OF ZAPPOS

IN TODAY'S competitive business landscape, organizations face the dual challenge of cultivating a high-performance culture while attracting and retaining top talent. This challenge is particularly acute for scaling great tech companies, where culture can make or break their ability to innovate, adapt, and succeed in a rapidly evolving market.

A strong, purposeful culture is the bedrock of organizational success, directly impacting employee engagement, productivity, and innovation. It serves as a powerful magnet for top talent; a crucial factor in an industry where skilled professionals are in high demand. Moreover, a well-established culture can significantly enhance an organization's resilience and adaptability, essential traits for navigating the complexities of scaling a tech business.

This chapter explores a blueprint for building a high-performance culture centered on mastery, autonomy, and purpose, underpinned by psychological safety. We'll examine strategies for clearly defining and consistently reinforcing your culture, from hiring practices to workplace design. The chapter will guide you through creating feedback loops, encouraging open communication, and aligning your actions with your stated values to create an environment where talent naturally gravitates and thrives.

By implementing the insights and strategies outlined in this chapter, you'll be equipped to forge a culture that not only attracts top talent but also inspires your team to consistently deliver exceptional results.

The Traditional Approach and Why It Falls Short

Many traditional IT organizations cling to outdated practices that hinder their ability to thrive in today's dynamic business landscape. These approaches now create environments that stifle innovation, demotivate employees, and prioritize internal politics over customer satisfaction.

One prevalent issue is the culture of maintaining the status quo. Organizations that discourage "rocking the boat" create an environment where innovative ideas are unwelcome, leading to stagnation and an inability to adapt to market changes. This mindset often stems from fear of failure and a lack of trust, resulting in rigid structures that resist innovation even when leadership calls for it. Consequently, these organizations struggle to attract and retain top talent who seek opportunities for creativity and growth.

Another problematic aspect is the reliance on "carrots and sticks" to motivate employees. This outdated approach, rooted in traditional management theories, creates a compliance-driven culture that sidelines intrinsic motivation. The consequences are far-reaching: low engagement, minimal innovation, high turnover, and a lack of initiative. By focusing on short-term gains through rewards and punishments, organizations fail to cultivate the true engagement necessary for long-term success and adaptability.

Furthermore, the belief that "failure is not an option" breeds a risk-averse culture that paradoxically increases the likelihood of failure overall. This mindset, often resulting from pressure to maintain a flawless track record, leads to a reluctance to take risks or experiment. As a result, organizations miss crucial learning opportunities and struggle to solve complex problems creatively. In an industry where innovation is key, this approach severely hampers an organization's ability to compete and evolve.

Together, these traditional practices create IT organizations that are ill-equipped to meet the challenges of the great tech world. The focus on maintaining internal power structures and short-term gains comes at the expense of customer satisfaction and long-term viability. As the tech industry continues to evolve at a rapid pace, it's clear that an innovative approach is needed—one that promotes innovation, embraces calculated risks, and puts customer needs at the forefront.

The General Blueprint

The Goal Is a Culture Where Purpose and Psychological Safety Inspire Everyone to Excel

The best modern workplaces strive to create a powerful culture. This culture combines two key elements—a strong sense of purpose and an environment of psychological safety. Together, they inspire people to truly excel.

Cultivating a sense of purpose involves aligning individual and organizational goals, and ensuring that employees understand how their work contributes to the larger mission. When employees feel a deep connection to the purpose of their work, they are more motivated, engaged, and willing to go the extra mile to achieve success. Purpose-driven cultures empower employees to see beyond individual tasks and understand the impact of their contributions on the company, society, and even the world.

Psychological security refers to creating an environment where employees feel safe to take risks, share their ideas openly, and be vulnerable without fear of judgment or reprisal. In such cultures, there is trust between colleagues and between employees and leadership. Mistakes are viewed as opportunities for learning, and feedback is given and received constructively. Psychological safety encourages creativity, innovation, and collaboration, as employees are more willing to explore new ideas and challenge the status quo when they feel supported and valued.

When purpose and psychological security are prioritized, employees are not only more engaged and motivated, but they also experience greater satisfaction and fulfillment in their work. This leads to higher levels of productivity, innovation, and overall performance, driving the organization toward its goals and creating a positive and inclusive work environment. Additionally, such cultures attract and retain top talent, as individuals are drawn to organizations where they can find meaning in their work and feel supported in their professional growth and development.

Mastery, Autonomy, Purpose, and Other Attributes of a Healthy Culture

In a successful organizational culture, several key attributes contribute to creating a fulfilling and dynamic work environment.

- Mastery: Employees are encouraged to pursue continual improvement and mastery of their skills and expertise. Opportunities for growth, such as training programs and challenging assignments, empower individuals to excel in their roles and drive innovation within the organization.
- Autonomy and Trust: Granting employees the freedom to make decisions and take ownership of their work enables autonomy. In this environment, individuals are trusted to manage their tasks independently, leading to increased creativity, initiative, and accountability.
- Purpose: A strong sense of purpose aligns employees with the organization's mission and values. When individuals understand how their work positively impacts the overarching goals of the organization and perhaps even society, they feel more motivated, engaged, and resilient, which encourages innovation and progress.
- Collaboration: Effective collaboration across teams and departments is encouraging to achieve common objectives. By leveraging diverse perspectives and expertise, employees can solve complex problems and drive innovation collaboratively, creating a sense of belonging and camaraderie.
- Transparency: Open and honest communication at all levels cultivates transparency within the organization. Leaders share information about goals, strategies, and performance, enabling informed decision-making and creating trust, feedback, and continuous improvement.

- Growth Mindset: Having a growth mindset is fundamental to success. Individuals with a growth mindset view challenges as opportunities for learning and development, persisting in the face of setbacks, and seeking feedback to improve. This mindset enables resilience, adaptability, and a culture of continuous learning and improvement.

Psychological Safety Boosts Creativity, Innovation, and Performance

In technology organizations where innovation is the lifeblood of success, psychological safety has emerged as a critical factor in driving creativity, innovation, and performance. At its core, psychological safety is a shared belief within a team that it's safe to take interpersonal risks and express oneself without fear of negative consequences.

The importance of psychological safety in tech organizations cannot be overstated. In an environment where rapid innovation and complex problem-solving are the norm, team members need to feel comfortable communicating openly and honestly. This openness leads to richer discussions and deeper insights, ultimately fueling the innovation process.

Google's Project Aristotle is a prime example of the impact of psychological safety. The study found it to be the single most important factor in team effectiveness, with highly psychologically safe teams more likely to harness the power of diverse ideas and produce innovative solutions.

The benefits of psychological safety go beyond innovation. In psychologically safe environments, employees are more engaged and motivated, willing to go the extra mile to achieve common goals. They're more likely to take calculated risks, propose novel ideas, and collaborate effectively across departments, and when team members feel safe to voice concerns or point out potential problems, issues are identified and addressed earlier, resulting in more efficient problem-solving processes.

Leaders play a critical role in establishing and maintaining psychological safety within their teams and organizations.

- They can start by setting the tone at the top, demonstrating vulnerability, and openly acknowledging their own mistakes or insecurities.
- Leaders should actively listen to their team members, validate their perspectives, and encourage open communication without fear of judgment.
- Providing regular feedback and recognition for contributions, enabling a culture of respect and inclusion, and encouraging collaboration are essential leadership behaviors that contribute to psychological safety.
- In addition, leaders should be transparent about goals, expectations, and decision-making processes to ensure that everyone feels informed and valued.

Often overlooked in discussions of psychological safety, middle managers also play a critical role. They serve as a bridge between top management's vision and front-line implementation, reinforcing psychological safety practices daily. Pixar's "braintrust" meetings, where middle managers and creatives provide candid feedback on films in progress are an example of how psychological safety can be integrated into regular processes.

The rise of remote and hybrid work models has created new challenges for maintaining psychological safety. Organizations need to adapt their practices to ensure that psychological safety translates to these new environments. This can include encouraging video meetings to promote nonverbal communication, using digital tools for anonymous feedback or idea sharing, and creating virtual "water cooler" moments for informal team bonding.

Companies like GitLab, which operates entirely remotely, have shown that strong psychological safety in distributed teams is achievable through intentional practices and tools. Their success underscores the importance of being mindful of time zone differences and creating asynchronous opportunities for input.

To reinforce psychological safety, organizations should consider implementing targeted training and development programs. Workshops on active listening and empathic communication can help team members develop the skills they need to contribute to a psychologically safe environment. Training on giving and receiving constructive feedback is also valuable, as are programs that help employees identify and mitigate unconscious biases.

Leadership development programs that focus on creating psychologically safe environments are especially important. These programs can help leaders at all levels understand the impact of their behaviors on team dynamics and provide them with tools to promote psychological safety.

For organizations looking to assess and improve psychological safety, several validated survey tools are available. Amy Edmondson's Team Psychological Safety Survey, a concise 7-item questionnaire, offers a quick assessment of team dynamics. For a more comprehensive evaluation, consider The Fearless Organization's Psychological Safety Index (PSI).

Google's Team Effectiveness Discussion Guide, which incorporates findings from Project Aristotle, provides a broader framework for team assessment. Culture Amp and McKinsey & Company also offer robust psychological safety surveys tailored for organizational use. These tools not only measure current levels of psychological safety but also provide insights for cultivating a more open and innovative work environment. By regularly employing these assessments, organizations can track progress and identify areas for improvement in their journey toward building a psychologically safe workplace.

Beyond surveys, organizations can track metrics such as employee turnover rates. The speed with which problems are identified and addressed can also be a powerful indicator of psychological safety.

Implementing psychological safety isn't without its obstacles. Here are some common challenges and strategies for overcoming them:

- Resistance to change: Some team members may be skeptical. Address this by sharing success stories and data about the benefits of psychological safety.
- Inconsistent application: Ensure that all levels of leadership are aligned and consistently modeling psychological safety behaviors.
- Cultural differences: In global teams, perceptions of psychological safety may vary. Provide cultural intelligence training and create flexible policies that can be adapted to different cultural contexts.
- Maintain for the long term: To prevent psychological safety from becoming a short-lived initiative, integrate it into your organization's values, performance reviews, and ongoing training programs.

Creating and maintaining a psychologically safe environment is an ongoing process that requires consistent effort and commitment from all levels of the organization. However, the payoff in terms of increased innovation, improved problem-solving, and enhanced team performance makes it a worthwhile investment for any technology organization looking to thrive in today's competitive landscape.

Describe Your Culture Clearly and Concisely

A clear description of the culture is essential because it provides employees with a clear understanding of the behaviors that are expected of them and that will make them and the organization successful. This clarity not only attracts and retains employees who align with the culture, but also creates a positive work environment where individuals are empowered to contribute their best efforts, leading to improved performance, productivity, and ultimately the organization's success and reputation.

Describing your culture is not easy. It involves articulating the core values, beliefs, and behaviors that define your organization's identity and guide its actions. It's about distilling complex concepts into simple, understandable terms and principles that resonate with employees and stakeholders. This description should capture the essence of what makes your culture unique and inspiring, and provide a clear framework for decisions, behaviors, and interactions within the organization.

The best and most pragmatic way to describe a company's culture is to focus on specific, observable behaviors and practices that exemplify the core values and principles that define the organization.

Here are some pragmatic steps to effectively describe an organization's culture:

- Identify core values and principles: Begin by clearly articulating the core values, beliefs, and guiding principles that serve as the foundation of the organization's culture.

- Describe observable behaviors: Translate these values into concrete, observable behaviors that employees are expected to demonstrate in their daily work. For example, if one of the values is "customer focus," observable behaviors might include actively seeking customer feedback, going the extra mile to resolve customer issues, and prioritizing customer needs in decision-making.
- Share real-life examples: Provide specific, real-life examples or anecdotes that illustrate how the company's cultural values are put into practice. These could be stories of employees going above and beyond, instances of collaboration and teamwork, or examples of innovation and problem-solving.
- Address decision-making processes (optional): Explain how the company's cultural values influence decision-making processes, resource allocation, and overall priorities. For example, if one of the values is "transparency," describe how the company shares information openly and involves employees in important decisions.
- Discuss leadership and management practices: Highlight how the organization's leaders and managers model and reinforce the company's cultural values through their actions, communication styles, and management practices.

In the context of our domain-driven organization, each domain and team can and should have its specific values, principles, and standards of conduct. Of course, these should not contradict the basic corporate culture. Rather, they should be more specific to the work of the domain or team.

Who You Hire, Reward, Promote, and Let Go Shows Your Real Culture

Who you hire, reward, promote, and let go reveals your true culture. An organization's culture is defined not only by written values or mission statements but also by the actual behaviors and decisions that are made within the organization, as well as the way the organization treats its current and potential employees.

The people chosen to join the organization reflect its cultural priorities and values. The hiring process, including the qualities and characteristics sought in candidates, reveals what the organization values in its employees and the type of culture it seeks to cultivate. We recommend that a significant part of the recruitment process focuses on the candidate's specific past behavior in relation to the desired culture. This involves describing specific situations in which the candidate explains how he or she behaved. The best way to do this is to use the STAR Scheme, describing the situation, the task, the actions taken, and the results achieved.

How employees are rewarded and promoted demonstrates the behaviors and achievements that are valued and recognized within the organization. This includes not only tangible rewards such as bonuses or promotions but also less formal forms of recognition and advancement.

REALITY TECH

Sophie led a very innovative and young organization. In one of the teams, an engineer reportedly refused to collaborate and demonstrated bad behavior toward other employees (especially less senior ones) such as being rude and showing bad morale. The individual had been known as technically outstanding. Overall, the person delivered above and beyond results in solving some of the most complex issues. Regardless of this overperformance, Sophie decided to let the person go with immediate effect. She wanted to make sure that the people understood that the organization was not only concerned about performance but also culture. One of the core values was 'being collaborative.'

In essence, these actions speak volumes about the true culture of an organization. They reveal what is truly important, what behaviors are encouraged or discouraged, and how aligned the organization's actions are with its stated values. Therefore, paying attention to who the organization hires, rewards, promotes, and lets go is critical to understanding and shaping its culture.

Practice What You Preach, Even When No One Is Watching

When leaders fail to align their actions with their words and the defined organizational culture, the result is a breakdown in trust, disengagement, and cynicism among employees. This disconnect undermines the cultural integrity of the organization, erodes morale, and can lead to a fragmented and ineffective work environment where stated values become meaningless.

It is critical for leaders to practice what they preach for several reasons:

- They serve as role models for their teams. When managers consistently demonstrate the behaviors and values they expect of their employees, they set a clear example for others to follow. This helps to establish and reinforce cultural norms within the organization.
- Consistency between words and actions builds trust and credibility with employees. When leaders act according to their stated values and commitments, employees are more likely to trust their leadership and feel confident in following their lead.

- When leaders hold themselves accountable to the same standards they expect of their employees, it creates a culture of accountability throughout the organization. Employees are more likely to take ownership of their work and responsibilities when they see their leaders doing the same.
- Consistent leadership behavior is essential to driving cultural change in the organization. If leaders do not align their actions with the desired cultural values, efforts to instill new norms or behaviors are likely to falter.

Reward Success, Effort, and Failure

Rewarding success, effort, and (some) failure is essential to strengthening organizational culture because it recognizes the value of both outcomes and the processes that lead to them. This approach promotes a culture of continuous improvement and resilience, motivating employees to strive for excellence, take risks, and innovate without fear of punitive consequences. Recognizing efforts and learning from mistakes helps create an environment where employees feel valued and supported, which in turn boosts engagement and morale.

There are several ways to effectively reward these aspects. Celebrating success can include bonuses, promotions, public recognition or awards, and highlighting successful domains, teams, and individuals in company communications. Recognizing effort can include verbal praise, thank you notes, or small tokens of appreciation, as well as offering professional development opportunities as a reward for continued effort. Encouraging learning from failure can be accomplished by holding debriefing sessions where lessons learned are shared openly, and by recognizing and rewarding constructive risk-taking and innovative thinking.

Without rewards for success, effort, and failure, employees can feel undervalued and unmotivated, leading to reduced engagement and productivity. This lack of recognition can create a culture of fear and blame, where mistakes are hidden rather than used as opportunities for growth. Such an environment stifles creativity and hinders the organization's ability to adapt and thrive in a competitive environment.

Of course, not all mistakes should be celebrated, especially those that result from negligence, misconduct, or repeated mistakes without improvement. These errors must be carefully managed to maintain accountability while preserving a positive organizational culture.

Negligence, such as ignoring safety protocols or failing to follow procedures should be addressed with clear policies and comprehensive training programs that emphasize care and responsibility. Constructive feedback and additional training can help prevent future occurrences.

Failures due to unethical behavior, dishonesty, or policy violations are harmful and require immediate and appropriate disciplinary action. Upholding organizational values and consistently enforcing policies are critical to maintaining integrity.

Repeated mistakes with no effort to learn indicate deeper problems. Identifying root causes and providing targeted support, such as training or mentoring, can help. Developing a mindset of continuous learning and improvement is essential, but employees must also take responsibility for their development.

Managing these errors requires clear communication about acceptable risks versus avoidable errors, constructive feedback focused on improvement, and investment in training to address knowledge or skill gaps.

Talk About Your Culture a Lot—Internally and Externally

Talk extensively about your organizational culture, both internally with employees and externally with the public, especially potential new joiners. This helps shape, reinforce, and sustain a positive, cohesive culture.

It also clarifies core values, beliefs, and expectations in your current and future staff. Regular discussions reinforce these and guide behaviors and decisions. It promotes consistency and alignment throughout the organization and builds awareness and understanding of what defines the culture. Employees gain a sense of belonging and shared identity, which builds team cohesion and morale.

External communication attracts talent that is aligned with the company's values and mission. Prospective employees seek cultures that align with their beliefs and aspirations. Clear communication supports recruitment and retention. It shapes the company's external reputation and brand image. Positive cultural narratives enhance attractiveness to customers, investors, and stakeholders whereas negative perceptions can damage trust and credibility.

Use internal channels—meetings, newsletters, intranets, town halls, etc. Discuss culture, share success stories, and reinforce values. Leaders must embody the culture and be vocal in their words and actions. Their visibility reinforces its importance. Recognize and reward employees who exemplify these values and contribute to the culture. Highlight their accomplishments to reinforce desired behaviors. Incorporate culture into training programs and new employee onboarding, and guide how to embody values in daily work.

Externally, use social media, press, websites, and recruiting materials. Highlight cultural initiatives, employee testimonials, and community involvement. This will attract like-minded talent and enhance reputation.

Employees can become disconnected from values and goals, leading to misalignment and confusion, which creates a loss of identity and cohesion, making it difficult to maintain a distinct culture. Prospective employees may be reluctant to join an organization with unclear cultural values, hindering talent attraction and retention. External stakeholders may form inaccurate perceptions, potentially damaging the company's reputation and brand image.

Establish Internal and External Feedback Loops to Sustain Your Culture

Establishing internal and external feedback loops is critical to creating, maintaining, and evolving an organizational culture. Feedback loops ensure continuous communication and improvement, enabling the organization to stay aligned with its values and goals. They encourage a culture of transparency, accountability, and continuous learning. By actively seeking and responding to feedback, organizations can identify and address issues early, promote employee engagement, and improve overall effectiveness.

Internally, organizations can use a variety of methods to gather feedback. Regular employee surveys can measure satisfaction, gather suggestions, and identify areas for improvement. Performance reviews that include 360-degree feedback allow employees to receive input from peers, subordinates, and managers. Regular team meetings and open forums provide a safe and constructive environment for sharing thoughts and feedback. Anonymous suggestion boxes encourage honest feedback without fear of retribution.

Externally, organizations can gather feedback from customers through surveys about their experiences and satisfaction with the company's products or services. Focus groups with customers or industry experts provide deeper insight into market perceptions and expectations. Monitoring social media channels helps gather real-time feedback and gauge public sentiment about the organization. Engaging with business partners and suppliers provides perspectives on working with the organization and identifies areas for collaboration and improvement.

Without feedback loops, organizations risk becoming disconnected from their employees and customers. This disconnect can lead to stagnation as the organization fails to innovate or adapt to changing circumstances. Employees may feel undervalued and unheard, leading to decreased motivation, morale, and productivity. Problems may go unnoticed and unresolved, leading to inefficiencies, decreased quality, and potential crises. Poor decision-making can occur when decisions are not aligned with the needs and expectations of employees and customers, damaging the organization's reputation and success.

Provide Work Environments That Encourage Social Interaction, Creative Group Work, and Individual Focus

The work environment serves as a tangible expression of organizational culture, reflecting values, beliefs, and priorities. Its design, layout, and atmosphere convey important messages about what the organization values, shaping employee experiences and perceptions.

Factors such as lighting, noise levels, and spatial layout directly influence mood, well-being, and especially productivity, impacting daily interactions and behaviors. An appealing work environment attracts and retains top talent, as candidates consider it when evaluating job opportunities.

In general, an organization should provide different work environments for different types of work:

- Social interaction: Encouraging social interaction helps build strong relationships among team members and creates a sense of camaraderie and belonging. This leads to better collaboration, communication, and teamwork, which are essential for achieving common goals. This requires rooms and spaces within the office that have the character of a French café or Scandinavian living room.
- Creative group work: Providing spaces and opportunities for creative group work allows teams to brainstorm ideas, solve problems, and innovate together. These environments spark creativity, encourage different perspectives, and promote forward-thinking solutions. This requires rooms and spaces with large walls for writing, painting, gluing, and other creative activities. These spaces must be easily accessible from both inside and outside the company.
- Individual focus: An environment that encourages individual focus allows employees to concentrate on their tasks without distraction. This encourages focused work, increases productivity, and allows employees to perform at their best. Employees should be able to choose where, when, and how they want to work. At home, at a remote workstation, or even in the office. In the office, however, small, quiet rooms for one or two people need to be available to enable focused, uninterrupted individual work.

Common Misconceptions and Mistakes

Your Culture Document Reads Like the 10 Things Everyone Should Have Learned in Kindergarten

Some culture documents read like "10 Things Everyone Should Have Learned in Kindergarten," presenting a view of organizational culture that is simplistic and superficial. Examples include those that emphasize vague platitudes such as "be kind" or "work together" without providing meaningful context or actionable guidance. This misconception can be damaging because it can leave employees without direction, undermine the organization's credibility, and limit the impact of its culture efforts.

To address this misconception, organizations should define core values with specificity, link values to behaviors, promote accountability, and encourage dialogue and feedback. By developing a more authentic and meaningful culture, organizations can drive employee engagement, performance, and business success.

A Well-Being Culture Kills Creativity and Performance

Some companies, especially traditional ones, misunderstand the importance of employee satisfaction, trust, and autonomy. They fail to find the right balance between employees, customers, and the company. These companies focus on perks and benefits for employees without considering how these affect productivity, innovation, and teamwork.

Without clear expectations or accountability measures, this could lead to decreased accountability, missed milestones, and decreased collaboration. Similarly, placing too much emphasis on individual happiness may result in a lack of focus on collective goals and shared values, leading to decreased alignment and cohesion. This can hinder creativity, performance, and organizational success.

To mitigate the negative effects of a well-being culture that undermines creativity and performance, organizations can take several steps:

- Give employees the freedom to work however they want, but make sure they know what's expected of them and how they'll be held accountable. Meet with them regularly to discuss their progress and make sure they're on track.
- Encourage cross-functional collaboration, knowledge sharing, and team-based problem-solving to create innovation and drive performance.
- Align well-being initiatives with organizational goals.
- Encourage open dialogue and feedback to improve well-being programs and use this feedback to make data-driven decisions.

A High-Performance Organization Kills Psychological Safety

In a high-performance software development team focused on meeting tight deadlines and delivering flawless code, psychological safety can inadvertently take a back seat to productivity and efficiency. For example, in an agile development environment where rapid iteration and problem-solving are critical, developers may feel pressured to prioritize individual contributions over collaboration or admit uncertainty.

This dynamic can lead to a lack of psychological safety, with team members reluctant to ask questions, share ideas, or voice concerns for fear of appearing incompetent or slowing progress. The consequences can be harmful, resulting in decreased innovation, increased stress, and lower morale among team members. Without a sense of psychological safety, developers may be less likely to experiment with new approaches or offer creative solutions to complex problems, ultimately hindering the team's ability to deliver high-quality software.

TL;DR and Further Reading

Creating a great place to work and establishing a great culture can only be achieved in the long term. To get started, you can make your culture a common discussion point, inviting people to participate and contribute, e.g., with culture ambassadors.

- The goal is a culture where purpose and psychological safety inspire everyone to excel
- Mastery, autonomy, and purpose are core attributes of a healthy culture
- Psychological safety boosts creativity, innovation, and performance
- Describe your culture clearly and concisely
- Who you hire, reward, promote, and let go reflects your real culture
- Practice what you preach, even when no one is watching
- Reward success, effort, and failure
- Talk about your culture a lot—internally and externally
- Establish internal and external feedback loops to sustain your culture
- Provide work environments that encourage social interaction, creative group work, and individual focus

For a more in-depth look at this topic, these are some of our favorite books:

- *The Culture Code: The Secrets of Highly Successful Groups*, by Daniel Coyle

- *Delivering Happiness: A Path to Profits, Passion, and Purpose,* by Tony Hsieh
- *Work Rules!: Insights from Inside Google That Will Transform How You Live and Lead,* by Laszlo Bock
- *Drive: The Surprising Truth About What Motivates Us,* by Daniel H. Pink
- *Remote Work Revolution,* by Tsedal Neeley

15

HOW TO LEAD AND MANAGE WITHIN A TECH ORGANIZATION

LEADERSHIP AND MANAGEMENT in great tech organizations face the challenge of balancing autonomy and alignment across different levels while cultivating innovation and agility. This challenge is critical as effective leadership directly impacts an organization's ability to adapt, innovate, and deliver value at scale. Poor leadership can lead to misaligned efforts, reduced productivity, and missed business opportunities.

This chapter explores a multi-tiered leadership approach tailored for agile, product-driven, and domain-oriented tech organizations. We'll examine how team-level leaders cultivate high-performing, self-organized teams, how domain-level leaders orchestrate strategy execution, and how executive leadership sets overarching direction. The chapter will delve into key concepts such as empowering others, optimizing the whole system, adapting to change, and forming cross-functional leadership teams that can effectively guide and sometimes overrule local decisions for the greater good.

By mastering the leadership strategies presented in this chapter, readers will be equipped to build and steer tech organizations that are both nimble and aligned, capable of thriving in today's rapidly evolving digital landscape.

The Traditional Approach and Why It Falls Short

In many traditional IT organizations, leadership practices often hinder rather than help technological progress and organizational growth. These approaches, rooted in outdated beliefs about control and efficiency, create a disconnect between intentions and results.

One of the most prevalent issues is the tendency for managers to become overly involved in day-to-day operations. This micromanagement stems from a lack of trust in employees' abilities and a desire for tight control. While intended to ensure quality and consistency, it instead creates decision-making bottlenecks, stifles creativity, and hampers innovation. Employees feel undervalued and restricted, leading to lower engagement and job satisfaction. Consequently, the organization becomes less agile and struggles to attract and retain top talent.

Another problematic aspect is the view of organizational optimization as a one-time, outsourced effort. This approach, driven by a quick-fix mentality and budget constraints, fails to address the dynamic nature of modern businesses. Improvements are often temporary and don't stick, as they're not embedded in the organization's culture. This cyclical pattern of decline and intervention wastes resources and lowers employee morale, as their insights are overlooked in favor of external solutions.

Furthermore, traditional management structures often prioritize personal status and empire-building over organizational efficiency. The focus on expanding one's kingdom through headcount and budget increases leads to political games and resistance to necessary restructuring. This mindset, coupled with the fear of becoming obsolete, results in bloated organizations that struggle to adapt to rapidly changing business environments.

These traditional practices collectively create an inefficient, inflexible organization ill-equipped to thrive in today's fast-paced, complex tech landscape. The disconnect between leadership intentions and actual outcomes highlights the urgent need for a new approach to managing and leading great tech organizations.

The General Blueprint

Team-Level Leaders Cultivate High-Performing, Self-Organized Teams

In tech organizations, the role of functional team leaders has evolved to meet the demands of a rapidly changing industry. These organizations are typically structured as loosely coupled systems organized around domains, using agile principles to increase flexibility and responsiveness. Within this framework, cross-functional, self-organized teams form the backbone of the company's operational structure. These teams bring together professionals from different disciplines to work together on specific products or services. In this context, team-level leaders play a critical role as functional managers responsible for nurturing talent and collaboration, and ensuring alignment with organizational goals, while respecting the autonomy of their self-organized teams.

Team-level leaders are functional managers, such as engineering managers, product managers, or design leads, who are responsible for specific job families within cross-functional product teams. They oversee the professional development, performance, and alignment of their job family's individual contributors who may be distributed across multiple teams. These leaders balance functional expertise with cross-team collaboration to support both specialized skill development and overall product team goals.

Team-level leaders work on the system, not in the system. Rather than getting involved in the day-to-day tasks, they focus on creating an environment that enables their team to self-organize effectively. They help establish agile and lean processes, remove obstacles, and provide the resources necessary for the team to function autonomously. This approach empowers team members to make decisions and take ownership of their work, enabling a sense of ownership and pride.

Operating at the most granular level, known as Flight Level 1 in organizations that use the Flight Level method, team-level leaders play a critical role in maintaining smooth day-to-day operations. They come from a variety of functional backgrounds such as engineering, user experience (UX), and product management, each bringing their unique expertise to the team. Their primary responsibility is to create an environment where team members can thrive and do their best work.

One of the key aspects of a team-level leader's role is to attract, hire, develop, and retain diverse bar-raising talent. They are at the forefront of talent management, continuously seeking individuals who can elevate the team's performance and contribute to the organization's success. Through regular one-on-one meetings, they provide feedback, offer guidance, and nurture the growth of individual team members. Beyond professional development, team-level leaders are deeply invested in the motivation and well-being of their direct reports, recognizing that a healthy, engaged team is fundamental to sustained high performance and innovation. This focus on high-caliber talent and team well-being ensures that the team continuously improves its skills and performance.

A critical aspect of their role is to help the team stay in flow, maintain motivation, and deliver expected results. They also work to align the team's efforts with broader domain and organizational goals, ensuring that their work contributes meaningfully to the organization's goals.

Team-level leaders play a critical role in cultivating and reinforcing the organization's culture at the grassroots level (see Chapter 14 under the section, Describe Your Culture Clearly and Concisely). Through their daily interactions and leadership style, they set the tone for the entire team and influence the broader organizational culture. They ensure that the company's values and behaviors are reflected in the team's day-to-day operations, cultivating a positive and productive work environment.

While nurturing autonomy in a loosely coupled organization, team-level leaders also play a crucial role in providing feedback, challenging the team when necessary, and occasionally exercising their authority to veto decisions. They offering constructive feedback to help the team improve and grow, challenge assumptions or approaches to push the team toward better solutions, and in rare instances, veto a team's decision if it conflicts with organizational goals or policies or poses significant risks. This delicate balance between empowerment and oversight requires excellent judgment and communication skills, ensuring that interventions are seen as supportive rather than undermining the team's autonomy.

The cross-functional nature of product teams adds an extra layer of complexity to the team-level leader's role. They must balance the needs of their functional area with the goals of the various product teams their reports are part of. This requires a broad understanding of the organization's objectives and the ability to navigate potential conflicts between functional and product priorities.

Domain-Level Leaders Orchestrate Strategy Execution

Product-driven technology organizations are typically designed as loosely coupled systems organized around business domains, using agile and lean principles to increase flexibility and responsiveness. Within this framework, cross-functional, self-organized teams form the backbone of the company's operational structure. These teams bring together professionals from different disciplines to work together on specific products or services.

In this context, domain-level leaders play a critical role in orchestrating strategy execution across multiple teams. Operating at Flight Level 2 in organizations that use the Flight Level method, these leaders act as conductors who harmonize the efforts of different teams within a given domain. They are functional leaders, such as Director of Engineering, Director of Product Management, or Head of UX/UI, who are responsible for overseeing team-level leaders within their domain and forming a cross-functional, domain-level leadership team.

The primary goal of domain-level leaders is to create and maintain a loosely coupled organization that effectively executes the business strategy and delivers value in alignment with the organization's North Star. They accomplish this by nurturing an environment in which multiple teams can collaborate effectively, innovate, and adapt to changing circumstances while ensuring that their collective efforts contribute to the domain's strategic goals and the organization's overarching objectives.

A core responsibility of domain-level leaders is to translate high-level organizational strategy into actionable plans for their teams. They break down strategic initiatives into manageable components, assign them to appropriate teams, and ensure that those teams understand how their work contributes to the bigger picture. This process of strategy translation and execution involves making critical decisions about resource allocation, prioritization, and trade-offs that directly impact the organization's ability to achieve its strategic goals.

Domain-level leaders define and continually optimize the domain's operating model to support effective strategy execution. They create a framework that not only enables efficient current operations but also promotes continuous improvement and adaptation. This includes regularly assessing the effectiveness of existing processes, identifying areas for improvement, and implementing changes that enhance the domain's ability to learn, innovate, and respond to changing strategic priorities.

To facilitate strategy execution, domain-level leaders oversee the domain's kanban board, which provides a high-level view of work progress across multiple teams. This enables them to identify bottlenecks, manage resources effectively, and ensure alignment with the overall business strategy. They use this visibility to make real-time adjustments, reallocate resources, and keep the domain's efforts on track with strategic goals.

By forming a cross-functional leadership team at the domain level, these leaders bring together diverse expertise to address complex, multifaceted challenges that cut across teams and disciplines. This ensures a holistic approach to strategy execution, enabling coordinated efforts that leverage the full capabilities of the domain.

Domain-level leaders support the development of team-level leaders and ensure effective talent management across the domain. They work with team-level leaders to attract, develop, and retain top talent across multiple teams by providing guidance, mentoring, and cultivating the growth of leadership capabilities that align with strategic needs. Crucially, domain-level leaders also prioritize the motivation and well-being of their people, recognizing that engaged and healthy teams are fundamental to successful strategy execution and long-term business success.

While respecting the autonomy of self-organized teams, domain-level leaders also provide feedback, challenge teams when necessary, and occasionally veto decisions that may deviate from strategic goals. This delicate balance requires excellent judgment and communication skills to ensure that interventions are seen as supporting strategy execution rather than undermining team autonomy.

Domain-level leaders play a key role in managing and reducing interdependencies between teams that could impede strategy execution. They work to identify areas where teams are overly dependent on each other and take steps to minimize these dependencies, increasing the overall agility and responsiveness of the domain in pursuit of strategic goals.

The cross-functional nature of their role requires domain leaders to balance the needs of different functional areas with the goals of the domain and the organization's strategy as a whole. This requires a broad understanding of the organization's strategic goals and the ability to navigate potential conflicts between functional, domain, and organizational priorities to ensure cohesive strategy execution.

By fulfilling these responsibilities, domain-level leaders ensure that their domain remains agile, innovative, and capable of effectively executing strategy while delivering significant business value. Their role is essential in maintaining the delicate balance between empowering self-organizing teams and ensuring that these teams' efforts contribute meaningfully to the organization's strategic success in a rapidly evolving technology landscape.

The Executive Leadership Team Sets Overarching Direction

The executive leadership team plays a pivotal role in guiding the company to success. This team typically includes the chief executive officer (CEO), chief technology officer (CTO), chief product officer (CPO), vice president of engineering, and vice president of product. Operating at Flight Level 3 in organizations that use the Flight Level methodology, they provide overarching direction while encouraging agility and innovation throughout the organization.

The primary objective of the executive leadership team is to establish and execute the overall strategy and vision for the company. Led by the CEO, they create a unifying direction that aligns different areas and teams. This includes managing the portfolio of initiatives across all domains, overseeing the organization-wide kanban board, and making high-level decisions that impact the company's ability to innovate and compete (see Chapter 7 under the section, Objectives and Key Results (OKRs) can Support Strategic Execution).

Executive Leaders shape the entire organizational system. The CTO and VP of Engineering focus on creating a technology environment that enables effective strategy execution (see Chapter 3 under the section, Cultivate Strategy through Continuous Dialogue and Adaptation), while the CPO and VP of Product ensure that the company's offerings meet market needs. They continually evaluate and refine the company's operating model and translate market insights into strategic initiatives.

A core responsibility of the executive team is talent management and culture shaping. They work to attract, develop, and retain top talent and nurture an environment of innovation and engagement. The CEO plays a critical role in defining and communicating the company's values and ensuring they are consistently reflected at all levels.

While respecting the autonomy of business units and teams, the leadership team provides feedback, challenges assumptions, and makes key decisions that affect the entire organization. They also work to manage and reduce dependencies between domains, increasing overall organizational agility.

The executive leadership team must balance the needs of multiple stakeholders, including employees, customers, partners, and investors. This requires a broad understanding of the business landscape, market trends, and technological advances.

By fulfilling these responsibilities, the executive leadership team ensures that the company remains adaptable, innovative, and able to effectively execute its strategy in a rapidly evolving technological landscape. Their collective role is essential to creating a resilient organization that can pursue its vision while responding adeptly to changing market conditions and emerging opportunities.

Leaders Empower Others to Excel

Servant Leadership is a leadership philosophy based on the idea that a leader's primary role is to serve others, especially his or her team members and colleagues, rather than to be served.

In a loosely coupled organization, a servant leader focuses on empowering his or her team members, nurturing their growth, and creating an environment where innovation and collaboration can thrive. The leader's success is measured not by personal accomplishments or the exercise of authority, but by the growth, well-being, and accomplishments of those they lead. It involves a shift from seeing leadership as a position of power to seeing it as a position of responsibility—responsibility for the success, growth, and well-being of others.

A servant leader spends a significant amount of time mentoring team members, helping them develop new skills and advance in their careers. They actively listen to understand the challenges and needs of individuals and teams and then work diligently to provide necessary resources or remove barriers to success.

This leadership style prioritizes creating a supportive, inclusive culture where everyone feels valued and heard. In practice, this might mean encouraging open communication, incorporating diverse perspectives, and ensuring that all team members have the opportunity to contribute their ideas and expertise.

Servant leaders also focus on building a sense of community within the organization. They work to break down silos between teams and departments, encouraging cross-functional collaboration and knowledge sharing where appropriate.

When making decisions, a servant leader considers the impact on all stakeholders, not just their immediate team or personal interests. They strive to make decisions that benefit the entire organization, even if it means sacrificing short-term gains for long-term success.

Servant leadership also means leading by example and demonstrating the behaviors and values you want to see in others. It includes a willingness to roll up your sleeves and help with hands-on work when needed, admitting when you don't have all the answers, and actively seeking feedback on your performance.

Leaders Optimize the Whole, Not Just the Parts

Systems thinking is a critical aspect of leadership in great tech organizations. It's an approach that views the organization as an interconnected system and network rather than isolated components. Leaders who embrace systems thinking understand that changes in one area can ripple throughout the organization, affecting overall performance and results.

In loosely coupled organizations, systems thinking helps maintain alignment while preserving autonomy. Leaders look beyond their immediate team or domain to understand how work flows across different domains and how decisions affect the entire system. This holistic view allows them to identify bottlenecks, inefficiencies, and opportunities that may be invisible when focusing on individual parts.

Applying systems thinking involves mapping entire value streams, from concept to customer feedback. Leaders consider not only immediate outcomes but also second-order effects, asking, "What will happen after this happens?" This forward-looking approach leads to more robust strategies and better problem-solving.

Systems thinking encourages addressing root causes rather than symptoms. When faced with challenges, leaders dig deeper to understand underlying systemic issues rather than implementing quick fixes. This approach leads to more effective, long-lasting solutions.

To cultivate systems thinking, leaders must develop a holistic perspective and a curiosity about connections. They should encourage cross-functional collaboration and knowledge sharing, and create opportunities for diverse teams to work together. Tools such as causal loop diagrams or value stream mapping can help visualize complex systems and communicate insights.

By embracing systems thinking, leaders can make more informed decisions, create resilient strategies, and promote a culture of holistic problem-solving. This approach enables organizations to navigate complexity more effectively and remain agile and innovative in pursuit of their goals. Ultimately, systems thinking enables leaders to manage their organizations as unified, adaptive entities rather than as collections of disparate parts.

Leaders Adapt to Change

"The measure of intelligence is the ability to change." —Albert Einstein

Adaptive leadership is about embracing change as a catalyst for growth and innovation rather than a threat to be avoided. Leaders who embody this principle view challenges as opportunities to learn, evolve, and improve. They understand that in the fast-paced world of technology, to stand still is to fall behind.

In practice, adaptive leaders create a culture of experimentation and calculated risk-taking. They create safe spaces where team members feel comfortable trying new approaches, knowing that failure is not only accepted but valued as a learning opportunity. This mindset cultivates innovation and helps organizations stay ahead of the curve in a competitive industry.

Flexibility is a key characteristic of adaptive leaders. They recognize that different situations and team dynamics require different leadership styles. Sometimes they need to be directive, sometimes facilitative, and they adjust their approach based on what will best serve their team and organization in a given context.

Adaptive leaders are also adept at challenging the status quo and are vocally self-critical. They continually question existing processes and assumptions and encourage their teams to do the same. This critical thinking helps prevent complacency and drives continuous improvement throughout the organization.

In the face of uncertainty, adaptive leaders are comfortable making decisions with incomplete information. They understand that in many situations, waiting for perfect data can lead to missed opportunities. Instead, they make the best decision possible with the information available, then remain agile and ready to change course as new insights emerge.

To implement adaptive leadership, tech companies are introducing regular retrospectives to reflect on processes and results. They encourage A/B testing of new ideas or guide teams through significant organizational changes. Adaptive leaders help their teams become comfortable with uncertainty, providing guidance and support as they navigate uncharted territory.

By embracing adaptive leadership, technology organizations can build resilience, nurture innovation, and maintain a competitive edge in a rapidly evolving industry. This approach enables leaders to guide their teams through challenges, seize new opportunities, and continuously evolve to meet the demands of an uncertain future.

Leaders Translate Between Agile and Traditional Parts of the Organization

In most organizations, the adoption of the methodologies discussed in this book is often uneven, creating a complex ecosystem where agile and traditional operating models coexist. In this mixed environment, leaders in agile-oriented parts of the organization play a critical role as the interface between these divergent paradigms.

These leaders act as cultural translators, bridging the gap between agile principles and traditional management approaches. They must deftly navigate the challenges of explaining agile concepts to those unfamiliar with them while understanding and respecting traditional practices. This role extends to managing expectations on both sides, aligning goals, and ensuring effective collaboration despite different methodologies.

Often, these leaders serve as a buffer, protecting their agile teams from unnecessary bureaucracy while ensuring compliance with essential organizational requirements. They become advocates for agility, demonstrating its benefits to other parts of the organization and potentially influencing broader organizational change.

The interface role requires exceptional flexibility in communication. Leaders must adapt their style to resonate with different organizational cultures, using more formal reporting structures when dealing with traditional IT departments while maintaining a collaborative approach within their agile teams. They also play a critical role in managing the risks that arise from the intersection of different operating models and negotiating resources in ways that make sense to traditional management structures.

This position comes with significant challenges. Leaders must maintain credibility and effectiveness in both agile and traditional contexts, avoid diluting agile principles when working with non-agile entities, and manage the stress of operating in two different organizational paradigms. Success in this role requires strong communication and diplomatic skills, a deep understanding of both agile and traditional management approaches, the ability to navigate complex organizational politics, and remarkable adaptability.

By effectively fulfilling this interface role, leaders in agile parts of the organization facilitate better collaboration, reduce friction, and potentially drive broader organizational transformation. They become the linchpin in creating a more cohesive, more understood, and ultimately more effective organizational structure that can leverage the strengths of both agile and traditional approaches.

Leaders Form a Cross-Functional Leadership Team

In organizations structured around loosely coupled, cross-functional teams, cross-functional leadership teams have become a necessity rather than an option. It aligns leadership structures with the cross-functional nature of teams and domains at the operational level.

Traditional siloed leadership, where each leader focuses solely on his or her functional area, is no longer effective in the fast-paced, interconnected world of technology. Cross-functional leadership teams bridge these silos, enabling faster decision-making, more innovative problem-solving, and better alignment with overall business goals.

The need for this approach becomes clear when you consider the complex challenges facing technology organizations today. These challenges often span multiple functional areas and require diverse expertise to address them effectively. A cross-functional leadership team brings together different perspectives, allowing for more comprehensive solutions and strategies. This collaborative approach also ensures that decisions made at the executive level consider the impact on all areas of the organization, reducing conflict and improving overall efficiency.

Key characteristics of such a leadership team are:

- Shared accountability: While each leader retains his or her functional expertise, they share responsibility for the overall success of the team, division, or organization.
- Collaborative decision-making: Decisions are made collectively, taking into account input from multiple functional perspectives.
- Holistic problem solving: Challenges are approached from multiple angles, resulting in more comprehensive solutions.
- Aligned Goals: The team works toward common goals, reducing conflicts between functional priorities.
- Improved Communication: Regular interaction between cross-functional leaders improves the flow of information and reduces silos.

In practice, cross-functional leadership teams operate at all levels of the organization. At the team level, roles such as engineering manager, product manager, and design lead work together to lead their agile team.

At the domain level, directors from different functions work together to oversee multiple teams. At the organizational level, C-suite executives and vice presidents form a cross-functional unit to guide the entire organization. For such cross-functional management teams, the same mechanisms for success apply as for the cross-functional development teams we described in Chapter 4, in particular, that they are co-located and share an office as a team.

The benefits of co-location are:

- Improved communication through frequent, spontaneous interactions.
- Stronger trust and relationships between leaders from different functional areas.
- Shared context and deeper understanding of cross-functional challenges.
- Rapid problem-solving and decision-making.
- Visibly modeling collaborative behavior for the rest of the organization.
- Informal knowledge sharing and serendipitous innovation.
- Increased accountability among team members.
- Better alignment with agile principles and culture.
- More empathetic and holistic decision-making.
- Faster response to emerging issues and opportunities.

However, implementing cross-functional leadership teams is not without its challenges. Leaders must balance their functional expertise with a broader organizational perspective. They must develop skills outside of their primary areas of expertise, becoming "T-shaped leaders" and adapting to a more collaborative, systems-thinking approach. This often requires a significant cultural shift away from traditional hierarchical structures.

Despite these challenges, the benefits of cross-functional leadership teams are substantial. They increase organizational agility, nurture innovation through diverse perspectives, and ensure more consistent execution of strategy. They also support employee development by exposing team members to a broader range of leadership perspectives and expertise.

Cross-functional leadership teams provide a structure that can effectively manage complexity, drive change, and maintain competitiveness in a rapidly evolving landscape. By aligning the leadership approach with the organizational structure and operational practices, these teams enable technology companies to fully leverage their agile, loosely coupled systems for maximum effectiveness and success.

Leaders Guide and Sometimes Overrule Local Decisions

Organizations, especially in the tech industry, are increasingly turning to autonomy and self-organized teams to increase agility and speed. This approach enables rapid, localized decision-making and promotes innovation. However, there are times when leaders need to guide or, in rare cases, override local decisions to ensure alignment with broader organizational goals and strategies.

This leadership intervention is necessary for several reasons:

- Leaders often have a broader view of the organization's strategy, market position, and long-term goals. They are privy to information that may not be available at all levels of the organization.

- Leaders are responsible for managing organizational risk and ensuring regulatory compliance—aspects that individual teams may not fully consider.
- Executives have insight into resource constraints and interdependencies across the organization, allowing them to anticipate potential conflicts or inefficiencies that may result from certain decisions.

Consider a few examples:

A product team might decide to refocus its development efforts based on recent user feedback. While this decision may seem good locally, it could conflict with a soon-to-be-announced strategic partnership of which the team is unaware. In this case, leadership guidance is critical to align the team's efforts with the broader organizational strategy.

In another scenario, a marketing team may propose a bold campaign that, unbeknownst to them, may violate industry regulations or conflict with the company's ethical standards. Here, executive intervention is needed to prevent potential legal or reputational damage.

At its core, leadership should be a collaborative process. Leaders should approach this responsibility with an attitude of support and facilitation rather than control.

Key methods for guiding decisions include:

- Clear communication: Regularly sharing organizational strategy, priorities, and constraints.
- Mentoring and teaching: Using decision-making scenarios as learning opportunities for teams.
- Asking probing questions: Encouraging teams to consider the broader implications of their decisions.

- Providing context: Providing insight into how local decisions might affect other parts of the organization.

In some cases, more direct intervention in the decision-making process may be necessary. Interventions can range from facilitating additional discussion to more actively steering decisions in a particular direction.

These situations can arise when:

- Decisions could result in significant misalignment with organizational strategy.
- There are serious unrecognized risks or compliance issues.
- The decision may create problematic dependencies or resource conflicts.

In rare and exceptional circumstances, leaders may need to override or veto a decision. This should be considered a last resort to be used only after other forms of leadership and intervention have been exhausted.

Situations that may warrant such action include:

- Legal or ethical concerns: When a decision could lead to legal problems or ethical violations.
- Existential risks: When a decision poses a serious threat to the organization's viability or reputation.
- Severe strategic misalignment: When a decision is fundamentally at odds with the organization's core strategy and could lead to significant negative consequences.
- Critical Resource Conflicts: When a decision would create unsustainable resource allocation issues affecting multiple parts of the organization.

When it is necessary, leaders must act with transparency, clearly explaining the reasoning behind the decision to overrule. They should be open to questions and feedback, using the situation as a learning opportunity for future decision-making.

The key to effective decision support is balance. Leaders should strive to create an environment where teams are well-informed about organizational strategy, constraints, and the potential impact of their decisions. This approach minimizes the need for intervention and makes overrides extremely rare. Leaders should regularly reflect on their decision guidance practices, solicit feedback, and adjust their approach to best serve their teams and the organization. By viewing decision guidance as a tool for empowerment rather than control, leaders can create an environment of trust, learning, and aligned autonomy.

Common Misconceptions and Mistakes

One Person from the Team Manages All Team Members Regardless of Function

In most organizations today, it's common to see functional and disciplinary leadership combined under one role. For example, a team lead is often responsible for both building and running an application while also managing a team of direct reports. However, many organizations are finding that this traditional structure may not be optimal for modern, agile environments.

Transforming this leadership structure by separating these responsibilities often meets significant resistance. The change can be challenging because many individuals define their status and identity through their reporting lines and span of control. The idea of reassigning people-management responsibilities to someone else can be particularly difficult for some to accept. As a result, many organizations end up with hybrid solutions that attempt to satisfy all parties. Unfortunately, these compromises often leave team members without clarity about leadership roles, leading to frustration and confusion.

Despite these challenges, we strongly advocate for this organizational change. Separating functional- and people-management responsibilities can bring a new balance of power to your organization with several key benefits:

- It encourages more open communication among team members.
- It allows individuals to interact on a more equal footing regardless of their role.
- It helps clarify priorities for everyone in the organization.

By implementing this change, organizations can create an environment where collaboration is more natural, hierarchies are less rigid, and the focus remains on achieving shared goals rather than maintaining traditional power structures.

While the transition may be difficult, the long-term benefits to organizational culture, employee engagement, and overall effectiveness make it a worthwhile endeavor for companies looking to thrive in today's fast-paced, collaborative business environment.

Self-Organized Teams with Minimal Disciplinary Leadership Results in Very Large Leadership Spans

A common misconception is that self-organized teams require minimal disciplinary leadership, leading to expansive leadership spans. However, this overlooks the crucial role of disciplinary leaders, especially in expert-rich environments.

Disciplinary leadership goes beyond basic management tasks. It involves fine-tuning job profiles, enhancing skills, encouraging collaboration, and organizing knowledge-sharing sessions. Crucially, it's about attracting and nurturing top talent—a task requiring far more than posting job descriptions online.

This leadership approach doesn't contradict self-organization; it complements it. By providing support and opportunities for growth, disciplinary leaders create an environment where professionals can thrive without undermining team autonomy.

Recognizing the importance of strong disciplinary leadership, even in self-organized teams, leads to a more skilled and engaged workforce. This balance ultimately results in stronger teams, innovative solutions, and a more adaptable organization.

Staff Engineers Provide Technical Leadership

Staff engineers are seasoned technical professionals who bridge the gap between hands-on engineering and organizational leadership in great tech organizations. Their role is critical in supporting self-organizing teams and complementing disciplined leadership.

These engineers provide technical guidance without direct managerial authority. They work across teams, aligning technical strategies and enabling collaboration. Their expertise informs decision-making at both the team and organizational levels, supporting the decision process we've discussed. In self-organized teams, staff engineers maintain technical excellence without imposing top-down control. They provide expertise and mentorship, supporting team autonomy while ensuring high-quality results. This approach is consistent with our discussion of balancing guidance with team independence.

Staff engineers also contribute to talent development, working with discipline leaders to identify skills gaps and lead technical mentoring initiatives. At higher organizational levels, they provide valuable input on technical strategy and help translate business vision into technical reality.

By driving innovation and providing technical leadership without formal authority, staff engineers exemplify how specialized expertise can be leveraged in flatter, more agile organizational structures. Their role supports the balanced leadership approach we've been exploring, where guidance and expertise coexist with team autonomy and self-organization.

Managers Not Getting Out of the Way After Setting Constraints and Direction

The concept of management in self-organized work environments often seems contradictory. A common misconception is that self-organization leaves no role for management. The key, however, is to find the right balance.

Effective management in self-organized teams involves setting clear boundaries and direction, and then stepping back. Micromanagement or excessive control can stifle team autonomy and efficiency. Instead, management should focus on working with employees to establish common goals and priorities, and clearly communicate their importance. Once these conditions are in place, teams can effectively self-organize and understand how to prioritize their work.

Successful technology companies like Netflix and AWS exemplify this approach. They hire exceptional talent, ensure they can operate within organizational boundaries, and then give them the freedom to excel.

This principle of setting direction and then "getting out of the way" has been critical to the success of these companies, allowing them to attract and retain the industry's top talent.

TL;DR and Further Reading

- Team-level leaders cultivate high-performing, self-organized teams
- Domain-level leaders orchestrate strategy execution
- Executive leadership teams set overarching direction
- Leaders empower others to excel
- Leaders optimize the whole, not just the parts
- Leaders adapt to change
- Leaders translate between agile and traditional parts of the organization
- Leaders form a cross-functional leadership team
- Leaders guide and sometimes overrule local decisions

For a more in-depth look at this topic, these are some of our favorite books:

- *The Manager's Path: A Guide for Tech Leaders Navigating Growth and Change,* by Camille Fournier
- *Become an Effective Software Engineering Manager: How to Be the Leader Your Development Team Needs,* by James Stanier
- *Managing Humans: Biting and Humorous Tales of a Software Engineering Manager,* by Michael Lopp
- *Leaders Eat Last: Why Some Teams Pull Together and Others Don't,* by Simon Sinek
- *The Fifth Discipline: The Art & Practice of The Learning Organization,* by Peter M. Senge
- *Management 3.0: Leading Agile Developers, Developing Agile Leaders,* by Jurgen Appelo

- *Reinventing Organizations: A Guide to Creating Organizations Inspired by the Next Stage of Human Consciousness,* by Frederic Laloux
- *Team of Teams: New Rules of Engagement for a Complex World,* by General Stanley McChrystal

An Ask from the Authors

Dear Reader,

Thank you for journeying with us through "All Hands On Tech." We hope our insights and strategies have inspired you to build and scale great tech organizations.

As self-published authors, we rely heavily on word-of-mouth and reader feedback. If you found value in our book, **we would be incredibly grateful if you could take a moment to leave an honest review on Amazon** or your preferred book platform. Your review, whether it's a few words or a detailed analysis, helps other potential readers discover our work and contributes immensely to the book's success.

Moreover, we're always eager to learn and improve. Your feedback, positive or constructive, is invaluable to us as we continue to refine our ideas and potentially work on future editions.

Thank you again for your support. Together, let's build a community of tech leaders committed to excellence and innovation.

Sophie & Matthias

Made in the USA
Las Vegas, NV
19 November 2024

12095979R00213